American Trails Series
IX

COAST LINE, SAN JUAN & LOS ANGELES U.S. MAIL STAGE
Painting by W. H. Hilton, San Francisco, 1876.
Courtesy Wells Fargo Bank History Room, San Francisco.

Stagecoaching

on El Camino Real

Los Angeles to San Francisco
1861-1901

the clouds on its origin —
its turbulent and boisterous
progress to the
completion of the rails

by
Charles F. Outland

THE ARTHUR H. CLARK COMPANY
Glendale, California, U.S.A.
1973

FOR

Ellie and Stan Taylor

Contents

Illustrations

Preface

When this research began, there was no intention on the part of the author of developing a book-length manuscript on coastal staging. A chapter to fit into an informal treatment of all facets of pioneer life in Ventura and Santa Barbara counties in the 1860s, '70s, and '80s was the original purpose. That idea evolved while indexing the newspaper files of the period and making the discovery that much of the later printed matter on the life and times of the pioneers, particularly in the so-called "mug books," was pure rubbish with a rank chamber of commerce flavor. Life as it really was had been made subordinate to life as the fast buck promoters wanted it to be, and which, if they could convince their readers, would result in rapid profits through expansionism run rampant.

Seldom were the seamier subjects – the saloon, the bawdy houses, street brawls and other unseemly but common behavior – mentioned in these extravagant two-bit *opera* of the nineteenth century. It was to fill this gap that the writer composed several chapters before making the further discovery that far more serious errors were being allowed to stand uncorrected insofar as stagecoaching was concerned. Here was an instance of repetition creating a belief in "those facts which really aren't," and being carried to the extreme where the best authorities were unwittingly confirming Napoleon's cynicism that history is but a fable agreed upon.

The problem then became one of correcting the recare simple and illustrate the importance of its avoidance. Someone commits the original error, usually unintentionally but on rare occasions with a deliberate intent to deceive for all time. Later, after years of painstaking research and scholarly writing, that "someone" becomes an acknowledged authority. His works are accepted by any university history department as accurate, and quotable in theses for advanced degrees. This is right and proper; it is manifestly impossible for each new scholar to recheck the sources of all past knowledge. The later student is concerned with new evidence or old records overlooked by his predecessors. It is his duty to fit this new material into the old pattern and possibly add to the old interpretations or formulate new ones.

It is at this point that the original error assumes monumental proportions. *If* the student bases his new interpretations upon the old error, or uses it in any manner as fact to reach final conclusions, he will have compounded the original "historical felony" and his own interpretations will in whole or in part be erroneous. If he in turn then becomes an authority to the next generation of scholars, the original error has, indeed, become a fable agreed upon; and the resulting shock waves spread in all directions to be picked up *ad infinitum*.

It was this very situation that confronted the author on Los Angeles to San Francisco stagecoaching and resulted in his discarding most of the written material available thereon and dusting off the ancient records in search of facts.

It is not always easy to delve deeply into basic records or even locate their whereabouts. I am indebted to Wells Fargo Bank and Wells Fargo Bank History

Room, San Francisco, for the assistance of its personnel, particularly in the matter of making available pertinent information from the Overland Mail Company Minute Book; and to Miss Dorothy Flint of Hollister for furnishing valuable records of Flint, Bixby & Company.

The staffs of the Clerks of the Boards of Supervisors of Santa Barbara and Los Angeles counties were most helpful and courteous in supplying the Supervisors' Minute Books and, in the case of Los Angeles, duplicated copies of important road records.

State Archivist Chief W. N. Davis, Jr. and David L. Snyder, Archivist II, have my sincere thanks for checking corporate records, or more specifically, the lack thereof where so-called stagecoach "companies" were concerned.

Courtesies extended the author by the library staffs at Santa Barbara, Ventura, Santa Paula, and Los Angeles City Library are greatly appreciated.

Thanks are due The Arthur H. Clark Company for permission to quote from *A County Judge in Arcady,* and *The Butterfield Overland Mail;* and to the Regents of the University of California for permission to quote rather extensively from William Brewer's *Up and Down California in 1860-1864.*

My thanks also to Mr. Robert Johnston of Hartnell College for filling in gaps and furnishing leads to information on coastal staging in the Monterey County area; to Miss Ynez Haase for similar favors and photographs in Santa Barbara County; to Supervisor Ralph "Hoot" Bennett for liaison assistance with the Clerk of the Board in Los Angeles County; to my brother, George E. Outland of San Francisco for assuming tasks that I was unable to travel to the Bay area to take care of myself; to Gus Ramirez and others at Title Insurance and Trust Company for furnishing copies of important maps of the staging era; and to my everlasting friend (I hope) the Sage of Chico, W. H. Hutchinson, for encouragement, friendly insults, and at least one invaluable lead. *Con Dios, Amigos.*

Stagecoach Corral Dust

In the beginning God created the heavens, the earth, and Gregory's Great Atlantic & Pacific Express; He then molded a group of historical exaggerators, lazy researchers, and outright plagiarists that the devil himself could gaze upon with admiration. At least, this might be the hasty opinion of anyone whose primary interest of the moment was the beginnings of stagecoaching between Los Angeles and San Francisco. If the authors of some of these "six-in-hand" and "throw-down-the-box" accounts had not become famous and authoritative over the years, their sins could be forgiven and forgotten; but their very prominence has given rise to repetition that creates a belief in those "facts which really aren't." It is incumbent, therefore, upon any narrator to untangle the twisted skein of their inaccuracies, distasteful though the task may be, before attempting to reconstruct the story of coastal staging between the two early populated centers of the state.

It was the Thompson & West *History of Los Angeles County, California* (1880) that appears to have started the tale about Gregory's Great Atlantic & Pacific Express being the first to introduce the stagecoach to Los Angeles. If there was any basis for the statement, it has eluded this researcher. The subsequent writers who copied from the Thompson & West history (without crediting or discrediting their source) were of such prominence in the field of history that the original version and the "plagiarisms" therefrom are worthy of notice.

Under the heading of "Stagecoaches" on page 74, the Thompson & West history stated:

The first intimation we have of this invasion of the *antique* by the *antique* is in 1851, when Gregory's Great Atlantic and Pacific Express brought the Eastern mails to Los Angeles in the hitherto unheard-of time – "one month and nineteen days." Yet saddle-horses were not altogether discarded, and the Express messenger who, in December, 1856, rode from San Pedro to Los Angeles (twenty-seven miles) in one hour and eighteen minutes, must have surely worn Mexican rowels. In the following year we find David Smith running stages semi-monthly to Visalia, and thence to San Francisco. In the same year Wells, Fargo & Co. established a branch office in Los Angeles.

Seventeen years after that prize-winning bit of historical redundancy appeared in print, the noted historian, J. M. Guinn, recorded in the Southern California Historical Society's *Annual Publication* IV, Part I, 1897:

"The first stage ever seen in Southern California arrived in Los Angeles in 1851. It was Gregory's Great Atlantic & Pacific Express from San Francisco and brought the eastern mails to Los Angeles in the unheard-of-time of 'one month and nineteen days.'"

It will be noted that Guinn added to the Thompson & West account to the extent of having San Francisco the point of departure, thus by implication inaugurating stagecoaching between the two cities in 1851.

However, it is to the oft-quoted Hubert Howe Bancroft in *Chronicles of the Builders of the Commonwealth,* Volume V, page 272, that one must bestow the golden loving cup for copying from the famous Los Angeles "mug book" and changing the wording enough to escape plagiarism:

The first mail wagon to come to Los Angeles was one owned by Gregory's express company, which in 1851 delivered the mail one month and nineteen days after it left New York; nevertheless, but for Gregory it might have been much longer on the way, or not have come at all. It was not until 1857 that David Smith ran a line of semi-monthly stages between Los Angeles and Visalia, and thence to San Francisco, or that Wells, Fargo & Co. established an office in the city of the Angels.

A comparison of the above quotation, and several paragraphs that followed, from *Chronicles of the Builders of the Commonwealth* with page 74 of the Thompson & West *History of Los Angeles County, California,* leaves no doubt that Bancroft utilized the latter without so much as a crosscheck with his own great collection of Californiana and without giving credit to his source.

If the original had been accurate, or even a reasonable facsimile of accuracy, there would be little quarrel with the copier. However, a careful check of page 74 of the Thompson & West history with the contemporary issues of the Los Angeles *Star* establishes so many errors on that one page it is hopeless to untangle the mess. Bancroft even fouled his own nest with contradictions, on page 270, Volume V, of his *Chronicles:*

"In 1855 the California company [California Stage Company] established a line to Los Angeles, which was the first overland communication had between that place and San Francisco."

One or two errors and *deliberate deceptions* in the Thompson & West history are worth noting. The reference to the express messenger riding from San Pedro to Los Angeles in one hour and eighteen minutes must come under the category of deliberate deception, the trick being performed by the omission of an important part of the original story. In order to hasten the news of the eastern presidential election results upon the arrival of the steamer, the Pacific Express Company had set up a relay of horses between San Pedro and Los Angeles. The *Star* of December 6, 1856, noted that "four fine horses" were used in the scheme. In an era when five-mile horse races were not uncommon, it should be obvious that the writer for the Thompson & West history had deliberately omitted facts in order to make sensational reading.

The erroneous statement that it was not until 1857 that Wells, Fargo & Company opened an office in Los Angeles was probably due to sloppy research rather than to deception. In view of the fact that Wells Fargo was to become so closely associated with all western stagecoaching, the correct version as it unfolded in the news columns of the Los Angeles *Star* will be given here.

The first germane reference to the famous express and banking house appeared in the *Star* on April 8, 1854, with an advertisement for Leland & McCombs Express "in connexion with Wells, Fargo & Co."

Eight and one-half months later the *Star* ran the following news item:

> Messrs. Wells, Fargo & Co. have purchased the entire interest of Leland & McCombs in their express business in this State and Oregon. Mr. Gilbert, to whom we are indebted for an abundant supply of papers, will be their messenger on the Southern coast, and Dr. H. R. Myles agent for this city. The long established reputation of this firm will impart confidence to our business men and the public generally.[1]

Thus it will be noted that Wells Fargo was active in Los Angeles three years prior to the date cited by Hubert Howe Bancroft in *Chronicles of the Builders of the Commonwealth.*

---

[1] Los Angeles *Star,* Jan. 4, 1855.

Several weeks after the purchase of Leland & McCombs by Wells Fargo, the *Star,* on February 22, 1855, ran the first reports of the failure of Page, Bacon & Company in St. Louis. The ensuing panic runs on the San Francisco banking houses resulted in the failure, among others, of Adams & Company, one of the pioneer express and banking companies in California. Out of the failure a new express concern was born, the *Star* reporting on March 10, 1855:

> The attaches of the house of Adams & Co., have associated themselves together under the title of Pacific Express Company for the purpose of doing an express business within the State of California. The members of the new firm enjoy the confidence of the principal business men in San Francisco. Their energy and perserverance is too well known to need comment. R. Hereford, Esq., will continue as messenger on the southern coast. Charles Johnson, Esq., will act as agent in this city.

Two weeks later, in the *Star* of March 24, 1855, Wells Fargo ran their first advertisement, listing H. R. Myles as agent in charge of the Los Angeles office. On April 21, 1855, Gilbert & Company advertised an express from Los Angeles to Great Salt Lake "in connection with Wells, Fargo & Co." The accompanying article stated:

> Mr. F. Gilbert, well known as a messenger in Wells Fargo & Co.'s express line, will leave this city for Salt Lake the 25th inst., and San Bernardino on the 1st of next month. Mr. Gilbert will connect with Wells, Fargo & Co. at this place, running through to Salt Lake City and intermediate towns, on the first of every month. From the well known popularity of Mr. Gilbert for his energy and promptness in the dispatch of business, we feel confident of his success.

On September 29, 1855, Wells Fargo ran a list of all their agencies from Portland, Oregon, to Honolulu and

Panama City, together with the resident agent for each city. Los Angeles was listed, with H. R. Myles still acting as agent. Despite this incontestable evidence, H. H. Bancroft in his *Chronicles* stated that Wells Fargo did not open an office in Los Angeles until 1857. Hereby hangs one of the more intriguing tales of these early express companies:

With several such concerns operating out of Los Angeles, but Wells Fargo and Pacific Express being the "top dogs," events ran their course until a surprising news item appeared in the October 25, 1856, issue of the Los Angeles *Star:*

> PACIFIC EXPRESS – This company have made an arrangement by which they now exclusively conduct the Express business on the Southern coast, Wells, Fargo & Co. having withdrawn. This company have throughout the State established for themselves a high reputation for promptness and attention to all business entrusted to them, and we are certain the same enterprising spirit will continue to characterize their proceedings in the future.   .   .

Precisely why Wells Fargo should have withdrawn from the express business in Los Angeles in October 1856, is unfathomable. Wells Fargo simply was not in the habit of "withdrawing" in favor of Pacific Express or anyone else. Many scholars have stated that considerable enmity existed between the two business houses, although there is room for suspicion here that insufficient research confused Pacific Express with the much later Pacific Union Express. If enmity did exist, it can be asserted with certainty that Wells Fargo did not quit Los Angeles because of it. There is far more reason to believe the company had found the claims of the *Star* respecting the vast mineral wealth of the southern California mines to be highly exaggerated and that there was not enough profit in the meager bullion shipments (by comparison with the northern mines) to justify an office in Los Angeles. Whatever the reason, the last Wells Fargo advertisement for the moment appeared in the *Star* on November 1, 1856.

The monopoly of Pacific Express was not long-lived. Early in April 1857, the San Francisco *Bulletin* reported that the sheriff had levied attachments upon the Bay City office of the company and was in possession of its assets. The Los Angeles *Star* copied the story on April 11, and the advertisement for Pacific Express expired for all time in the same issue. The *Star* then ran the following news item:

"Wells, Fargo & Co. – Our friend 'Buck' of this old established express and banking house, arrived here this week, for the purpose of establishing a branch office in this city, in the place of Pacific Express which has stopped operations." [2]

In a related story the *Star* noted with undisguised pleasure the arrival of Mr. Buchanan with "an abundant supply of papers from all parts," and added that the company could not have made a more fitting choice. Wells Fargo had arrived in Los Angeles to stay, but it was the above cited news items that were responsible for so many historians quoting 1857 as the date of the company's beginnings in Los Angeles instead of 1854.

The mention of "an abundant supply of papers" brought by Buchanan for the *Star* calls attention to what was probably the most important contribution to the popularity of Wells Fargo during these early years, one that even exceeded its financial reliability. In the days before the telegraph the local newspaper editor

---

[2] *Ibid.,* Apr. 11, 1857. This refers to the express side of the Wells Fargo firm only. It was not until May 28, 1859, that the *Star* announced Wells Fargo had completed arrangements for a banking and exchange business in Los Angeles.

was almost wholly dependent upon his "exchanges" to gather enough news to get out a weekly paper. It was the express companies, in lieu of an almost non-existent mail service, that took care of this item for the fourth estate. No cheaper form of advertising has ever been invented by anyone, the editors always acknowledging the receipt of favors from the express companies in the most glowing terms.

So far as Los Angeles was concerned, Gregory's Great Atlantic & Pacific Express started the practice; and Adams & Company continued it upon opening an office in Los Angeles in 1853. Wells Fargo had purchased Gregory's in late 1852, and naturally continued to supply "favors," as newspapers and other printable matter were called, to the *Star* upon assuming Leland & McCombs' office in Los Angeles. In time the rivalries to see which express company could reach the local newspaper office first with "eastern intelligence" and other "favors" resulted in some of the greatest stagecoach races ever seen in California, both in the mining camps of the north and between San Pedro and Los Angeles.

While many of the past errors in respect to the beginnings of stagecoaching between Los Angeles and San Francisco can be traced to the Thompson & West *History of Los Angeles County, California,* another and much more highly respected source today was equally as guilty. Harris Newmark's *Sixty Years in Southern California* (1916) page 153, under the dating of 1855, stated:

> Shortly after my arrival in Los Angeles the transportation service was enlarged by the addition of a stage line from San Francisco which ran along the Coast from the Northern city to the Old Town of San Diego, making stops along the road, including

San Jose, San Luis Obispo, Santa Barbara and San Buenaventura, and particularly at Los Angeles, where not only horses, but stages and supplies were kept. . .

With such an unimpeachable source from which to quote, it is little wonder that a later authority of the caliber of Oscar O. Winther would write that "before the close of 1853 stage connections were made for the first time between the two sections of the state by way of San Luis Obispo, Santa Barbara, and San Buenaventura."[3]

The misquotation of 1853 for 1855 can be attributed to a typographical error, but it is much more difficult to understand how Professor Winther could then about face and contradict himself forty-five pages later, when referring to the California Stage Company in 1855: "This concern extended, according to Bancroft, a new route between San Francisco and Los Angeles during this year; the opening of this line provided the first direct communication between these points."[4]

Of such ingredients are skepticism and cynicism made. Authorities of the renown of Bancroft and Newmark influencing later generations of authorities and repetition creating beliefs in "facts which really aren't." For let there be no misunderstandings; if there was *any* stagecoaching between Los Angeles and San Francisco by *any* route prior to the advent of the Overland Mail Company in 1858, it was the best kept newspaper secret in the history of southern California. Strangely enough, it was a fine definitive work on the Overland Mail Company that was guilty of one of the worst errors of all. Roscoe and Margaret Conkling in *The Butterfield*

[3] Oscar Osburn Winther, *Express and Stagecoach Days in California* (Stanford, 1936), p. 91.   [4] *Ibid.*, pp. 135-136.

Overland Mail (1947) stated in Volume II, page 259:

In august, 1858, through the energy of Kinyon, the Company acquired a one-half interest in the Coast line from Charlie McLaughlin, who at the time controlled nearly all the stage lines running out of San Francisco. This branch operated under the name of Charles McLaughlin & Company. The Coast route diverged from the Inland route at Cahuenga station, much the same as Ventura boulevard diverges from Cahuenga boulevard and follows the approximate line of the old Mission route up the coast at the present time. The principal stations on the route were: San Buenaventura, Santa Barbara, San Luis Obispo, San Miguel, and San Juan. A junction was again made with the Inland route at Gilroy, and the regular stops made from there to San Francisco.

The road up the coast at the time was little more than a rough winding trail, in some places following along the shore of the ocean. It was not until april, 1861, that Santa Barbara county expended $40,000 to improve the road south to Los Angeles and north to San Luis Obispo.

In june, 1859, the service on this route was increased to a three-times-a-week service, the mails leaving Los Angeles on tuesdays, thursdays, and saturdays. . .

With the possible exception of that portion of the account dealing with the purchase of a one-half interest in McLaughlin's stage line, the whole of the above quotation is in error.

Here, indeed, are authorities that the occasional historian would be rash to challenge: Bancroft, Guinn, Thompson & West, O. O. Winther, Harris Newmark, and the Conklings. Yet challenged they must be and evidence contrary to their findings presented so that the reader may judge for himself the truth of the beginnings of stagecoaching between Los Angeles and San Francisco via the Coast Route.

Ironically, the least important of the various assertions in respect to the first staging between northern and southern California is the one most difficult to impeach. It is possible, although most improbable, that Gregory's Great Atlantic & Pacific Express did bring such a vehicle to Los Angeles in 1851. The first issue of the Los Angeles *Star* appeared on May 17, 1851, and subsequent issues carried advertisements for Gregory's Express. The advertisements clearly indicate that Gregory's was a nautical enterprise: "To the Atlantic States and Europe by semi-weekly steamers, and to the Sandwich Islands and China by American clipper-built sailing vessels. Valuable papers insured, and forwarded by every steamer. . ." There followed a list of towns and cities, all of which were either river towns or ports of call on the coast. The only indication that Gregory used overland travel in California was the statement: "and to all parts of the mines on the arrival of each steamer." While Gregory emphasized that he had no connections with any other company, there was nothing to indicate his concern operated stages from the wharves to the mines.

Precisely when the cliché originated that Gregory brought the eastern mails to Los Angeles "in the unheard-of-time of one month and nineteen days" is uncertain to this writer. It may have appeared in one of the numerous missing issues of the *Star* during 1851. A careful search of all available issues of the newspaper through 1851 and 1852 revealed a number of similarly worded notices:

> We received our papers and letters last week through Gregory's express, which arrived in advance of the mail. We improve the present opportunity to tender thanks to Mr. Gregory for this and similar favors. His energy and enterprise have placed him ahead of his competition. . .[5]

[5] Los Angeles *Star*, May 17, 1851.

We are indebted to Gregory's Express for files of New York and Boston papers to the 20th January, and for San Francisco papers to the 26th ult.[6]

We owe the great Gregory many thanks for his attention. In the absence of any mail by the steamers, his express has proved the greatest convenience to our citizens.[7]

(At this time the mail was unloaded at San Diego and carried to Los Angeles on muleback semi-monthly.)

One thing is conspicuous by its absence in all the above quotations: No mention is made in any form to stagecoaching being involved in Gregory's promptness. If the express company brought any wheeled vehicle to southern California in 1851, it was probably a primitive spring wagon for the purpose of transporting express from San Pedro to Los Angeles. At no time was there any report made in the *Star* of stagecoaches or of Gregory transporting passengers to or from San Pedro. Less than a month before Wells Fargo bought out the great Gregory, the *Star* copied an article from the New Orleans *True Delta* which documented well the man's operations:

Only three years ago, when Mr. Gregory landed at San Francisco, an Express on the Pacific Ocean was entirely unknown. By his industry and reliable regularity exerted to meet the wants of California, he has established offices of his Express in this city, Boston, Honolulu, Hong Kong, New York, Liverpool, London, and Paris, to each of which Gold Dust, Letters, etc., are forwarded via Nicaragua, in charge of special faithful agents. But the fame of this Express has been acquired chiefly by the two facts that, running via Nicaragua and New York, they have delivered gold at the Bank of England in thirty-eight days! and also delivered a chest of tea to President Fillmore, at Washington, only seventy-two days from Hong Kong, China, via San Francisco.[8]

---

[6] *Ibid.,* Mar. 6, 1852.   [7] *Ibid.,* Sept. 18, 1852.   [8] *Ibid.,* Oct. 16, 1852.

WELLS FARGO ADVERTISEMENT
This Wells Fargo ad of March 24, 1855, refutes H. H. Bancroft's assertions that the express company did not open an office in Los Angeles until April 1857.

GREGORY'S EXPRESS ADVERTISEMENT
This Los Angeles Star ad for Gregory's Great Atlantic & Pacific Express began May 17, 1851, and ran until purchase by Wells, Fargo in 1852.

Before consigning the great Gregory back to obscurity, one final reference must be cited. It is important, not only because it gives every indication of being the source from whence the Thompson & West *History of Los Angeles County, California,* distorted the information on that infamous page 74, but for the exasperating omission of knowledge concerning Gregory which must have been known at the time but that appears to have become lost through the years. The author was Judge Benjamin Hayes writing in his portion of *An Historical Sketch of Los Angeles County, California* (1876):

> Certainly we have not violated the maxim – "hasten slowly." The *Senator,* Capt. Thomas Seeley, three times a month, and the overland stages three times a week, in the Summer of 1859, were god-sends to the public. At sea, we were glad to have parted with *Ohio, Goliath,*[9] *Sea Bird,* and *Southerner,* although memory is true to the pleasant companionship of their Haleys and other officers. On land we hailed Wells, Fargo & Co., April 11, 1857, when "Buck" – A. W. Buchanan, Esq. – came down to establish a branch; and have pardoned Gregory's great Atlantic & Pacific Express of 1851, and the mails – a month and nineteen days from the East. . .[10]

For what "crime" had the great Gregory been "pardoned?" Was the Judge merely being facetious over the notoriously slow ship-isthmus-ship-muleback mail service of the period? Certainly the *Star* during the entire span of Gregory's existence in Los Angeles had nothing but the highest praise for the express company. What then was the Judge's meaning? *Quien sabe.*

There are too many missing issues of the Los Angeles *Star* during the first three and one-half years of its pub-

---

9 This ship is always listed as the *Goliah* in the *Star.*

10 Col. J. J. Warner, Judge Benjamin Hayes, and Dr. J. P. Widney, *An Historical Sketch of Los Angeles County, California* (Los Angeles, 1876), p. 100.

lication to be overly positive about any assertion. These gaps, while exasperating, are not such as to preclude reasonably accurate deductions in respect to most events. For example, the first advertisement for the stage line of Alexander & Banning from San Pedro to Los Angeles appeared in the issue of February 12, 1853, the first issue available for that year. It is dated January 29, in the lower left hand corner, indicating the date when it was originally inserted.

An advertisement for Banning's rival, B. A. Townsend, appeared in the *Star* on April 2, 1853, emphasizing an "Accomodation line of stages, Los Angeles and San Pedro." It was Townsend, so far as the *Star* was concerned, who brought the first vehicle worthy of the name "stagecoach" to Los Angeles:

> Mr. Townsend, whose advertisement will be found in another column, has brought down from the north a fine Troy Coach, which he is running between this city and San Pedro. This looks like enterprise and we like to see it. Every thing which increases our travelling facilities is deserving of praise, and we wish all such success.[11]

On April 22, 1854, Alexander & Banning advertised semi-monthly stages between San Pedro and San Bernardino; and on August 24, 1854, Lanfranco & Sepulveda advertised a line of stages "leaving Estero de San Pedro for Los Angeles, and vice versa, on the arrival of every steamer or sailing vessel when there are passengers."

A. W. Timms, a forwarding and commission merchant, advertised "a line of stages will leave San Pedro for Los Angeles immediately on the arrival of each steamer." By the time this appeared, on June 23, 1855,

---

11 Los Angeles *Star*, May 7, 1853. The *Star* of Apr. 24, 1858, reported that Phineas Banning was manufacturing his own stagecoaches and using harness made in Los Angeles by E. Workman.

the continuity of the *Star* files is excellent, with only an occasional missing issue. It is inconceivable that any such venture as a stagecoach line between Los Angeles and San Francisco could have escaped the notice of the editor or that he would have considered it unworthy of reporting.

On April 18, 1857, the previously noted stage line of David Smith from Los Angeles to Visalia via Fort Tejon and Kern River was announced. Contrary to the statements made in the Thompson & West *History of Los Angeles County, California,* and H. H. Bancroft's *Chronicles of the Builders of the Commonwealth,* Smith's advertisement made no claims in any form to going beyond Visalia, or of making connections at that point for through travel to San Francisco.

It is difficult to tell just how long Smith's line was in operation. The week prior to his initial advertisement, the *Star* had reported in a news item that: "The contract for carrying the U.S. Mail on route 12544, Los Angeles to Visalia, semi-monthly trips, is let to David Smith, of Kern Fiver, and will go into operation immediately. The mail will leave here immediately after the arrival of each steamer." [12]

Smith's advertisement ceased after May 16, 1857, a deletion of no significance. Of far more interest is the fact that the United States Post Office Department had originally advertised, beginning March 14, 1857, Route 12,544 as Route 12,575, and specified that bidders had until June 15, 1857, to submit bids. However, in the *Star* of April 11, the contract was announced as let, two months before the bids were supposed to be closed. Truly, there were queer business methods in the United States Post Office Department in those days.

[12] Los Angeles *Star,* Apr. 11, 1857.

There were, of course, other venturous souls willing
to gamble on making a fortune by running out of Los
Angeles with six-in-hand and, if lucky, one or two inside: H. W. Osborne with a daily line from Los Angeles to the San Gabriel Mission in 1857; Allen &
Brazleton to San Bernardino, and Henry Roberts' San
Gabriel Mines Stage Line in 1859. There were others,
but one outstanding fact is always evident: At no time
during this period was any mention made or implied of
a stage line from Los Angeles to San Francisco via the
Coast Route. A news item appearing in the *Star* on
February 8, 1855, is the only one giving pause for
serious consideration:

> CALIFORNIA STAGE COMPANY – The Superintendent of this
> Company, Mr. W. H. Hall, arrived on the last steamer. The
> horses came down by land and arrived here last week in good
> condition. One fine Concord coach was brought down on the
> *America,* and three more will be received by the next steamer.
> Such enterprise has a cheering effect, as it gives us the assurance
> that we shall soon have a stage route to the States, either by way
> of Salt Lake or the Gila River and El Paso.

In the weeks that followed, not one follow-up item of
news appeared explaining what happened to those
horses and the "one fine Concord coach." No mention
was ever made of the arrival of the other three coaches
expected on the next steamer. If Warren Hall and the
California Stage Company had any intentions of opening a line between the north and Los Angeles at this
time, they changed their collective minds upon Hall's
examination of the rough terrain and lack of roads surrounding Los Angeles. However, it was probably this
news item copied in a San Francisco newspaper that
was responsible for Bancroft's assertion concerning the
California Stage Company opening a line to Los Angeles in 1855.

What possibly occurred was revealed in the very next issue of the *Star,* when an advertisement appeared for the "Southern Express, for Kern River Mines, Tejon Reservation, Elizabeth Lake, and San Fernando. Arrangements have been made and horses placed on the line for an Express to leave on the arrival of every steamer from San Francisco. This express will carry nothing but light packages, and go through with dispatch. Every effort will be made to deserve patronage. Heavy packages forwarded by stage or wagons." [13] The advertisement was signed by A. Bell, Jr.

It is possible that Bell had purchased the coach and horses from the California Stage Company, and Hall had merely made the delivery. It is also possible that Hall was readying a line from San Bernardino to the Colorado River. It was here on the desert he would meet death a few years later, actively involved in staging to the end.

If any lingering doubts haunt the reader respecting stagecoaching between Los Angeles and San Francisco prior to 1858, two news items in the *Star* during 1857 should clarify the picture for all time:

STEAMER DAY – This is an institution generally supposed to be peculiar to San Francisco, but such is not the fact, for with us "steamer-day" is of even more importance than it is in the Bay City. *Here we are cut off from all communication with the outer world, except bi-monthly, on steamer-day.* With our "neighboring" coastal cities, with the more remote inland cities, the great commercial mart of the State, the "capital" city, the mining cities, as well as the busy world outside our State limits, with all its ramifications of friendship, business and pleasure – with all these *we can communicate only on steamer-day.* And for the dispatch of all these requirements, we are generally allowed about a couple of days. When, therefore, our merchants and business men re-

13 *Ibid.,* Feb. 22, 1855. The advertisement is dated Feb. 15, an issue which is missing.

ceive their correspondence, their bills, and all have to be answered and attended to in the brief time allowed – it may easily be conceived that steamer time is a busy time here, and steamer-day one of no little importance. Hence the hurry and bustle of that day, the running to and fro, the galloping in hot haste, the loading and departure of the long lines of monster wagons, with their ten and twelve-mule teams, the coursing of gaudy stages [the steamer stages are meant here] the driving fast and furious, of the numerous expert "whips," the rush to the Post and Express offices and the eager pleadings for "one moment longer" – in short, the thousand and one circumstances which attend hasty dispatch of all business matters. Then follow the meeting and treating, and parting of friends, the jingling of glasses and "pop" of champagne, when the cry "all aboard" stops the revelry; then comes a rush for seats, crack goes the whip, off go the horses, and amid adieus and waving of hats and hands, away dash the stages, leaving us for two more weeks to tranquillity and repose. After a while, the next arrival is alluded to – talked of – looked for, and finally, in her own time, she is at hand; when the same scenes are reenacted, the same bustle and hurry, the same crushing and crowding. And so we go all year around – and so it is with us the arrival and departure of the steamer are the great events of our business life.[14]

Stagecoaches? Yes, but only for transportation to the steamers.

It has been (to us) three weeks since the arrival of the steamer. During that time, the budget of news then brought, has been discussed in every phase; all kinds of conjectures have been hazarded on the progress of events then in embryo – and in fact, every possible effort has been made to come to a satisfactory conclusion on the various interesting topics engaging the attention of our more favored friends elsewhere. But all to no avail. We must await steamer day, which will not be till tomorrow; bringing us a three weeks installment of interesting events, political sayings and doings, and all the varied incidents of busy life. When will the time come when we shall enjoy daily communication with the busy marts of commerce? Oh for the realization of that system of

---

[14] *Ibid.*, Mar. 21, 1857. The italics are added.

"speedy communication" with the great cities of the east, so often spoken about, so long promised but still so distant! As for the telegraph – that is something we may dream of! [15]

How is it possible to read a contemporary description of that nature and still believe Harris Newmark's story of transportation being facilitated by a San Francisco to San Diego stage line in 1855? How is it possible to reconcile the above description of "steamer-day" with Bancroft's assertion that the California Stage Company opened overland communications between the north and Los Angeles in 1855? Most important of all, how is it possible to accept the Conklings' version of the Overland Mail Company's purchase of a one-half interest in an operating line of stages up the coast via the present 101 Highway Route in lieu of the following news item which appeared *after* the Butterfield line was in operation:

Proposed Stage Route – The inhabitants of the coast towns of San Luis Obispo, Santa Barbara, and San Buenaventura, and the adjacent country, are very much in want of mail facilities by land with the cities and towns north and south of them. *This locality is perhaps the only one in the State possessing so large a population, without the accomodation of a stage route.* These cities are dependent on the coast steamer for their mail matter, which they obtain only twice a month, as heretofore, while those on the interior line of travel have tri-weekly communication with San Francisco, and semi-weekly with the Eastern States. This state of affairs calls loudly for redress, and we think the Post Office authorities should establish a route to connect the above named cities with the great Overland Mail Line. Stages connecting San Luis, via Santa Barbara, with Los Angeles, would effect this object; and we believe it is proposed to organize this route, should the Department assist by establishing a mail on it. With this reasonable request, in view of the pressing necessity of the case, we have no doubt the authorities would gladly comply. If so, we

---

[15] *Ibid.,* June 6, 1857.

understand that Mr. Banning of this city, would accept the contract, and at once open up this line of communication. The citizens immediately interested should make representation of their wants to the Department, and we have no doubt they will meet with immediate attention.[16]

At the time this article was published, the Overland Mail Company had been running from St. Louis and Memphis to San Francisco for about seven weeks. From Los Angeles the route led through Cahuenga Pass, San Fernando Valley, San Fernando Pass, San Francisquito Canyon, Elizabeth Lake, and Fort Tejon into the San Joaquin Valley, and thence over Pacheco Pass to Gilroy. However, it should be abundantly clear from the above article of November 1858, that there was no such thing as a "Coast Line" in operation that "diverged from the Inland route at Cahuenga station, much the same as Ventura boulevard diverges from Cahuenga boulevard and follows the approximate line of the old Mission route up the coast at the present time. The principal stations on the route were: San Buenaventura, Santa Barbara, San Luis Obispo, San Miguel, and San Juan. A junction was again made with the Inland route at Gilroy.   ." [17]

This matter of the Overland Mail Company and the Coast Route is of such importance because of later developments that a thorough impeachment of the stories concerning its use in the 1850s is paramount.

In February 1859, the Santa Barbara *Gazette* published a short news item to the effect that a group of Los Angeles business men were in town endeavoring to persuade the citizens of the Channel City to repair the

[16] *Ibid.,* Nov. 6, 1858. The italics are added.

[17] Roscoe Conkling and Margaret Conkling, *The Butterfield Overland Mail* (Glendale, 1947), vol. II, p. 259. Permission to quote by courtesy of The Arthur H. Clark Company.

county road to Los Angeles, "promising that they will in such case establish a regular stage line between the two towns." [18]

It will be recalled that the Conklings in *The Butterfield Overland Mail* had asserted that an existent semi-weekly stagecoach service via the Coast Route was increased to tri-weekly service in 1859. The following letter published in the *Star* of May 12, 1860, should put to rest for all time *any* claims of coastal staging between Los Angeles and San Francisco in the 1850s:

> San Francisco, May 2, 1860. Editor *Star* – According to promise, I write, but I am sorry I cannot write more interestingly. I arrived here in four weeks by way of the Coast route – the grass excellent all the way. It is raining today, and the prospect for the farmer, grazier, horticulturist is said to be better than ever before.
>
> The good people of Santa Barbara and San Luis Obispo are nursing what I consider the vain hope that the Overland Mail line will be changed from the present to the Coast route. As a friend of the overland mail, without any special interest in the route, I should regret to hear of the change. *I consider the latter named route as being impracticable in its present condition for a stage road,* and it will require a greater expenditure of money to put it in a passable condition than can possibly be raised by the settlements along the route. I question very much whether the country can be made equal, topographically, by any probable amount of expenditure, to that by which the mail is at present conveyed.

How was it possible for so many prominent historians to be so badly in error on this matter of coastal staging? It should be noted at the outset that it has only been within recent years that a microfilm file of all known issues of the Los Angeles *Star* has been available for research. It should also be noted in rebuttal thereto that many eminent scholars would have scorned the news-

---

[18] Los Angeles *Star*, Feb. 26, 1859. Reprinted from the Santa Barbara *Gazette*.

paper as a research tool even though it had been at hand. The Thompson & West histories had obviously used the newspaper files, although much of their information was misinterpreted or distorted; and Bancroft in his *Chronicles* had just as obviously copied from the Thompson & West. Later scholars accepted Bancroft at face value, little realizing that they were, in essence, quoting second and third-hand information which they would have belittled in its more accurate, original form.

If these later generations of scholars had only stop- to rationalize upon the logistics of starting a five hundred-mile stage line, probably each would have smelled the proverbial mouse. The enormity of the job of locating and building stations with an unfailing water supply every fifteen to twenty-five miles, stocking them with horses, harness, and feed – supervised by competent station-keepers, with blacksmiths and wheelwrights in close proximity – all this together with the best available drivers had to be in working order before the first stagecoach turned a wheel.

Then if our scholars had merely checked the census records for 1850 and 1860 in the counties south of Santa Clara, suspicions regarding the claims of Harris Newmark, H. H. Bancroft, and J. M. Guinn would have surfaced. Even as late as 1860 Santa Barbara County (which then included Ventura County) could boast of but 3,543 persons; San Luis Obispo County had 1,782, and Monterey 4,739. If the 4,385 inhabitants of the "City" of Los Angeles are added, the total was less than 15,000 souls to which a stage line could look to for patronage; and most of these were using the coastal steamers whenever travel was necessary.

Conclusions that are based upon false information or

misinterpretations of correct information will invariably be in error or partially so. The assumption by historians that a Los Angeles to San Francisco coast line of stages was in operation merely because Harris Newmark and H. H. Bancroft said so, and because the Overland Mail Company purchased a one-half interest in Charley McLaughlin's line running south out of San Francisco, is a fine example. At the time this transaction was made, McLaughlin's line reached no farther south than Monterey; but because it was popularly known as "The Coast Line," many writers concluded it continued on to Los Angeles and even San Diego. They had Newmark and Bancroft to sustain their contentions.

The purpose behind the Overland Mail Company's purchase should be readily apparent. From Gilroy to San Francisco the line of McLaughlin would overlap that of the Overland Mail. By purchasing a one-half interest in McLaughlin's line, the Overland would acquire operating stations, stock, and personnel, thus avoiding a duplication of effort. Since the original Butterfield contract did not provide for a way mail service, there would have been little competition involved between the two lines, McLaughlin holding the mail contract from San Francisco to Monterey. Subsequent friction which may have developed after way mail service was established would have been irrelevant to the facts at the time of the purchase. The Overland Mail would have had no use for a line from Gilroy south along the Coast Route. The transaction makes sense, then, only if one understands that the terminus of the McLaughlin line was at Monterey.

The statement of the Conklings respecting the increase of service on the Coast Route in June 1859, was another example of a wrong conclusion reached because of their erroneous assumption that such a line existed. The Los Angeles *Star* of June 18, 1859, had reported:

"The stages of the overland mail company now leave and arrive in Los Angeles, to and from San Francisco, three times a week, leaving here on Tuesdays, Thursdays, and Saturdays."

The Overland Mail had been operating tri-weekly over the Inland Route to San Francisco from the beginning, usually on Mondays, Wednesdays, and Fridays. The authors of *The Butterfield Overland Mail* apparently concluded that the above quotation had to mean the Coast Route. It was in fact a change of departure day notice for the regular Inland Route.

Another fine example of an error which resulted from the almost universal acceptance of the "fact" that an operating stage line existed up the coast was Vernette Snyder Ripley's "The San Fernando Pass and the Traffic That Went Over It":

> Right up to the time the first stage of the Butterfield Overland Mail took the New Pass, *on its way up the coast,* for two months, three times a week, the company's stages from San Francisco had labored over the Pass on their way down, then struggled up it on their way back.[19]

It was just not true. The Overland Mail Company did start operating between San Francisco and Los Angeles some two weeks prior to the time their contract

---

[19] Vernette Snyder Ripley, "The San Fernando Pass and the Traffic That Went Over It," Southern California Historical Society *Quarterly*, xxx (March 1948), p. 52. The italics are added. The reader should not confuse "New Pass" as used here with Williams Pass, which was also called "New Pass." It is now Soledad Canyon. The author was distinguishing between the new route over the San Fernando Hill and the old route, or *El Camino Viejo* (also *Cuesta*), which was farther to the east.

with the Post Office Department was due to go into effect on September 15, 1858; but the runs were made over the regular Inland Route, not "up the coast."

Most authors who committed this and similar errors based their contentions on the wording in the Waterman L. Ormsby narrative. Ormsby was a New York newspaper correspondent and the only through passenger on the first westbound Overland Mail run:

> I should have mentioned, before, that the Overland Mail Company, through the energy of Mr. Kinyon, have been running a tri-weekly stage between San Francisco and Los Angeles, for nearly two months, using the Concord coach to San Jose and the canvass-covered thoroughfare wagons the rest of the distance.[20]

From that one slightly faulty paragraph grew some mighty erroneous conclusions.

One of the more interesting sources of errors involves semantics. *El Camino Real* to the Californian meant something entirely different than that which was conjured up in the mind of the American translator. The former was a citizen of the saddle; the latter was an addict of the wheel. At this time the word "road" could be defined as a corridor or right of way over which it was legally permissible to travel, usually on foot or horseback, without interference from adjoining landowners. When such a right of way was improved to permit wheeled vehicles to pass, it was invariably referred to in the newspapers and supervisors' minutes as a *"wagon* road." Early American maps showing "Old Conejo Road" were veritable tar pits for the researcher who took the word "road" literally. It was not until 1874 that a writer to the Ventura *Signal* suggested building a *wagon* road up the present 101 Highway

---

[20] Waterman L. Ormsby, *The Butterfield Overland Mail*, edited by Lyle H. Wright and Josephine Bynum (San Marino, California, 1942), p. 127.

Route into the Conejo: "I do not know if this trail I speak of has ever been prospected with a view of securing a wagon road through it, but I am satisfied a good easy grade can be secured.   .   ." [21]

It was all very well for those writers who insisted upon the existence of a stage line up the coast to excuse the road conditions on *El Camino Real* with descriptions such as: "The road up the coast at the time was little more than a rough winding trail, in some places following along the shore of the ocean." [22] *Of course* stagecoaches could have rolled over the "trails" of the San Fernando and Pleasant valleys, as well as the Las Posas, Simi, Carpinteria, Santa Maria, Santa Ynez, or any of the other numerous valleys and rolling hills on the Coast Route; but no wheels would ever cross that boulder-strewn Santa Susana Pass until the first wagon road was completed over it in 1861.

Despite the "easy grade" in the imagination of the letter writer to the *Signal* in 1874, the mere thought of dropping over the declivitous point of the Conejo with a stagecoach where ranchos Guadalasca, Calleguas, and Conejo meet should have brought early writers and researchers to an abrupt halt.

The beach road, while a nuisance at times, was more of a thrill than a danger. The exception was the mile of road south of Rincon Point, where more often than not huge beach boulders were a hazard at high tide. It was passable, but ahead lay the Gaviota and La Cuesta passes to be crossed before any Jehu with four or six-in-hand could breathe with ease.

"El Camino" can only be translated intelligently as "The Route" when referring to events prior to 1850, or even 1860. The lone reference found by this writer to a

[21] Ventura *Signal*, Dec. 12, 1874.   [22] Conkling, *op. cit.*, p. 259.

lengthy journey on wheels before the American occupation appeared in volume XXIX, no. 1, of the Southern California Historical Society *Quarterly,* which described a trip of "a train of carretas" on two occasions from Santa Barbara to Los Angeles. It is noteworthy that the route taken was via the Santa Clara Valley and over the San Fernando Pass, *not* by Conejo Valley or Santa Susana Pass. The route over the San Fernando Pass used at that time was later known as *El Camino Viejo* (also *Cuesta*) or the Old Road (or Hill) to distinguish it from the newer route that crossed the mountains at the point where Beale later made his famous cut. The old cuesta was probably the most dangerous and notorious mountain crossing in the West at the time. The route taken by the carretas was a dozen miles longer than either the Conejo or Santa Susana Pass routes. It can, therefore, be assumed with a certainty that neither of the latter routes was passable for a carreta or any other wheeled vehicle.

Another problem in semantics concerns the usage of "Santa Susana" as it was applied by early explorers and cartographers to the connecting range of mountains from Calabasas to the San Gabriel Range. At least three early references were noted to "a pass over the Santa Susana mountains" where the writer obviously had the San Fernando Pass in mind. The unwary researcher, however, would logically assume that the present Santa Susana Pass was intended and arrive at erroneous conclusions thereby. The Los Angeles *Express* in August 1871, called attention to the report of Lieutenant Parks of the United States Army, noting: "The Santa Clara river, of which the Simi is tributary, is called Simi above the junction of that stream; and the San Fernando Pass is called the Simi Pass in the Lieutenant's report." [23] In view of the fact that Simi Creek comes no closer than seven miles to the Santa Clara River (and that as the crow flies over the intervening 2000-foot-high South Mountain), it would be difficult to judge between the greater error – the Lieutenant's or that of the *Express!*

It was probably a similar circumstance that resulted in J. R. Knowland stating in *California, A Landmark History* (1941), that the Santa Susana Pass stagecoach road was started in 1822. It is doubtful if there was enough blasting powder in all of Alta California in 1822 to have constructed one hundred yards of that solid rock road.

The key to the correct answers to all California stage-coaching, except in the Sierra mining country, lay in the United States Mail contracts. No stage line of any length outside of the rich mining areas could begin to operate at a profit without such a subsidy. Writers of Western history have made much ado and glamorous glory out of Butterfield's great Overland Mail Company, and James Birch's San Antonio to San Diego Mail of the previous year. The recent centennials of these favorites of historians are still fresh in most minds, but seldom if ever were the financial consequences of those famous mail routes mentioned by the banquet speakers. The Overland Mail Company received $600,-000 per annum for the semi-weekly mail service from St. Louis and Memphis to San Francisco. The first year of operation the Post Office Department received in revenue $27,229.94. [24]

The San Antonio to San Diego mail contract was let to James Birch, famed as the man who "put an empire

---

[23] Santa Barbara *Press*, Aug. 19, 1871. Reprinted from the Los Angeles *Express*.   [24] *Report of the Postmaster General, 1859, pp. 25 & 40.*

on wheels," for $196,000. The Post Office Department received in revenue from the line the princely sum of $601.00.[25] Little wonder it was called "The Jackass Mail," although few Western history buffs are willing to concede who the jackasses were.

One man that did grasp the significance of such enormous deficits was Postmaster General Joseph Holt, who had succeeded Aaron Brown, the United States Postmaster General at the time of the letting of the contracts for the Overland Mail and the San Antonio to San Diego Mail. Holt expressed his philosophy on such matters in most lucid terms in *The Report of the Postmaster General, 1859:*

> There are those who maintain that the adjustment of the mail service should be made subservient, if not subordinate, to the interests of commerce and travel, and that the rapid and cheap conveyance of passengers, and the support of railroad, steamboat, and stage companies, should be as carefully looked to and as anxiously provided for by the department as the transportation of the mails. This is a fatal fallacy, whose bitter fruits may now be seen in the enormous sums paid to these companies for mails, some of which are so light as scarcely to yield a revenue sufficient to defray expense of carrying them on horseback. . .

There are those who would argue that considerations other than money entered into the case. The rabid Western American history fan would consider it treason even to mention filthy lucre where the Overland and Jackass mails were concerned. The Conklings, while devoting three pages in *The Butterfield Overland Mail* to Holt's "lack of friendly feelings towards the Californians," secured a moot revenge by not listing the man's name in their index, except in an inconspicuous sub-note under the "California" index heading.

---

25 *Ibid.*

It remained for a later Postmaster General, Alexander W. Randall, to define the opposing viewpoint:

> Large sums of money are paid every year to contractors for carrying mails beyond our frontiers, across the central wilderness, to the Pacific States; and other large sums are paid for service on lines tributary to the main lines, to accomodate as yet sparse settlements. From these, comparatively small returns come back in the shape of postal revenues. Yet these very agencies invite settlement and encourage enterprise in material development, so that there comes back to the people in real wealth almost as many millions of dollars as the government expends thousands in this particular branch of the service.[26]

If Randall had been content to state his case and let it rest, there would have been only the two sides to the coin and at most a nice loud discussion on the merits of each; but the Postmaster General had to go "all out" for the postal service: "It has done more to aid in enlightening and Christianizing the people than anything else except the spelling-book and Bible."[27]

The Christianizing capabilities of the United States Postal Service must be considered as argumentative at best.

Regardless of one's philosophy on such matters, the fact remains that without a contract to carry the United States Mails, few stagecoach lines in the old West could have survived. A closer look at the California mails in the late 1840s and the 1850s is therefore in order.

---

[26] *Report of the Postmaster General, 1866,* p. 15.   [27] *Ibid.,* p. 14.

2

The California Mails, 1847-1861

The parsimonious gunfire of the Mexican War in California had barely ceased its puny reverberations from the Sierra Madres when Brigadier General Stephen Watts Kearny issued an Army order establishing a fortnightly mail "service" between San Diego and San Francisco. A party consisting of two soldiers on horseback was to leave each city on Monday, April 19, 1847, carrying letters and papers free of charge. The parties were ordered to meet at Captain Dana's ranch at Nipomo the following Sunday, exchange sacks, and return to their respective starting points by the next Sunday. The process was to be repeated beginning the following Monday and so continuing.

Historian J. M. Guinn noted that the soldiers were discharged during the latter part of 1848 and a "semioccasional" mail service established between San Diego, Los Angeles, and San Francisco by sailing ships.[1]

The Postmaster General in Washington, D.C. looked upon this thing called "California" more formally and with no little bewilderment, noting, "The laws regulating the post office duties and services are in many respects ill adapted to the circumstances and conditions of that country."[2]

Citing an Act of Congress approved August 14, 1848, whereby he was authorized to appoint postmasters in California and "places on the Pacific," and to appoint

---

[1] Southern California Historical Society *Annual Publication,* IV, Part I, 1897.
[2] *Report of the Postmaster General, Executive Document I,* Dec. 3, 1849, p. 785.

postal agents for making arrangements to establish post offices, the Postmaster General continued:

> Under this Act, as early as November 1848, a postmaster was appointed for San Francisco, and agents were appointed and sent on that business. That postmaster entered on his duties, and for a time attempted their discharge; but finding, as he writes, no sufficient income from the postage to pay the expense of room and assistance, or even for his support, he resigned. No report from those agents has ever been received. In April last another agent was sent, who immediately departed and entered upon his duties, and also another postmaster for San Francisco, who has also arrived there; and from information received from them and others, there is good reason to believe that all reasonable exertions are being made to give the people there all the mail facilities the limited means legally applicable will afford. . .[3]

The Postmaster General's confusion was unabated the following year, when he noted in his annual report that the mail service in California was still in an unsettled state and only partially reported. He then continued by mumbling something incoherent about "the very peculiar state of affairs in that distant region. . ."[4]

Obviously, the head of the United States Post Office Department could not grasp a very simple fact, one that was devoid of any peculiarities whatsoever: It was impossible to run the San Francisco Post Office or establish a line of postal facilities on the Pacific coast and at the same time shovel pay dirt into a cradle or Long Tom in the Sierra foothills.

It is regrettable that the Postmaster General failed to give a detailed report concerning the activities of that second agent, who had in turn appointed still another special agent to establish those post offices from San

---

[3] *Ibid.*

[4] *Report of the Postmaster General, Executive Document 1,* Nov. 30, 1850, p. 407.

Francisco to Los Angeles. This new agent was J. Ross Browne, who would gain fame and $10,000 for recording and transcribing the proceedings of the convention in September and October of 1849, to form the State Constitution. It is to Browne himself that we owe the record of his commission "to establish a line of Post-offices on the land route to Los Angeles, and enter into contracts for the carrying of the mails." [5]

Browne's account in "A Dangerous Journey" made no further reference to post office business, although the shadow of sinister events to come permeates the tale. He did not travel farther south than San Luis Obispo during the trip in the summer of 1849, and the only post office established was at San Jose. One wonders if he or that special agent ever reported to Washington his findings on the dangerous conditions he encountered. It is inconceivable that contracts for carrying the mails on horseback from Monterey to Los Angeles would even have been considered if the conditions described by Browne in "A Dangerous Journey" had been presented to the United States Post Office Department.

If ever a land was infested with cutthroats, murderers, thieves, and desperadoes of every description, that portion of the future Coast Line Stage Route between Mission Soledad and Santa Barbara was it. Browne reported that in 1849, several drovers who had started from San Francisco to purchase cattle on the southern ranchos had never reached their destination.

[5] J. Ross Browne, "A Dangerous Journey," *Harper's New Monthly Magazine,* XXIV (May 1862), p. 741. See also: *Muleback to the Convention, Letters of J. Ross Browne,* Book Club of California, 1950, and David Michael Goodman, *A Western Panorama 1849-1875, the travels, writings and influence of J. Ross Browne on the Pacific Coast, and in Texas, Nevada, Arizona and Baja California, as the first Mining Commissioner, and Minister to China* (The Arthur H. Clark Company, Glendale, California, 1966), p. 33.

In two instances the mutilated remains of the bodies were found, and the others were presumed to have been victims of foul play.

> At that period the laws existing were those administered by the Alcaldes, under the Mexican system, which had been temporarily adopted in connection with the provisional government established by General Riley. The people generally were too deeply interested in the development of the gold regions to give themselves much concern about conditions of other parts of the country; and the chances of bringing criminals to punishment in the southern districts were very remote.[6]

Not that Santa Barbara, San Luis Obispo, and Monterey counties had a monopoly on lawlessness. The Los Angeles *Star* for the first twenty years covered by the files contains some of the most shocking crime reading imaginable. The difference lay in the fact that there were more "white hats" in Los Angeles to assist in the application of justice, not infrequently handed down by "Judge Lynch," than there were in the central counties. The latter were fast learners, however. The *Star* for July 10, 1858, reported that three *more* desperadoes had been killed in San Luis Obispo County by citizens attempting to cure the infection that festered in their midst. Here in Santa Barbara, San Luis Obispo, and southern Monterey counties the Old West was more than wild. It was evil, it was hideously insane, and *it was damned dangerous:*

> Supposed Murder – We alluded last week to the disappearance of Mr. John Caldwell, the mail contractor between Monterey and San Diego, and the supposition that he had been killed by Indians. Mr. Caldwell was last seen at Mission Santa Ines, thirty miles from Santa Barbara, on the 21st June. He stopped at the Mission all night, and two Americans who had slept at the same

---

6 *Ibid.*

house, followed Mr. Caldwell about an hour after his departure. The distance between the Mission where Mr. Caldwell was last seen, and the next rancho, is about four miles. The owner of the ranch knew him and would have seen him had he passed. Mr. Caldwell was from Ohio and about 50 years of age.[7]

An advertisement offering a $500 reward for information leading to the discovery and conviction of Caldwell's murderers appeared in the *Star* on August 2, 1851. An additional "liberal reward" was offered for the discovery of his body and the mail, the advertisement furnishing the further information that the United States Mail contractor was last seen on June 22, 1851, riding "an ordinary sized grey mule."

No further mention of the missing mail rider ever appeared in any of the issues of the *Star* now available, nor could any information on the subject be found in the records of the United States Post Office Department. It should be noted, however, that the Special Agent for postal matters in California accepted on a temporary basis on October 16, 1851, Caldwell's low bid to carry the mails on Route 5084 from Los Angeles to Santa Barbara, and as late as January 15, 1852, a notation appeared on the worksheet for Route 5084 that the contract had been accepted in Washington on a permanent basis. Nothing could more perfectly illustrate the inconvenience of the slow communications of the times – acceptance of a government contract seven months after the death of the low bidder.

At this time the mail arrangements from the east were rather novel to say the least. It was carried by steamers

---

[7] Los Angeles *Star*, July 12, 1851. Neill C. Wilson in *Treasure Express* (New York, 1936), p. 17, claimed that Caldwell was shot by Indians "who left him where he fell." Wilson cited no source for this statement. The appearance of a $500 reward for the finding of Caldwell's body six weeks after his disappearance would seem to refute Wilson's version.

twice monthly to Aspinwall or Chagres on the east coast
of Panama, then across the isthmus by the Government
of New Granada under a treaty agreement which provided for compensation according to the weight of the
mails. On the west coast the Pacific Mail Steamship
Company contracted to carry the mails *monthly* from
Panama to Oregon, with stops at San Diego, Monterey
and San Francisco. Thus the eastern mails were delivered bi-monthly but picked up only monthly at the
isthmus. From San Diego and Monterey it was supposed to be delivered north and south respectively by
horseback riders. The Postmaster General in his report
of November 29, 1851, noted that the delivery-pickup
discrepancy at the isthmus had been corrected through
a new contract with the Pacific Mail Steamship Company for bi-monthly deliveries on the west coast.

For years following Caldwell's murder, however, the
picture is blurred and confused insofar as the mail riders
from Monterey to Los Angeles are concerned. The
fuzzy image can be attributed to many factors, not the
least of which are the Post Office records that have been
lost, strayed, or stolen, and the Department's innumerable combinations of mail routes and re-advertisements
for bids. Add to this the submission of "straw bids,"
plus the sale and transfer of routes by the contractors,
and a veritable jigsaw puzzle emerges out of the postal
arrangements. In this maze of bureaucratic bungling,
and contractual juggling for profits, the chronologically
arranged news items from the contemporary newspapers
are an invaluable aid to decipher the puzzle. Caution
must be used, however, because of editorial prejudices
and policies, and constant checks made with *available*
postal records to insure some degree of accuracy. It will

be conceded that the end result may produce errors in specific cases, but the general picture should reflect a fairly accurate portrayal of the era.

The Los Angeles *Star* on March 27, 1852, reported disappointment that the expected visit of the California Mail Agent had not materialized:

> The report has got to be such an old story now, that we fear the agent has given up all idea of coming, if, indeed, he ever had any such intention, and we must jog along at the same old rate, and take comfort from the reflection that the steamers running up and down the coast, will keep us tolerably informed of what is going on. The last mail brought us San Francisco dates to the 12th instant – the *Sea Bird,* which arrived the day before, brought us papers as late as the 19th.

The above news item conveys the information that the mails were still coming down from the north by horseback riders, while the express shipments via the Steampship *Sea Bird* were able to beat the rider's time by one week.

Again, on June 26, 1852, the *Star* helps fill in the gaps with the following news report:

> A fortnight ago, the mail rider arrived from San Diego with the letters for this place and *the towns above,* but without a single newspaper; alleging as an excuse, that they were not ready when he left, and he couldn't wait; and our Postmaster informs us that by the last arrival he received papers which had been mailed from this office in January last for the States, and moreover, that such occurrences are very frequent.[8]

It will be noted that insofar as the editor of the *Star* was concerned, the prime evil of the mail arrangements as cited above was the arrival of the carrier without the eastern newspapers which he had relied upon for reprint material to fill up the columns of his Los Angeles

---

[8] Italics added.

newspaper. The Postmaster General presented the other side of the case in 1853:

> The most striking discrepancy appears, on comparing these prices which the government pays in California with those which it receives for the same work – I mean the rates of postage. The one is graduated to the highest scale of prices, and the other to the lowest. For a single letter of half an ounce the department receives six cents when prepaid, and ten cents when unpaid; and for each pound of printed matter, which comprises a very large proportion of the contents of the mails, about five cents a pound, the cost to the department for transportation across the isthmus alone being twenty-two cents a pound. The necessary consequence is, that the cost of mail service in California greatly exceeds the revenue it yields.
>
> And not withstanding the government incurs a heavy unrefunded expenditure in supplying citizens of that State with his letters, newspapers, and other mail matter, the citizen himself employs other facilities for the conveyance of his letters, and pays therefor at a rate from twenty to forty-fold greater than the government charges for similar service.
>
> The facilities referred to are the expresses   .   .   .[9]

The newspaper editors might well have asked for a definition of the word "service." If one is to believe only a portion of the criticism in the contemporary newspapers, Uncle Sam's postal bureaucrats could have taken several lessons from Wells Fargo and the other express companies. The new Californian wanted news from home, and he was willing to pay any price to get it as rapidly as possible. Twenty or forty times the postal rates seemed reasonable enough under the circumstances; and the express companies, which were getting ample free advertising from the newspapers by bringing along as much reprintable matter as possible (the same material which the Postmaster General was com-

---

[9] *Report of the Postmaster General, 1853,* p. 9.

plaining about) and *giving* it to the editor, were more than willing to oblige and expedite. But God pity the poor mail rider:

> "Long looked for come at last." Sure enough our newspaper mail came straggling along last Monday about twenty days after it should have arrived according to what purports to be the mail arrangements for California. The letters came in a few days ahead. The news (!) of which we are in receipt by this most gracious arrival has a very ancient and fishlike smell. . .[10]

When Postmaster General Randall reported that the United States Mail Service had done more to "Christianize" the American people than anything except the Bible, he did not have newspaper editors in mind.

The *Star* made it clear that one of the problems was the habit of the mail steamers passing by San Diego and carrying the southern California mails to San Francisco for unloading. From there they had to be returned to Los Angeles "by the mail or one of our coastal steamers." "By the mail" was meant the cumbersome mail rider.

The California mail service reached its probable all time low in June 1853, when the *Star* reported the arrival of the mail rider from San Diego bearing letters and newspapers from the east with "the date of a year now passed." That might have been poetic justice in retaliation for some of the *Star's* "Christian" remarks of April 2, 1853, wherein the editor had stated:

> Of what earthly use to us is a horde of well paid imported office holders, who instead of attending to the duties which they were sent here to perform, pay no regard to them at all, but sit quietly and suck their thumbs, regardless of everything but their own interest?

---

[10] Los Angeles *Star,* Apr. 2, 1853.

Previously, the *Star* had inferred (much the same as Postmaster General Holt would later define) that the mail contractors were actually an unnecessary burden on the taxpayers and where efficiency was concerned, a damned nuisance: "Our land mail is a fine speculation for the persons who have the contract for transporting it, but further than that, we can conceive of no possible good which it accomplishes." [11]

The uncertainty and unreliability of the mail rider system was brought out again in the October 22, 1853, issue of the *Star:* "Sometimes the rider brings two mails, sometimes one, and sometimes none. . ."

By late 1853, even the northern newspapers were haranguing the Post Office Department in respect to the mail service between San Francisco and San Diego, calling it "a mockery" that should "be at once abandoned for the more certain, speedy and regular route by water." [12]

Most of the criticism at this particular time was generated by the knowledge that the new mail contracts would be advertised for bids in early 1854. The propitious time to prod the Post Office Department into a change of methods would be prior to the letting of those contracts. All during 1853 the *Star* would "ride herd" on the postal authorities and with an utter disregard to where it was stepping:

> We notice that the Post Office Department has advertised for proposals to carry the mails to and from this place for the next four years, in the same manner as during the last four. We suppose this implies that the mail rider may bring the bags just as it suits his convenience – once or twice a month, or not at all. And that he may have the privilege of lounging along the road from San Diego for fifteen or twenty days upon a trip, with from one

[11] *Ibid.,* Feb. 12, 1853.   [12] *Ibid.,* Nov. 12, 1853.

to two hundred pounds of mail matter, provided he can find some disinterested friend to swear he had a necessity for so doing. All this is very well, and if the government is satisfied to pay a man for carrying empty bags along the road we won't complain. As the thing is now managed, the mail matter is first transferred to Adams & Co.'s Express, whose agent in this place is accomodating and prompt in all his transactions. The slow motions of the government will drive all its business into the hands of individual enterprise. We did expect our Democratic friends would pay some attention to our afflictions, but our prospects are no better now than under the Whigs.[13]

Little did the editor realize it at the time, but a new system of mail distribution for California was just over the horizon. Ironically, the idea had first been proposed by the *Star* itself on June 25, 1853, wherein it was advocated that the steamship mail contractors be permitted to drop San Diego and Monterey as ports of call and allowed to proceed directly to San Francisco with the mails. It was thought the steamship line could save enough money thereby to put on speedy, first-class coastal vessels to service the only post offices on the coast: Monterey, San Luis Obispo, Santa Barbara, Los Angeles (San Pedro) and San Diego. Under this system the plodding mail rider could be dispensed with and the Los Angeles mails deposited at San Pedro instead of San Diego.

It has been impossible to ascertain precisely when this change took place, but it was during 1854. Unfortunately, 1854 was one of those periods where there are now serious gaps in the *Star* files.[14] *The Report Of The Postmaster General, 1854,* makes it clear that the change had been accomplished during the year:

---

13 *Ibid.,* Feb. 11, 1854.

14 The cynic who derides the newspaper files as sources of historical information can only learn to appreciate their value when missing issues occur at critical points in a research program.

> On the Pacific line the company are permitted to omit Mon-
> terey and San Diego by their ocean steamers, and thus expedite
> the through mails, on condition of their supplying those offices,
> together with Santa Cruz, Santa Barbara, San Luis Obispo (if
> practicable) and San Pedro, semi-monthly, by a coastwise steamer
> from San Francisco, in due connexion with the through route,
> without change of pay.

There are reasons for believing that a bit of conniving
on the part of steamship owners, California postmasters,
and possibly a newspaper editor or two, resulted in some
"extra-curricular" activities in the California mail arrangements which were designed to bring about this
new system. The *Star* had reported on January 21, 1854,
that the San Francisco Postmaster, Colonel Henley, had
"bestowed a favor" upon Los Angeles by forwarding
the mails via the s.s. *Goliah*. Early in March the paper
reported: "The mail rider came in on Sunday. No one
was disappointed that he brought no mail." [15] The inference was that no one expected any mail by the rider
in lieu of a cooperative San Francisco postmaster.

Nothing further on the subject appeared in any of the
available issues of the *Star* for 1854; but the first number in 1855, January 4, carried an advertisement (dated
November 30) for the "Independent Line" of steamships "Carrying The United States Mail." One of the
two ships listed was the *Goliah*.

Any dreams that the mail millenium had arrived in
southern California, however, were soon shattered. The
Independent Line "Carrying The United States Mail"
had contracted to deliver said mail at San Pedro, *not*
Los Angeles, and that was precisely where it was delivered:

> Strange as it may appear – although we have a post office here,
> and a contract exists for carrying the mail to two points *from* Los

---

[15] Los Angeles *Star*, Mar. 4, 1854.

Angeles, there is no provision for delivering the mail *at* this city. There is a contract for a semimonthly service to San Pedro, a point on the coast thirty miles distant, but no provision whatever is made for the transportation hither! When the contractor throws the bags on the beach, his work is accomplished – how they are to reach this point, is a subject which seems not worth the consideration of the Department. Probably, they are expected, in this fast country, to pick themselves up and walk off to their destinations – or, it is hoped, that some good Samaritan passing by may take compassion on their helplessness, and "give them a lift" homeward. And this is just how we receive our mail matter. Messrs. Alexander and Banning take the mail from aboard the steamer, and carry it here of their own good will, there being no provision whatever for this service.   .   .[16]

The *Star* was not alone in condemning the new arrangements. The Monterey *Sentinel* pointed out the injurious nature of the infrequent mail communications to business interests in the southern part of the state, adding: "It appears that at this time there is no land mail of any kind, with the different connecting points between Monterey and San Diego.   .   ."[17]

The newspaper editors had harangued the mail riders and screamed for a steamer mail service along the coast. Now they were screaming because there was no land mail as in the "good old days" of the muleback mail rider! Verily, it took a heap of doing to "Christianize" the nineteenth century newspaper editor.

If one is inclined to agree with the fourth estate on this question, let him consider that as of January 2, 1858, the only post offices between San Francisco and Los Angeles along the future route of the Coast Line Stage Company were: Santa Clara, San Jose, Gilroy, San Juan Bautista, Natividad, Salinas, San Luis Obispo, and Santa Barbara. All but Santa Barbara and San Luis

---

[16] *Ibid.,* June 21, 1856.
[17] *Ibid.,* Jan. 26, 1856. Reprinted from the Monterey *Sentinel.*

Obispo were being serviced by the stage lines of Charlie McLaughlin running south out of San Francisco and San Jose.

In the meantime, the steamers continued to leave the mail bags on the sands of San Pedro, figuratively speaking, and the only difference insofar as Los Angeles was concerned was a change of Good Samaritans to deliver them into town. "Buck" Buchanan, ever-popular messenger and sometimes agent for Wells Fargo in Los Angeles, could always spot a good advertising medium for his company and be depended upon to carry it through. Uncle Sam's mail pouches at San Pedro were "sitting ducks" for Buchanan:

> This gentleman invariably takes charge of the letter mail on board the steamer, brings it off in his boat, and conveys it to town on his wagon, without any fee or reward, or expectation thereof. This is a favor conferred on our business men, and the public generally, of which, perhaps, they are not aware, and which, when known, will, we have no doubt, be duly appreciated. Such an act speaks highly for Mr. Buchanan, and entitles him to the thanks of the entire community, as, but for his exertions, the mail might be delayed for hours.   .[18]

"Buck" Buchanan had more friends in Los Angeles than Editor Henry Hamilton of the *Star* had commas. With that kind of free advertising it is little wonder the expeditious Wells Fargo Express was doing a lucrative business in carrying private letters at far higher rates than the United States Post Office Department.

This in brief was the state of affairs communication-wise in California when, on a beautiful fall afternoon in 1858, a celerity stage wagon rumbled into town – not from the north or south, but from the east. The first Overland Mail Company stage from the Mississippi

---

[18] *Ibid.*, Apr. 24, 1858.

ELIZABETH LAKE STAGE ROAD
The Butterfield Overland Mail passed this way.
Nineteenth Century view of the old stage road at Elizabeth Lake.

had arrived with "The Butterfield Mail" from St.
Louis and Memphis. It was one o'clock on the afternoon
of October 7; The Overland Mail was twenty-one days
out of Memphis and ahead of schedule.

"The joyful and important event of the arrival of the
first through stage from Memphis, was hailed with
great satisfaction by our citizens, and a salute of a hundred guns was fired in honor of the event, during the
afternoon." [19]

It is enlightening to compare this account in the *Star*
of the arrival of the first Overland Mail with that written by Roscoe and Margaret Conkling in *The Butterfield Overland Mail:*

> Although the city was wide awake and growing with a re-
> ported mixed population of about six thousand at the time, the
> arrival of the Mail passed almost unnoticed, los Angelenos ex-
> hibiting the same attitude of indifference and skepticism as other
> communities along the route, refusing to believe the time of
> twenty-one days made by the Mail until confirmed when some of
> their surprised eyes read a Saint Louis newspaper brought by the
> Mail containing dates several days later than those brought by
> the last steamer mail.

In fairness to the authors of *The Butterfield Overland Mail,* it should be pointed out that a one hundred
gun salute in Los Angeles in 1858 would not have been
considered an unduly excessive display of gunnery for
a "normal" afternoon. In all probability the first fifty
rounds weren't even noticed.

Waterman Ormsby, the New York correspondent
aboard and the only through passenger, reported that
the Overland Mail stopped in Los Angeles only long
enough to change coaches.

There has always been some question in respect to

[19] *Ibid.,* Oct. 9, 1858.

whether or not Los Angeles was originally intended to be on the Overland Mail Route. The contract wording was vague regarding the intent of the government after the mails left Fort Yuma, merely stating that the contractors were to proceed to San Francisco by the best passes and along the best valleys. The evidence indicates that the original intent of Postmaster General Brown had been to route the mail straight through from Fort Yuma to San Bernardino and the Cajon Pass, thence via Elizabeth Lake and Fort Tejon to the San Joaquin Valley. A cursory glance at any suitable map will establish that such a route would have been miles shorter than the one finally forced upon the company by the drifting sandhills northwest of Yuma, and the inability to find water by drilling wells on the desert. With only weeks remaining before the contract was to go into effect, the route was changed to the Temecula-Warner's Ranch line, resulting in San Bernardino being dropped from the original timetable schedule and Los Angeles added.

It would still have been possible to have by-passed Los Angeles, used the Cajon Pass, and reached Elizabeth Lake, saving almost as many miles as Brown's originally projected route. In essence it would have been a short-cut via the hypotenuse of a great triangle which rejoined the eventually adopted route where San Francisquito Canyon emerged into the high desert country. No great water problems presented themselves here, as the sag ponds of the San Andreas Fault line formed a natural chain of watering stations. The route had the further advantage of by-passing the notoriously steep San Fernando Hill and the very rugged going through San Francisquito Canyon.

There were other considerations, however, which entered into the eventual route selection, considerations that are seldom mentioned by writers on the subject. Primarily, the Los Angeles route gave promise of an ever increasing express business; and Wells Fargo was deeply involved in the Overland Mail Company. To have saved mileage at the expense of the lucrative express income would have been a classic example of thrift at the spigot and waste at the bung.

There was undoubtedly much fascinating scheming and behind-the-scenes maneuvering that have long since been obscured by time. The Los Angeles *Star* had been conspicuously uninterested in the enterprise as late as May 15, 1858, when it copied an article from the San Antonio (Texas) *Herald,* which scorned the Butterfield contract, doubted that it would ever be put into operation, and suggested the only feasible route was the one pioneered by James Birch the previous year between San Antonio and San Diego. The *Star* concurred in this opinion as late as the middle of May 1858.[20]

There is one intriguing aspect to this Texas article. No mention was made of the "Butterfield" contract; rather, the San Antonio *Herald* stated: ". . . a contract exists between the Post Office Department and the firm of Wells, Fargo & Co. of New York City to carry a semi-weekly mail from St. Louis to San Francisco. . ." Few editors of the day had such sharp eyes.

The following three weeks saw a complete reversal in the *Star's* viewpoint. Whoever was responsible for the change had accomplished no small feat where Editor Henry Hamilton was concerned. There is nothing to

---

[20] This is an interesting refutation of certain San Diego claims that Birch's mail was deliberately ridiculed by Los Angeles newspapers as the "Jackass Mail" because of sectional jealousies.

support the supposition but one can almost see the handiwork on Hamilton of "Buck" Buchanan, Wells Fargo's plenipotentiary extraordinary to Los Angeles.

The *Star* of June 12, 1858, reported the presence in Los Angeles of Warren Hall and E. G. Stevens of the Overland Mail Company for the purpose of purchasing horses and establishing stations between San Bernardino and Fort Yuma. M. L. Kinyon was expected momentarily to accomplish the same task from San Bernardino to San Francisco. It is important to note that San Bernardino, *not* Los Angeles, was the pivot point at this time. The *Star* continued:

> It is the desire, we believe, of the State directors of the company that the stages should pass through our city, provided the only obstacle to that arrangement, and a very serious one it is, be removed – namely the San Fernando Hill and San Francisco Pass [San Francisquito Canyon]. The subject has been brought before the Board of Supervisors of the county, who held a special meeting to consider the matter, and promptly and very wisely took action on the proposition.[21]

The uncertainty of the routing with only ninety days remaining before the Overland Mail contract was to become effective, the sudden change of attitude on Hamilton's part, and the special meeting of the Los Angeles County Board of Supervisors are strongly indicative of hasty, behind the scenes maneuvering to secure the Butterfield Mail for Los Angeles.

The special meeting of the supervisors was held on June 7, at which time $3000 was appropriated to make the San Fernando Hill and San Francisquito Canyon passable, *provided* enough citizens could be found to

---

21 Los Angeles *Star,* June 12, 1858. San Francisquito Canyon at this time was more often than not referred to as "San Francisco Pass."

put up the money and accept warrants at par on the County Treasury in exchange. A second stipulation called for a competent survey, set up a committee to oversee the work, and spelled out the bidding technicalities. The $3000 was immediately subscribed by prominent Los Angeles citizens.

By June 26, the *Star* could report the arrival of Mr. Kinyon, who supplied the editor with a list of stations and mileages from Gilroy to San Bernardino. It was noted that the stations between Gilroy and San Francisco could be decided upon at any time. Apparently, Marcus L. Kinyon was already negotiating for the purchase of a one-half interest in Charlie McLaughlin's so-called "Coast Line," which would automatically settle the station locations on this section of the route. Kinyon expressed the opinion that by August the stages would be running between San Francisco and Fort Yuma bi-monthly.

This optimism was based upon the conviction that well drillers in the desert would be successful, and repairs to the San Fernando Hill and San Francisquito Canyon would be completed. Neither happened. On August 21, with only three weeks remaining before the great trans-Mississippi Overland Mail was due to commence operations, the company admitted through the columns of the *Star* that the well drillers had failed in their efforts to find water in the desert. It was with obvious reluctance that the newspaper reported:

> In consequence of this untoward circumstance, the stations of the overland mail company have been changed, and the stages will run on the old road, by way of Temecula and Warner's Ranch. The longest distance on this road without water, is about twenty-five miles. The people of San Bernardino, as well as the com-

pany, have expended a great deal of money in the undertaking, but it is to be hoped that the effort will be renewed, and that it will yet be found practicable.   . .[22]

To this day no major road crosses the desert northwest of Yuma on the line originally contemplated by the Overland Mail Company.

Meanwhile, up at the San Fernando Pass Mr. G. Allen had been awarded the contract for improving the road to the extent that $3000 would permit. Insofar as the *Star* was concerned, the project was not without a bit of ironic humor. At least twice in 1855, and as many times in 1857, the newspaper had reported the Pass in excellent condition and being used constantly by heavy freight wagons with no problems whatsoever. There was nothing to indicate that any of the several chamber of commerce-type editors had ever been within telescopic sighting distance of San Fernando Pass until Hamilton made the journey in 1858. Favorable comments about the Pass stopped immediately:

> The repair to this road was greatly needed; indeed, we do not know how such an obstacle to the traffic of the country could be allowed to exist so long, by any community. We lately passed over this road, and were surprised to find so monstrous an evil existing on the great leading thoroughfare of the southern country.[23]

Not since the *Star* had punctured Senator Merritt's bill to make the San Joaquin River navigable the year round between Stockton and Fort Tejon had Hamilton displayed so much concern over travel routes.[24]

By July 31, work on the San Fernando Pass was progressing rapidly, but the $3000 appropriation was obviously not sufficient to make a suitable road over the hill. What was worse, nothing would be left to put the San

22 Los Angeles *Star*, Aug. 21, 1858.   23 *Ibid.*, July 3, 1858.
24 See the *Star* of Apr. 4, 1857, for this rare bit of editorial lampooning.

Francisquito Canyon road in shape for staging. With the deadline for the Overland Mail operations approaching, the situation called for drastic action. The Los Angeles County Board of Supervisors had gone too far to turn back. At the regular meeting the first week in August a further appropriation of $5000 was made for the work on the great natural barriers to stage-coaching in the northern portions of the county. The dust arising from San Fernando and San Francisquito passes must have been prodigious during the next three weeks. On August 28, 1858, under the heading *The Overland Mail,* the *Star* reported:

> This company, we are happy to say, is now fully ready for operations, giving by its promptitude, energy, and enterprise, assurance of punctuality in all details and permanence of its organization. The road from Memphis to Tucson is fully stocked, stations fixed, corrals built, horses and carriages supplied, and everything ready.
>
> The stock arrived here to be placed on the road from Fort Yuma to Tucson. From Los Angeles to Fort Yuma, the stations have been located and the road stocked.
>
> Yesterday the carriages for the road, and a band of 220 horses arrived here. The coach is an elegant and substantial Concord coach to run from here on the San Francisco line. The San Fernando mountain was crossed without the least difficulty, by a six-horse coach. The contractor, Mr. G. Allen, has made this a good road.
>
> The company will commence running the line on the first of September, from San Francisco to Los Angeles, and from here to Fort Yuma. On the 15th of the month, the company come under contract. . .
>
> We append the following list of stations, with the distance in miles apart, for which we are indebted to our obliging and very popular friend W. A. Buchanan, Esq., of Wells, Fargo & Co.'s Express, who has lately passed over and measured a portion of the road. . .

When honors are bestowed for transforming Los Angeles from total indifference to an enthusiasm which resulted in the appropriation of the then significant sum of $8000 to make possible the passage of the Overland Mail through Los Angeles, this writer suggests that Mr. Hamilton's "obliging and very popular friend, W. A. Buchanan, Esq." and his employers, Wells, Fargo & Company, not be overlooked. Such transformations in the space of seven weeks do not just happen. The subtle hand of "Buck" Buchanan was evident throughout the entire proceeding.

The coming of the Overland Mail to Los Angeles, with its bi-weekly service from the east and tri-weekly deliveries from San Francisco, was bound to make the deepest impressions upon a population that had suffered through years of an almost non-existent mail service. Although there were originally no provisions for way mail drop off and pick up service, this was soon adopted and in excellent working order by the first of November.

Even before the Overland Mail contract became effective, the company was operating on a regular basis between San Francisco and Los Angeles, the *Star* of September 11, reporting that the public was already taking the stage arrivals and services for granted. Hamilton noted on September 18, that "The public are taking advantage of them, not only as a means of conveyance, but for the express facilities afforded."

The Overland Mail at this time did not carry printed matter, but there was nothing to prevent the always-popular Wells Fargo from sending the newspapers and delivering them to local editors. Soon the *Star* was thanking the express company for favors from San Francisco and the east "by the Overland Mail."

Despite any legitimate criticism of the large postal

subsidy that favored the line, it must be conceded the company's record for performance and dependability was probably never equaled. As early as October 9, 1858, the *Star* reported: "The stages of this company arrive here on their appointed days with the regularity of an old established line. . ." Long after the Overland Mail had been forced to move to the Central Route because of the Civil War, it was still the yardstick by which all other lines and mail services to and from Los Angeles were measured.

One oft-quoted authority differed drastically from the contemporary accounts of the Overland's reliability. Harris Newmark in *Sixty Years In Southern California,* page 235, wrote:

> So uncertain, indeed were the arrival and departure of the stages, that not only were passengers often left behind, but mails were actually undelivered because no authorized person was on hand, in the lone hours of the night, to receive and distribute them. Such a ridiculous incident occurred in the fall of 1858, when bags of mail destined for Los Angeles were carried on to San Francisco, and were returned by the stage making its way south and east, fully six days later.

This incident was reported in the Los Angeles *Star* on October 16, 1858, but Newmark's recollections of the affair represent a good example of the fallacy of the human memory. Further, Newmark made no allowances for the fact that the Overland Mail had been in operation but a month and it was only natural a few "bugs" would make their appearance. Nor was he justified in using this one isolated instance to convey the impression that such occurrences were commonplace. Even the principal antagonist of the Overland Mail, Postmaster General Holt, conceded in his report for

1859 that "The service upon this extended route has been performed with great regularity. . ." For the benefit of the "oral history" convert, the contemporary account in the *Star* is given here for comparison with Newmark's recollections:

> On Wednesday night the through stage arrived here, bringing a way mail. On proceeding to the post office to have the bag opened and the letters for Los Angeles taken out, the Co.'s agent found the office closed and no one in attendance. Our postmasters will, we hope, make an arrangement by which an attendant will always be ready to take charge of the way mail. In consequence of the above circumstances, our mail was carried on to be returned probably from Fort Yuma.[25]

For two years and six months Los Angeles luxuriated in the knowledge that twice weekly from the east and thrice weekly from the north the mails would arrive "with great regularity." The gathering clouds of that "little unpleasantness" between the northern and southern members of the American family were far away and of little concern to southern Californians. And then the moment of truth arrived, but the Butterfield Overland Mail from St. Louis and Memphis did not and would not again.

---

[25] Newmark's comments represent the weakness of the research medium now called "Oral History," for *Sixty Years in Southern California* is but oral history set to type. Given the choice of personal recollections of events more than fifty years past or contemporary descriptions of those same events, particularly when sustained by official government documents, the latter must always prevail.

3

The Beginnings of Coastal Staging
San Francisco - Los Angeles

If one were to dislike history so much as to reduce the most intriguing true stories to their lowest common denominators, the beginnings of coastal staging between Los Angeles and San Francisco could be condensed into seven sentences written by two contemporary observers whose veracities were unimpeachable. On February 20, 1861, Judge Charles Fernald of Santa Barbara wrote a letter to his wife Hannah in which six of those seven sentences were penned – six simple sentences pregnant with local, California, and American history:

> The overland mail stages are soon to pass this way. Our road is nearly completed, too. We are anticipating much advantage from it. It would be fine for us to have an opportunity of sending letters twice a week. . .
>
> We are in receipt of very ill tidings from the East. If reports are true, Civil War is imminent. . .[1]

One sentence from the April 7, 1861, entry of William Brewer's journal, if added to those excerpts from Judge Fernald's letter, makes an accurate but abbreviated record of the actual beginning of Los Angeles to San Francisco stagecoaching via the coast route: "The first *Overland* through Santa Barbara, on Monday eve-

[1] Charles Fernald, *A County Judge in Arcady, Selected Private Papers of Charles Fernald, Pioneer California Jurist,* ed. Cameron Rogers (Glendale, California, 1954), p. 180. Permission to quote courtesy of The Arthur H. Clark Company.

ning, April 1, was celebrated with the firing of cannon, etc." [2]

It is all there: The Overland Mail Company which would inaugurate the first stagecoaching by the Coast Route, together with the correct date; the famous Santa Barbara County road from the top of the Santa Susana Pass to the San Luis Obispo County line that was an absolute necessity before any regular staging could be maintained; and the Civil War, which would be used as the excuse for the Butterfield Mail's forced abandonment of the Southern, or "Oxbow Route." It is all there *except* the myriad human interest items that make up history and which, if not recorded, became so obscured behind several coatings of poor literary paint that the most clever restorer cannot be sure that what is uncovered is dream or reality. It is all there *except* the passions and hatreds which would influence so many vital decisions of those last pre-Civil War months.

The unquestioned antipathy of those who from the beginning detested the southern routing of the Overland Mail for provincial reasons is not there; and missing, too, is what must have been relentless, behind the scenes maneuvering and conniving by those interests that felt the Coast Route from Los Angeles north would have superior advantages over the Inland Route. Yes, it is all there *except* the fear in men's hearts which prohibited them from entering into the records and minute books those germane items that the historian relies upon to secure accurate information. For who could foresee the

[2] William Brewer, *Up and Down California in 1860-1864: The Journal of William Brewer, Professor of Agriculture in the Sheffield Scientific School from 1864 to 1903,* ed. Francis P. Farquhar (Berkeley, 1966), p. 74. Originally published by the University of California Press; reprinted by permission of The Regents of the University of California.

outcome of the struggle – who could prejudge the consequences of a decision made in a directors' meeting if the wrong side won the war? Some matters were best left off the record.

One thing that emerges clearly to the researcher in this historical smog of the last pre-Civil War months is the vital importance of dates. They are the links that make up the chain of the story and prevent misinterpretations in ambiguous situations. Where no reliable records exist, it is the date that supplies the "educated" portion of the "educated guess."

The Butterfield Overland Mail had been in operation but seven weeks when the Los Angeles *Star* published the previously cited article on the need for a stagecoach line up the coast – at least as far as San Luis Obispo. It is a sound educated guess that some preliminary talk and ideas had been exchanged concerning the use of the Coast Route for the Overland Mail as early as November 1858, if, in fact, the line had not been given a crude reconnaissance survey months before the final Inland Route was adopted.

It had been but four and one-half months after the inauguration of the Overland Mail that the Santa Barbara *Gazette* published the news item concerning the Los Angeles gentlemen being in town, "endeavoring to persuade our citizens to repair the road between here and Los Angeles, promising that they will in such case establish a regular stage line between the two towns." [3]

The May 14, 1859, issue of the Los Angeles *Star* reported the return to Los Angeles of General Drown,

who has been on a visit to Santa Barbara, in regard to the con-

[3] Los Angeles *Star,* Feb. 26, 1859. Reprinted from the Santa Barbara *Gazette.*

struction of a road hence to that city. . . The people are to vote on Monday next, on the question of appropriating $15,000 for the accomplishment of the work. The supervisors of this county [Los Angeles] have appropriated $2000 for the purpose.

The *Star* in its enthusiasm for the road had failed to note two qualifications written into the $2000 appropriation by the Los Angeles County Board of Supervisors: "Provided, that the County of Santa Barbara make a good & passable road from Santa Barbara to the said dividing line, and further provided that parties can be found to take the Scrip issued for said amount of $2000 at face value. . ." [4]

The Los Angeles County Auditor was instructed and empowered to issue the $2000 in scrip when the conditions had been fulfilled. From the wording in the Minute Book of the Los Angeles County Board of Supervisors it is clear that no route had been selected for the road at this time, the entry merely stating, "the road leading from Los Angeles in the direction of Santa Barbara. . ."

The idea of using the Coast Route for the Overland Mail had several advantages. It avoided the always dangerous San Fernando Hill and San Francisquito Pass, as well as the awkward, long-distance, "dog-legged" detour to Elizabeth Lake and then back to Fort Tejon. It also avoided the none-too-easy Pacheco Pass east of Gilroy. From the viewpoint of Los Angeles the Coast Route also put off on to Santa Barbara County the cost of major road maintenance, although it is doubtful if General Drown and the other "gentlemen from Los Angeles" explored this angle with their northern neighbors. Instead of paying for the upkeep of the stage

4 Los Angeles County Board of Supervisors, Minutes, Book 2, p. 266.

road from Los Angeles to Fort Tejon via San Francisquito Canyon, the Coast Route would require maintenance by Los Angeles County only to the Santa Barbara
County line, a distance of less than thirty miles.

The Coast Route, however, offered one serious draw-
back: For all practical purpose there was no road from
Los Angeles to San Luis Obispo. The Santa Susana
Mountains stood squarely athwart the route on the south
end, while the main Coast Range offered only the Gaviota and San Marcos passes north of Santa Barbara.

That Santa Barbara County was giving serious consideration to using the San Marcos Pass as early as the
late 1850s is testified to by a report submitted to the
Board of Supervisors on May 3, 1859, by County Sur-
veyor Nidever, respecting a "waggon road" over the
Pass. The report was tabled.[5]

The Santa Barbara County road proposition that
General Drown was pushing, and upon which the State
Legislature had authorized the balloting, carried the
stipulation that the money, if voted, was to be matched
by State funds. The vote, although light, was heavily
favorable to the project; but it was not until March of
the following year that Senator de la Guerra introduced
a bill in the Legislature authorizing the appropriation
of the State funds. In reporting the story, the Los Angeles *Star* gave a clear insight into the reasons for the
road and its ready acceptance by the voters of Santa
Barbara County:

> The coast road to the southern line of the State is interrupted
> by the mountain range of Santa Barbara, and hence *the Overland
> Mail cannot traverse that route.* Mr. de la Guerra contends that
> if the road be improved, *the overland mail would arrive one day*

---

[5] Santa Barbara County Board of Supervisors, Minutes, Book A, p. 221.

earlier in San Francisco. The citizens of Santa Barbara agree to pay $15,000.[6]

English so plain as that would not qualify as an educated guess. Obviously, the proponents of the Santa Barbara County road had it in mind from the beginning to secure the Overland Mail for the Coast Route. The previous November the Santa Barbara Supervisors meeting in regular session appointed one of their members, Francisco Puig, Esq., "as a committee *to confer with the overland mail company, in relation to the opening of the main road running through this county,* and report back to the next session of the board." [7]

If Francisco Puig, Esq. reported back to his fellow board members at the next session, the contents were not spread on the minutes. The usual procedure in such cases was for the report to be made and that fact recorded in the minutes. The report itself was then ordered filed. It was not the general practice to divulge the contents of reports or communications in the minutes. It cannot, therefore, be asserted with certainty that Puig ever conferred with any representative of the Overland Mail Company; although a warrant was ordered issued to him for expenses. The point is academic in any event. It was the intent that is germane to the present subject matter, and there can be little question that the intent of the Santa Barbara County Board of Supervisors was to work closely with the Overland Mail Company in order to secure its services upon completion of the road.

It was during this same session that the Santa Barbara Supervisors voted to request their representatives in the State Legislature to have the taxes "collected in this

---

6 Los Angeles *Star,* Mar. 17, 1860. Italics added.

7 Santa Barbara Supervisors, Minutes, Book A, p. 254. Italics added.

SANTA SUSANA PASS ROAD

The San Fernando Valley side of the old stagecoach road into the Simi Valley.
Note the almost solid rock nature of the road.

SANTA SUSANA PASS ROAD
The Simi Valley side of the stagecoach road.
The present freeway is out of view on the left side of the picture.

SIMI VALLEY STAGECOACH ROAD
The old stagecoach road in the Simi Valley west of Larry's Station
at the foot of the Santa Susana Pass.

county for the state the present year, placed to the credit of the county for road purposes."[8]

It is not clear what the board had in mind. Possibly this approach was to supercede the agreed upon $15,000 in State matching funds that had been stipulated in the bond issue, or possibly it was to be in addition thereto. In any case, three weeks later Senator de la Guerra introduced the previously noted bill to authorize the $15,000 appropriation of State funds.

Regardless of what route was eventually adopted for the road, it was essential that there be complete liaison between the two counties to insure a proper junction up among the rocks and clouds where the Los Angeles-Santa Barbara County line ran. Immediately after the success of the election in Santa Barbara County, the Board of Supervisors appointed a Road Commission to meet with the Los Angeles County Supervisors to formulate the details. The meeting was held in Los Angeles on June 8, 1859, and the following action taken:

> Messrs. Pablo de la Noriega, Jose de Arnaz, & Charles Fernald, Commissioners on the part of Santa Barbara County, appeared and presented their credentials, which were accepted & ordered filed, and said Commissioners proceeded to state to the Board the views entertained by Sta. Barbara Co. as regards the route, cost of repairs & Etc.
>
> Whereupon, on motion, It was resolved that R. Emerson with the Co. Surveyor be appointed a Committee on repairs of said road with instruction to select a route from Los Angeles to the Sta. Barbara Co. line, and make a report of the same with the estimated cost of opening the same to be filed with the Clerk of Board within ten days from date hereof.[9]

It can be assumed that the report of the committee was filed with the Clerk of the Board as directed, al-

[8] *Ibid.,* p. 256.

[9] Los Angeles Supervisors, Minutes, Book 2, p. 270.

though nothing pertaining to it appears in the Minute Book. The only entry involving the Los Angeles portion of the road to appear for another two years was a minor amendment to the original $2000 appropriation order. The absence of pertinent information was nicely in keeping with the entire project.

Probably no public work of such major importance to a large area of California has been so obscured by conniving, poor records, and overshadowing cataclysmic national events, as that road from Los Angeles via the Santa Susana Pass to the San Luis Obispo County line. The Minutes of the Santa Barbara County Board of Supervisors reveal only enough to tantalize. The terms of the contract, the correspondence, Road Commissioners' reports, maps, and other pertinent data, have long since been destroyed or hopelessly buried in local archives.

To make matters worse, at the time Santa Barbara County began construction in June 1860, Los Angeles County had not moved a wheel, driven a stake, or held a meeting with the Santa Barbara group since the June 1859, meeting to determine where the road should run, nor would such a meeting be held until May or June of 1861.[10] So far as Los Angeles County was concerned, that original proviso in the $2000 appropriation was still valid: "Provided, that the County of Santa Barbara make a good & passable road from Santa Barbara to the said dividing line. . ." Someone in Los Angeles must have been endowed with marvelous foresight or nagging suspicions.

---

[10] The Santa Barbara Supervisors' minutes for May 29, 1861, record the order for a warrant for $100 payable to Pablo de la Guerra to defray expenses of meeting "to negotiate with Board of Supervisors of Los Angeles County concerning road over the Cuesta of Santa Susana."

It is under these circumstances that the "educated guesser" comes into his own and can have a holiday attempting to reconstruct the past by reading between the lines of the available records. The serious student should make careful note of that fact, however, and be prepared to adjust the findings if new information is uncovered in the future.

The plan got under way in earnest on June 6, 1860, when the Santa Barbara County Treasurer was ordered by the Supervisors to turn over to George Black, engineer for the road, bonds amounting to $15,000 whenever Black posted adequate bond in equal amount. From this entry it would appear that Black was either authorized or had contracted to build the road. A Road Commission was appointed at the same meeting to oversee the project.[11]

Three days later Dr. S. B. Brinkerhoff, and others, presented a petition to the Santa Barbara Supervisors praying for the privilege of constructing a toll road over the San Marcos Pass. It should be obvious that such a road would have been in direct competition to the county road under consideration, yet the petition was granted. Nothing came of the proposal for another decade, however.

In the meantime, T. Wallace More had made an offer to the Supervisors to build the road from the Los Angeles County line to the San Luis Obispo County line in exchange for the $15,000 in bonds. The newly appointed Road Commissioners recommended that the offer be accepted. This action, at least on the surface, appears to have been in direct contradiction to that of June 6, when the bonds were ordered turned over to

[11] Santa Barbara Supervisors, Minutes, Book A, p. 263.

Engineer George Black. Probably some compromise had been arranged, as Black remained on the job as engineer.

The original line of the road had been surveyed by William H. Leighton in 1859, and the portion north of Santa Barbara adopted by the Board of Supervisors at their meeting of August 5, 1859. Black (or More) would disregard much of this survey line when the road was built, an action that came to light ten years later.

Leighton's report of his reconnaissance of the line from Santa Barbara to the Los Angeles County line was tabled by the Board on August 12, 1859.[12] This action is revealing and probably had more significance than meets the eye at first glance. It must be remembered that at this time Los Angeles was taking no action whatsoever in respect to actual road construction. It would have been the height of stupidity for Santa Barbara County to build a road through the Las Posas and Simi ranchos to the county line at the summit of the Santa Susanas, and then have Los Angeles County decide that the Conejo Route was better. Precisely when the final agreement was reached to use the Santa Susana, or Simi, Pass is unclear; but it probably took the form of a gentleman's agreement, as no record on the subject appears in the minutes of either supervisorial board.

That original stagecoach road over the Santa Susanas was the nearest thing to an escalator without power that has ever been constructed. The summit was crossed some six-tenths of a mile south of the later Santa Susana Pass Road at a point almost at the end of present Lilac Lane. On the west side of the Pass the road dropped straight down the bottom of the canyon and emerged at what is

12 *Ibid.*, p. 236.

now Smith Road, passing just to the south of the west portal of where the Southern Pacific railroad tunnel now stands. It was here that the famous Larry's Station, or Mountain Station as it was sometimes called, was located, Lawrence Howard, "Host."

The road then went straight through the Simi Valley and the Tierra Rejada, over the mesa on the south side of Calleguas Creek (which it crossed just to the east of present day Somis) proceeded on a beeline through the Las Posas Rancho, buttonhooked around the end of Punta de la Loma (South Mountain) and then ran diagonally across the Santa Clara Valley, passing just to the north of Saticoy Springs and crossing the line of the future Santa Paula Freeway at Saticoy Avenue. The route of the road into San Buenaventura was approximately the same as Loma Vista Road of today. From San Buenaventura to Santa Barbara the "road" went where it could. Interestingly enough, this famous stagecoach road was not declared a county road until February 6, 1868.[13]

North of Santa Barbara no description of the road could be found in the Supervisors' Minute Book. The

---

[13] *Ibid.*, Book B, p. 130. For a detailed drawing of the Santa Clara Valley portion of the road see W. H. Norway's Plat of the Rancho Santa Paula y Saticoy, filed for record in Santa Barbara on Oct. 15, 1867. From Punta de la Loma to Los Angeles see the map of the Wheeler Expedition Surveys, 1875 and 1878, Atlas Sheet No. 73 (C). A map in the Santa Barbara Mission Archives entitled, "Topographical Map of the Valley of the Santa Clara River," shows the ranchos Santa Paula y Saticoy, Sespe, San Francisco, plus ranchos Simi, Las Posas, Conejo, Colonia, del Norte, etc. The More Brothers are listed as "Proprietors." (!) This map shows "New Road to Los Angeles" connecting with the old road near present day El Rio instead of crossing the Santa Clara River at Punta de la Loma. Many features on the map indicate that it was "anticipatory" rather than factual, and probably drawn before the Santa Susana Pass Road was constructed. The route as shown on the More map was commonly used during dry weather, while the Norway map indicates the route used during wet weather.

point is academic in any event since More or Black had
changed the route in places. Leighton's original map is
missing. In general, however, the road followed westward to Gaviota Pass, at places along the beach, and
then via Santa Ynez Mission and Foxen Canyon to the
future station of Suey and the Santa Maria River.

This was the road, in excess of 150 miles, that T.
Wallace More had contracted to build for $15,000 in
bonds. Whether or not the State matching funds were
intended to be included is unclear. What is worse, nothing in respect to the terms of the contract can be found –
the time allotted for the construction, specifications for
grading and quality of materials to be used in culverts
and bridges, allowances for inclement weather, etc. It is
inconceivable that More, the Santa Barbara County
Board of Supervisors, and the Road Commissioners,
were so naive as to overlook or neglect these matters;
and yet the farce that followed would indicate that they
were.

More took the job, one that from its very magnitude
would require considerable preparatory work, on June
9, 1860. By the first week in December he had appealed
to the Road Commissioners for an extension of time on
his contract. The Commissioners recommended to the
Supervisors that the extension be granted with reserva-
tions; but the implications would appear to be that the
original agreement called for the completion of the
road, all 150 miles of it, in so short a period of time that
even with the modern equipment of today it could not
have been accomplished.

Then the rains came – gentle, slow-soaking showers,
followed by those tempestuous, "gully-washing" down-
pours that only southern California can produce at

times. More appealed to the Road Commissioners for the suspension of all road work until March 15, 1861. The Santa Barbara County Board of Supervisors rejected the request.[14] More then presented a petition to have Road Engineer Black discharged (as though that might tame the elements!). The petition was denied; the rains continued.

T. Wallace More had never gained fame for being the easiest fellow in the world from whom friendly cooperation could be expected. It is a well documented fact that he seldom got along with his neighbors; the evidence indicates he had considerable trouble cooperating with his brothers; and some people, particularly in the Sespe area, claimed he could not even tolerate himself. As early as August 28, 1860, there were signs of trouble between More and Black. The Santa Barbara Supervisors' Minutes for that date recorded: "A communication was received from Geo. Black, Road Engineer, which was referred to the road committee with instructions to examine the matter and report thereon to the Board with all convenient dispatch." [15]

The committee made the report "with all convenient dispatch" on September 6, their report being filed and with no hint in the minutes respecting its contents.[16] Never let it be said that these 1860 supervisors did not know what to file, what to table, and what to spread on the minutes.

Road matters continued to deteriorate, mostly due to bad weather; although More claimed he was unable to secure adequate labor. What does not appear in the Santa Barbara Supervisors' Minute Books, but will be

---

[14] Santa Barbara Supervisors, Minutes, Book A, pp. 289-290.
[15] *Ibid.*, Book A, p. 271.   [16] *Ibid.*, Book A, p. 276.

found in the Los Angeles *Star,* is the fact that by January 12, 1861, the rains had reached such proportions as to melt down adobe houses in Los Angeles and inundate the plain below the city. Even the indomitable, indefatigable, irrepressible Phineas Banning had been forced to abandon an empty stagecoach between Los Angeles and San Pedro.

In the face of weather conditions of this nature, the Santa Barbara Supervisors called a special meeting for January 14, 1861, "to consider and regulate matters concerning the county waggon road." [17] It is not surprising that no quorum could be present or that none appeared until the 19th.

On the 19th a quorum was present, but Don Jose Arnaz, member from the First Township or that portion of Santa Barbara County which now comprises Ventura County, was absent. Don Jose probably considered himself lucky to get to the barn to say nothing of journeying to Santa Barbara. The Board would not be placated by weather conditions, however, and ordered a citation issued upon Arnaz as soon as possible "as matters of importance have been presented to the Board respecting the county waggon road and that the sheriff serve said citation forthwith." [18]

Even the most blasé student or researcher would have to pause at this point and ask himself: "What in the name of all that's holy was so important as to require the sheriff of Santa Barbara County to drag poor old Jose Arnaz over the mountains through the rain and mud to a special meeting of the Supervisors?" Had T. Wallace More become so obstinate as to necessitate such extreme measures? More was certainly capable of excessive ob-

---

[17] *Ibid.,* Book A, p. 291.   [18] *Ibid.,* Book A, p. 292.

stinancy, but subsequent developments indicate that far more important considerations were involved.

The most plausible answer (and it will be conceded that there may have been others) to all the frantic haste, asinine confusion, and near-hysterical panic over a fouled-up road contract, could be found on the United States Post Office Department's worksheet for Mail Contract No. 12,578, the Overland Mail Route to California, under the date of January 10, 1861:

> Accept proposition of contractor to convey from 1 April next the printed matter between Fort Yuma & San Francisco (789 miles) and to supply San Diego 1 a w [once a week] by side supply, on horse, at $12,000 additional per annum with privilege of changing their road between Los Angeles & Gilroy so as to run by way of Santa Barbara, San Luis Obispo and San Juan, omitting present offices.

With privilege of changing their road between Los Angeles & Gilroy so as to run by the way of Santa Barbara, San Luis Obispo and San Juan. . ! And that road from the top of the Santa Susana Pass to the Santa Maria River was in far better condition for steamboat navigation than it was for stagecoaching.

It is not suggested that the Santa Barbara Supervisors had received any notification of the Post Office Department's actions concerning the privilege granted the Overland Mail Company to change their route from the San Joaquin Valley to the Coast Route. This would have been impossible, even with the Pony Express-telegraph communication system. It was not until March 2, 1861, that the Los Angeles *Star* reported the authorization for the Overland Mail to carry the "printed matter" and the once a week horseback supply to San Diego. The Washington dispatch did not mention the change of route privilege.

It *is* contended that the Santa Barbara County Board of Supervisors knew with an absolute certainty the Overland Mail Company was going to make the proposition to the Post Office Department and that the key to its success was the road under consideration. It is further contended the plan had been agreed upon tentatively as early as the bond election of May 1859, and that it was common knowledge to the inhabitants of Santa Barbara County. It will be recalled that in May 1860 (before the road contract had been awarded), the letter writer to the *Star* reported the people of Santa Barbara and San Luis Obispo counties were "nursing what I consider the vain hope that the Overland Mail line will be changed from the present to the Coast route." [19] It was three weeks *prior* to the signing of the contract between the Post Office Department and the Overland Mail Company respecting the carrying of the mails between Los Angeles and Monterey via Santa Barbara and San Luis Obispo that Judge Fernald wrote his wife the Overland Mail was soon to pass that way. Fernald, as one of the original Road Commissioners, was in a position to know the precise plans.

It must be noted further that if the above evidence is valid the decision to use the Coast Route had been taken long before the fast developing Civil War crisis was a factor. Congress did not pass the act curtailing the Southern Overland Mail Route until March 2, 1861. It is clear from the report to the Board of Directors of the Overland Mail Company by the committee which had been representing it in Washington, D.C. that the decision to move to the Central Route in no manner originated with the Overland Mail Company:

19 Los Angeles *Star*, May 12, 1860.

. . . in view of the existing state of affairs upon the route occupied by your line [Southern Route] your committee acting also under the advice of other members of the Board were *forced to submit* to some action that would either abrogate our contract entirely . . . or, so modify it as to change our line to the Central or Salt Lake Route.[20]

At the March 8, 1861, meeting of the Overland Mail Company Board Of Directors when the above report was submitted, an enlarged committee was appointed to work out the details with the Postmaster General relative to the move to the Central Route. It was this enlarged committee that agreed to the terms for the mail service between San Diego and Monterey that actually inaugurated stagecoaching via the Coast Route. The letter of notification addressed to E. S. Alvord, Superintendent of the Overland Mail Company, from Second Assistant Postmaster General Childs, read:

Sir: The Postmaster General orders that a contract be made with your company at $40,000 per annum for carrying the mails between Monterey and San Diego via San Antonio, San Luis Obispo, Santa Barbara, and Los Angeles, three times a week, with certainty, celerity & security as far as Los Angeles, and once a week on horseback, the residue, service to begin when that on route 12578 ceases and to expire July 1, 1864. (Route to be No. 12,592) Respy Yours, E. L. Childs.[21]

The contract itself reads differently from the above letter, no mention being made therein that service would begin when Route 12,578 ceased functioning. Rather, the contract, dated March 12, 1861, called for service to commence on the Coast Route April 1, 1861. It should be noted that under the same date on the worksheet for the new route (12,592) the clause respecting service

[20] Minute Book of the Overland Mail Company, entry of Mar. 8, 1861. Italics added.   [21] *Ibid.,* Mar. 16, 1861, p. 156.

commencing when that on Route 12,578 ceases *is* present.

One wonders if the officials of the Overland Mail Company in New York City had any conception of the confusion existing on the Coast Route road when they signed that contract. Engineer Black had resigned on February 9, and T. Wallace More "threw in the towel" on March 5. The Santa Barbara County Board of Supervisors confiscated all More's equipment, with his approval and cooperation, and turned the project over to the Road Commission to untangle; while the Sheriff of Santa Barbara County was still being called upon to serve Supervisor Arnaz with citations in an effort to improve Don Jose's attendance record at meetings. The ranking officials of the Overland Mail Company on the Atlantic seaboard could not have known of this farce across the continent when they signed a contract to deliver Uncle Sam's mails "with certainty, celerity, & security" from Los Angeles to Monterey, three times a week, beginning in nineteen days.

Nor could William Brewer, camped with the Whitney survey party in Santa Barbara, have been endowed with supernatural powers of clairvoyance when he wrote on March 10, 1861, *two days before that contract was signed:*

> Santa Barbara lies on the seashore, and until lately it was isolated from the rest of the world by high mountains. No wagon road or stage route ran into it from without, only mere trails or paths for horses over the mountains. For a few years they had had a mail once in two weeks by steamer from San Francisco – two mails per month was the only news of the world outside. But *the Overland has been working the road – or the county has – and will run this way after the first of April.*[22]

22 Brewer, *op. cit.*, pp. 55-56. Italics added.

There was nothing secretive about it at all. Even in Los Angeles the *Semi-Weekly Southern News* announced the change on March 13, 1861, only one day after the contract was signed on the east coast. There was no possible manner by which the *Southern News* could have obtained the information from the Atlantic seaboard.

When the plan was formulated and by whom can only be surmised. Bearing in mind the tediously slow communications between the Atlantic and Pacific, and the wording on the January 10, 1861, entry on the Post Office Department's worksheet for the Overland Mail Route, it seems certain that an agreed upon formula and the date for its implementation had been arranged by officials of the Overland Mail Company on both coasts as early as the fall of 1860.

There is nothing in the Overland Mail Company Minute Book to sustain this assertion, nor is there any entry that provides a clear answer as to whether it was the company or the Post Office Department which first proposed the Coast Route.[23] The question would have little importance except for the statements made (and generally accepted) by the Conklings in their work, *The Butterfield Overland Mail:*

"On january 10, 1861, the Post Office department *ordered* the Company to abandon the stations on the Inland route in California between Los Angeles and Gilroy, and confine the service to the Coast route. . ."[24]

It will be recalled that the Post Office Department's

---

[23] The writer is indebted to Wells Fargo Bank, San Francisco, for compiling a resumé of the Overland Mail Company Minute Book concerning this phase of the case. The bank also supplied photostatic copies of pages from the Overland Mail Company Minute Book that were critical to this research.

[24] Conkling, *op. cit.,* p. 337. Italics added.

entry began, "Accept proposition of contractors. . ."
and continued in respect to the route, ". . . with
privilege of changing their road between Los Angeles &
Gilroy. . ." [25]

It is submitted that an *order* to abandon a route, as
per the Conklings, and the *privilege to change to a new
route,* as the actual Post Office Department records
state, are two different matters. The *Semi-Weekly
Southern News* made the point unequivocally clear in
its article of March 13, 1861, respecting the change:
"The route has been changed at the option of the company and because they will receive additional compensation, and not by order of the department."

The evidence would seem to indicate that the idea
originated with western personnel of the Overland Mail
Company, probably William Buckley, in collaboration
with Santa Barbara and Los Angeles County officials;
that it was approved by eastern officials of the Overland
and a firm date agreed upon for implementing it; but
the fast developing Civil War crisis, the unexpected
"unusual" weather in California, and the Santa Barbara
road difficulties were of such a nature that the slow
communications of the period would not permit any
readjustments to a previously agreed upon schedule.

William Brewer's contribution to solving the riddle
of the beginning of coastal staging did not cease with
his firm record of dates and events. His rather uncertain suggestion that the Overland Mail Company might
be working on the road is intriguing in view of the fact
the Los Angeles County Board of Supervisors rejected
a claim for $731.00 submitted by the company.[26]

[25] Italics added. It hardly needs to be pointed out that the Conklings' error
stems from their acceptance as fact that there was such a thing as an operating
line of stages up the coast at the time this privilege was granted.

[26] Los Angeles Supervisors, Minutes, Book 3, p. 33.

No clew was written into the minutes respecting what the claim was for; however, it came at a time when the Santa Susana Pass road was nearing completion, which would indicate that road work was involved.

Brewer is the only source known to this writer that left any information relative to the quantity or the quality of the work done by T. Wallace More on the Santa Barbara road before he reneged on his contract. It is apparent from Brewer's descriptions that the road had been completed from Santa Barbara to the northern county line, and it is even more obvious that the contractor had constructed an excellent wagon road by the standards of the times:

> Tuesday, April 2, early in the morning, we started north. Santa Barbara County until now has been nearly isolated from the country around by rugged mountains. During the last few months thirty or forty thousand dollars has been expended by the county on getting a good wagon road through from San Luis Obispo on the north to Los Angeles on the south. The southern part of the road is not yet finished but the north is, and a fine road connects it with San Luis Obispo. This road we are following – sometimes it is a mere obscure trail across the grassy plain, scarcely visible yet for want of travel, at others well engineered, built over and along high hills and through deep canyons at great expense and labor. Fine bridges of wood span the streams and gulches, the first bridges we have seen in the southern country. Our mules shy of these, to them, strange structures.   .   .
>
> At the Gaviota a rent or fissure divides the ridge, but a few feet wide at the narrowest part and several hundred feet high. The road passes this "gate" and then winds up a rocky canyon, the wildest pass I have seen here.   .   .   A horrible trail ran through this formerly but now the road is good.[27]

After the Whitney survey party crossed the dry Santa Maria River into San Luis Obispo County, Brewer's descriptions took a radical turn for the worse. There

[27] Brewer, *op. cit.*, pp. 73-75.

was no road, only a trail "like a cow path, hardly marked by the tracks of wheels. . . In one place for some distance the road descended at *an angle of twenty-nine degrees!* Yet this is the 'better' road to San Luis Obispo." [28]

Brewer made no mention, either good or bad, of road conditions between San Buenaventura and Santa Barbara. There is some evidence that appeared several years later to the effect that a road had been cut on the steep cliffs south of Rincon Point to avoid the rocky beach. It is possible that T. Wallace More had reached this point by March 5, 1861, when he turned everything over to the Road Commissioners. The Noachian floods of 1862 would have obliterated it in any event.

In truth, it has been impossible to determine how much road work, if any, More had completed on his contract south of Santa Barbara. The one difficult section that appears to have been untouched in both counties was the Santa Susana Pass.

The Los Angeles *Star* was much too busy calling "Uncle Abe" Lincoln sarcastic names to keep abreast of road developments, and it was not until mid-summer of 1861 that Henry Hamilton got around to reporting:

NEW ROAD — The repairs on the road from Los Angeles to Santa Barbara, in this county, in connection with the new road to Santa Barbara county, approved by the Board of Supervisors, are nearly completed. A new road was made over the Santa Susana mountain, and the road through the Cahuenga Pass is now being repaired. As soon as finished, the stages of the overland mail will take this route, as it will be one of the finest on the line. The work has been executed under the supervision of Mr. James Thompson of this city, who has performed his duties in a most credible manner.[29]

---

[28] *Ibid.*, p. 79.   [29] Los Angeles *Star*, July 20, 1861.

GAVIOTA PASS

The great fissure of the Gaviota Pass as it looked to stagecoach
travelers on the Coast Route, circa 1880.

If ever there was a news item of historical interest in which the researcher would be justified in extreme skepticism, this one from the Los Angeles *Star* would be it. Remembering that it was published on July 20, 1861, a cross check with the Minute Book of the Los Angeles County Board of Supervisors for the previous five weeks reveals the following interesting facts:

On June 14, 1861: "In the matter of the road in the Simi Pass between the Counties of Santa Barbara & Los Angeles Counties [*sic*]. This being the day fixed for the report of Mr. W. T. B. Sanford, in the above matter, the same was taken under advisement by the Board until the 20th inst." [30]

Commissioner Sanford's report was not acted upon until the meeting of July 8, 1861, at which time it was "Ordered that the report of Cmr. Sanford in said matter be accepted and filed, and that the further consideration of said matter be continued until Wednesday, July 10th, A.D. 1861." [31]

On July 10, 1861, the Los Angeles County Board of Supervisors took the final action on the Simi Pass road:

> In the matter of the road between Santa Barbara and Los Angeles City – The board having considered the report of the Comr. hereinbefore filed – Whereupon it is ordered that T. G. Barker and W. T. B. Sanford be and they are hereby appointed Commissioners to contract for the building of said road PROVIDED that the cost of the same shall not exceed the sum of Four thousand, eight hundred dollars.
>
> And it is further ordered that said Comrs. shall during the progress of the construction of said road be empowered from time to time, as parts thereof shall be completed to their satisfaction and accepted by them, to give to the contractor a certificate of the acceptance thereof, and the value of the work at the time com-

[30] Los Angeles Supervisors, Minutes, Book 3, p. 17.   [31] *Ibid.,* p. 29.

pleted; And thereupon the County Auditor is authorized to draw
his warrant on the Co. Treasury for said sum, in such amounts as
said contractor may elect.[32]

Henry Hamilton had inferred on July 20, 1861, that
the new road over the Santa Susana mountain had been
completed; the Los Angeles County Board of Supervisors did not authorize its construction or appropriate
the money until July 10. Under these circumstances
skepticism is not unwarranted.

Earlier, the Santa Barbara Road Commissioners had
turned their portion of the road over to James Thompson to complete. Before the final Los Angeles authorization was taken on July 10, the Santa Barbara Commissioners had met with the Los Angeles group in an
obvious liaison session. It is not surprising, therefore, to
find Thompson accepting the contract to build the road
on the Los Angeles side of the Pass, also.

It would be interesting and historically important
to be able to pinpoint the date of completion of that
famous stagecoach road over the Santa Susana Pass. On
August 3, 1861, the *Star* reported the Los Angeles portion was completed, and expressed astonishment that the
Santa Barbara County section was still unfinished. Hamilton may have been correct this time, although it would
seem incredible to anyone who has ever walked up that
solid rock road to the summit. Was it possible to blast
out this road in so short a period of time? At the regular session of the Los Angeles Board of Supervisors of
August 5, 1861, the Los Angeles Road Commissioners'
Report was accepted and the Commissioners discharged
with the thanks of the Board.[33] No further reference to

[32] *Ibid.*, pp. 30-31.
[33] *Ibid.*, p. 34.

the matter could be found, indicating that the work was completed.

The Santa Barbara portion of Thompson's contract is more complex to unravel. On August 8, 1861, the Santa Barbara Supervisors "relieved" their Road Commissioners of all further duties "with the thanks of the Board." Up to that date the records show payments to Thompson totaling $2765.89. However, sixteen days after dismissing their Road Commissioners, the Board ordered the Santa Barbara County District Attorney to draw up a contract with Thompson "respecting the wagon road, subject to the direction of Supervisor Jose de Arnaz."[34]

As an educated guess it could be assumed that the Santa Barbara Supervisors were not trusting anyone after their experience with T. Wallace More.

The Santa Barbara Supervisors' Minutes show the final payment to Thompson was made on September 14, 1861, "as per report of Jose de Arnaz." Insofar as the Santa Barbara County records reveal, Thompson's fee for completing More's contract was $3915.89. The date would indicate that the Santa Susana Pass road was operational after the middle of September, 1861.

It was probably only natural that the prevailing national crisis would result in considerable confusion in the matter of records at all levels of government. The United States Post Office Department records for the Coast Route, No. 12,592, are a fine example:

Under the date of June 11, 1861, the entry on the worksheet for Route 12,592 reads: "P.M. of Los Angeles reports service began 22nd April, 1861."

---

[34] Santa Barbara Supervisors, Minutes, Book A, p. 312.

Under date of September 10, 1861, the entry reads: "P.M. of San Francisco has reported that service begin 1 April, 1861."

There was nothing unique, of course, about a bureaucrat from Los Angeles disagreeing with one from San Francisco. It is surprising, however, to find the Los Angeles Postmaster backing down and retracting his original report:

Under date of October 30, 1861, the entry reads: "Report to Auditor that certificate of P.M. of Los Angeles as to date of commencement of service was erroneous and that the one from the P.M. in San Francisco makes the proper statement in the case."

The odd part of this little misunderstanding is that both postmasters were partially correct in their original statements. News accounts in the Los Angeles *Star* and the *Semi-Weekly Southern News* establish that triweekly service as called for in the contract did not commence until April 22; but service of some sort did start on April 1, as the San Francisco Postmaster contended. Brewer's descriptions of the road conditions in San Luis Obispo County might indicate that the first two or three weeks of staging via the Coast Route were sporadic at best. It was not until April 19, that the *Semi-Weekly Southern News* reported discontinuance of service via the old Inland Route, indicating a few trips were still made on that line after April 1.

That the company was functioning with precision on the Coast Route by the end of April despite road difficulties is apparent from a news item in the Los Angeles *Star* of April 27, 1861:

When the *Senator* left San Pedro on her last trip, Mr. Hinchman, of the firm of Banning & Hinchman, left this city and reached her at the coast as she was just starting; went up on her to Santa Barbara; remained there some hours transacting business; and the Overland stage passing there from above bound to this city, he took passage in it and arrived home within 30 hours after the time he left here for San Pedro. These facilities of travel will furnish a great accomodation to merchants and others who have business along the coast, and desire it done expeditiously.

The story of the beginning of through coastal staging on April 1, 1861, thus arrives at an all-engrossing question: If the Santa Susana Pass road was still five months from completion, and the first wagon road down the present Highway 101 Conejo Grade route was not built until the mid-1870s, by what route was the Overland Mail Company traveling from Los Angeles to San Buenaventura?

The first reaction to the question would be the Santa Clara Valley. The *Star's* comment on August 3, 1861, that fifteen miles would be saved traveling to Santa Barbara when the Santa Susana Pass road was finished would point to the Santa Clara Valley Route. However, Henry Hamilton was a notoriously poor judge of distances (as well as a few other things) and all other evidence points to another route – the same that the Whitney survey party under Brewer has traveled a month earlier. Brewer's description is unmistakable:

> February 27, we raised camp and went about eighteen miles, first passing the lovely Triunfo Ranch, a large grassy valley surrounded by high hills. Then we crossed a high rocky ridge and descended a hill about five or six hundred feet. It was terribly steep, but Peter managed the wagon with a skill to be praised – all down safely. We then struck west a few miles in a valley, and by a stream near Cayeguas Ranch [sic].[35]

---

[35] Brewer, *op. cit.,* p. 49. Brewer's "high rocky ridge" is still a conspicuous outcropping, although the latest subdivision knocked down the portion crossed by the party.

The party had rounded the point of hills later known as Triunfo Corners and proceeded over the undulating terrain on an almost straight line to approximately the present intersection of Moorpark and Olsen roads. Here, instead of swinging to the right and down the canyon where Nils Olsen, *et al,* later built the Norwegian Grade, they continued straight ahead to the saddleback in the hills behind the present Lutheran College football field and down the steep slope into the Santa Rosa Valley. Traveling west for a few miles alongside Santa Rosa Creek they camped near the Calleguas Ranch.

For many years this was the principal wagon route down from the Conejo. The map of the Wheeler surveys of 1875 and 1878 shows the road clearly and marks it "Old Road." Later surveyors' maps frequently show the road and occasionally it will be found marked "Old Butterfield Road," or "Butterfield Grade." During the thirty-two days between the time Brewer and his party made the descent and the first Overland Mail stagecoach traveled the route, William Buckley, the great quartermaster general of staging, would have had little trouble cutting a serviceable road that swung around the contours of the hill and emerged by the spring at the present Santa Rosa School. It would have been a far easier grade than the Santa Susana Pass road proved to be on either side of the summit.

From this point the Overland Mail could have followed Brewer's route out of the Santa Rosa Valley, or it could have continued northward and joined the new Santa Barbara County road (still under construction) near the present Tierra Rejada Road. Although longer, the latter alternative appears preferable as it would have avoided the problem of constructing two stations which would have to be discontinued when the new Santa Susana Pass road went into operation.

That this is the correct route instead of the Santa Clara Valley is established by a little episode which occurred some nine years later. At the regular meeting of the Los Angeles County Board of Supervisors in August 1870, a committee that had been appointed to examine the Santa Barbara stage road over the Santa Susana Pass and hopefully find an alternative route, made its report:

> The committee consisting of Hayes & Forsman heretofore appointed to visit the Santa Susana Mountain for the purpose of ascertaining the feasibility of making said road passable, the opinion of the committee is that to repair said road in a substantial manner would require a large outlay of money. In view of the request heretofore made on this Board, your committee would recommend no appropriation. *We passed over what is known as "the original Stage road" or the "Butterfield route."* This road we found to be better and shorter; leaving the present travelled stage road at Encino Rancho, this road runs along the foothills of the Coast Range reaching the summit through a pass with an easy grade, intersecting the present road this side of San Buenaventura – the distance saved is about three miles. With a small outlay of money the road can be put in very good condition.
>
> On motion the report was accepted and it is ordered that a copy of this report be sent to the Board Of Supervisors of Santa Barbara County, and ask their cooperation in repairing *the original stage road* in a good and substantial manner.[36]

So far as Los Angeles County was concerned, there was nothing new about the route proposed by the committee. The Court of the Sessions, County of Los Ange-

---

[36] Los Angeles Supervisors, Minutes, Book 4, pp. 354-355. Italics added. In truth, the Santa Susana Pass Route was shorter than the Butterfield Route but much more difficult to cross the mountains.

les, State of California, at its May 1851, term had declared this a public highway:

"*Santa Barbara Road* – From Los Angeles to Cahuenga, from Cahuenga to Encino, from Encino to Las Virgenes, from Las Virgenes to Triunfo." [37]

While legally a public "highway" it is doubtful if anything more than horses' hoofs had ever traversed it before the Whitney party of 1861. In all probability the declaration of the Court of the Sessions had long since been forgotten.

Any change of stagecoach routing up the coast required the cooperation of Santa Barbara County, the same as when the Santa Susana Pass road was built. The letter from the Los Angeles Supervisors came before the Santa Barbarans on January 6, 1871, and was promptly put off until the next meeting while Thomas R. Bard investigated the proposition. At the next regular session the Santa Barbara County Board of Supervisors disposed of the Los Angeles proposal in short form:

> In the matter of the communication from a Committee appointed by the Board of Supervisors of Los Angeles County suggesting the advantage to the public of reopening *the old Butterfield Road*. The report of Supervisors Bard [?] Committee appointed by this Board to examine the route of the said road was taken up and acted upon by communication addressed to the Board of Supervisors of Los Angeles County declining to concur with said Los Angeles Board, for reasons stated in said communication.[38]

Briefly put: In answer to "said" communication, the Santa Barbara Supervisors said, "No!"

No reasons for not concurring with the proposal appear in the Santa Barbara Supervisors' Minutes, nor are

---

[37] Los Angeles *Star*, May 24, 1851.
[38] Santa Barbara Supervisors, Minutes, Book B, p. 303. Italics added.

the reasons germane to the present subject; but Supervisor Thomas R. Bard was opening up the Simi and Las Posas ranchos for settlement, and it was through this territory that the Coast Line stages were passing in 1871. Bard would have had little interest in routing them through the Conejo and Santa Rosa Valley, although the latter was partially in the Simi Rancho.

It would not be until 1875 that the coastal stages switched back to the Conejo Route and then only for a short time. By then the first wagon road down the present 101 Highway Route had been built. When the Santa Susana Pass was opened for staging in September 1861, the Butterfield Grade (so far as is known) had witnessed its last stagecoach.

4

The Confusing Years

The change of routes for the Overland Mail Company between Los Angeles and San Francisco was now an accomplished fact; through staging had begun along the coast. The problems of the company, and there must have been many, have all but vanished from the historian's view in the overshadowing dust of the War of the Rebellion. Few stagecoaching news items appeared in Henry Hamilton's *Star,* with the exception of those reports of dubious accuracy concerning the Santa Susana Pass road. Henry was much too busy explaining the Constitutional rights of the Secessionists to be bothered with such mundane subjects as how the "cradle on thorough braces" got from Los Angeles to San Francisco.

Hamilton's contemporaries over at the Los Angeles *Semi-Weekly Southern News* were more cooperative from the researcher's viewpoint. On April 19, 1861, the *Southern News* announced that the Overland Mail via Fort Tejon had been discontinued, and all future mails would be sent by the Coast Route. Tri-weekly service was to commence April 22, 1861.

The very absence of complaints respecting the mail service for the next few months was indicative of the dependability which the population had come to expect from the Overland Mail Company. Later in the summer the *Southern News* did deplore the lack of "side service" along the Coast Route, and the complete absence of any mail service in the Tulare Valley after the withdrawal of the Overland Mail; but no general criticisms were in evidence concerning the contractor's performance on the new road.[1]

If it had been common knowledge that Wells, Fargo & Company was the dominant factor in the Overland Mail Company by this time, there would have been no astonishment on the part of anyone. To the contrary, it would have explained the reasons for the Overland's reliability – that was what they expected and admired most about the great express company.

Nor would there have been any cause for concern when the Los Angeles *Star* copied a news item from one of the northern papers respecting the departure of E. S. Alvord, Superintendent of the Overland Mail Company, for Washington:

> Mr. Alvord is one of the most experienced and successful mail contractors in the United States. He has been for some weeks past on this coast engaged in perfecting arrangements which he hopes will impart all desirable speed and regularity to conveyance of the letter and newspaper mail, as well as the Express. . . Mr. Alvord goes directly to Washington, where he will make it his business to see that the mail interests of California are properly cared for. . .[2]

There might have been a general uneasiness, however, if Alvord's true motives in California had been known. Those readers who noticed a small advertisement on page three of the *Star* a number of weeks later could be excused if they expressed concern or even mild alarm over this new development:

> Office Of The Overland Mail Company, San Francisco, Aug. 3rd, 1861. NOTICE IS HEREBY GIVEN, that the Overland Mail Company have sold their line of stages between San Francisco

---

[1] Los Angeles *Semi-Weekly Southern News,* July 12 & 24, 1861.
[2] Los Angeles *Star,* Aug. 24, 1861.

and Los Angeles, and Los Angeles and San Diego, to Charles McGlaughlin [*sic*] and Owen Fuller, the sale to take effect from the 1st day of July, 1861. Said McGlaughlin & Fuller assume all liabilities of said line, created since that date, and the Company cease to be responsible from that date. E. S. Alvord, Sup't o.m.c.[3]

The man must have been a blood relative of Honest John Allman if this was Alvord's concept of "perfecting arrangements" and imparting "all desirable speed and regularity to conveyance of the letter and newspaper mail. . ." The truth of the matter was that the sale by the Overland Mail Company of its San Francisco to San Diego line marked the beginning of an era of confusion, rapid changes of ownership, and erratic service, which would not be wholly corrected until the arrival on the staging scene in 1866 of William Lovett, prominent state politician from Monterey County.

No small part of the confusion from a researcher's viewpoint was the tendency of the records to be smudged with semantics. For the next quarter of a century the newspapers of the coast would continue to refer to the Coast Line stages as "The Overland Stages," "The Overland Mail Stages," "The Overland Company," and numerous other variations of that magic word — *Overland*. The usage of "Butterfield" in conjunction therewith had diminished after W. B. Dinsmore replaced John Butterfield as President of the Overland Mail Company in 1860, but a West that had been hypnotized by the performance of the company still clung to the name *Overland*. No less a scholar of Western history than LeRoy Hafen had been deceived by this phenomenon when he quoted a letter from the San Francisco *Bulletin* of March 2, 1864:

[3] *Ibid.*, Sept. 14, 1861.

In 1864 the Overland Mail Company was running the mail from San Francisco southward to Los Angeles. The service was complained of. One passenger writes: "Their stages are old, rickety, mud wagons. . . If the Stage Company, for $25 through fare, and enormous way fare (at which prices they run full) in addition to the $44,000 paid them by the government for carrying the mail, cannot give better coaches and teams they had better sell out."[4]

Even while the notice of the Overland's sale of their Coast Route to McLaughlin & Fuller was running in the *Star,* the new "fireproof" Bella Union Hotel was advertising, "The stages of the Great Overland Mail Stages to and from San Francisco and St. Louis. . . arrive and depart from this hotel."[5]

The management of the Bella Union was living in a dream world of the past so far as the Overland Mail Company was concerned. On November 1, 1861, the *Semi-Weekly Southern News* observed with poetic sadness, "The last remaining glimmer of the ever memorable Butterfield Overland Mail has at last flickered out. . ." The article continued by noting that the stagecoaches from San Francisco were arriving in Los Angeles at all hours and very irregularly. No express was being carried and very little mail. "We have good reason to believe that matters in respect to the mails south of San Francisco are carried on loosely and have been tampered with. . ."

[4] LeRoy Hafen, *The Overland Mail* (Cleveland, 1926), p. 279. The use of this quotation is in no manner intended as a criticism of Hafen, whose contributions to Western history are far in excess of anything this writer could ever hope to accomplish. The intent is to illustrate how deceiving the indiscriminate use of the word "overland" could be to the best of researchers.

[5] Los Angeles *Semi-Weekly Southern News,* Oct. 25, 1861. This advertisement is dated Oct. 11; the final appearance of the Overland Mail Company's sale appeared in the *Star* on Oct. 18, 1861. The Bella Union advertisement was also running in the *Star.*

On November 6, and November 8, the *Southern News* continued its criticisms of the new management, going so far as to accuse the owners of deliberately performing poor service in order to put the mails back onto steamer contract. The accusation made little if any sense in view of the fact that the steamship line had refused to accept a mail contract at the time terms were offered to it on January 10, 1861. It was then that the Post Office Department granted to the Overland Mail Company the privilege of changing their route from the Tulare Valley to the coast. It is unclear whether or not there was any relation between the two acts.

On November 29, 1861, the *Southern News* conceded with no little sarcasm that, "We have mail occasionally. The buggy and four now used for conveyance of the mail bag arrived on Wednesday last, five days and eight hours from San Francisco." The *News* suggested that the United States Postal Agent investigate, "*IF* he is *NOT* a party to the swindle."

The newspaper had failed to consider that on the southern portion of the route heavy rains had commenced in mid-November and were continuing. No one could foresee that this was but a prelude to coming events of horrendous proportions.

It would be hard to imagine a more difficult "act" to follow than the Butterfield Overland Mail. The complaints in the *Semi-Weekly Southern News* directed at Charlie McLaughlin's operations of the Coast Line of Stages were but a reflection of this point. The Post Office Department's records for the Coast Route (12,-592) also mirror the problems of the various contractors in running the line, as well as the confusion generated in the researcher's mind while attempting to untangle the maze:

March 12, 1861: The Overland Mail Company contracts to carry the mails from San Diego to Monterey.

September 14, 1861: The Overland Mail Company announces the sale of the Coast Route to McLaughlin & Fuller, effective July 1, 1861. (There is no note of this transaction in the Post Office Department's records.)

November 13, 1862: Contract No. 12,592 is transferred to E. S. Alvord of Indianapolis, Indiana. Alvord appears to have made this transaction as a mail contractor on his own initiative and not in any official capacity he *may* still have had with the Overland Mail Company. The change was to be effective October 1, 1862, with Monterey dropped from the route and the line extended to San Juan Bautista. The contract was readjusted downward to $39,658, retroactive to April 1, 1861.

July 27, 1863: The Contract for Route 12,592 is transferred back to Charles McLaughlin of San Francisco effective July 1, 1863. With McLaughlin and Alvord playing beanbag with the Coast Route mail contract, it is not surprising to find the Post Office Department advertising for new bids a few months earlier than usual.

September 3, 1863: The Coast Route is ordered advertised for new bids, to go into effect July 1, 1864. Route 12,592 is re-numbered as Route 14,894. Only two bids were submitted: John Ashley & W. C. Adams submitted a bid of $26,000 for tri-weekly service, or $36,500 for six times a week service. B. F. Mann submitted a bid for tri-weekly service at $24,000 and was awarded the contract. This appears to have been a "straw bid" in lieu of the following entry.

February 15, 1865: "Accept Charles McLaughlin of

THE OLD BUTTERFIELD GRADE
The old stagecoach road came through the saddleback in the hills (center),
swung around the contours to the right (arrows) and emerged into the Santa
Rosa Valley at a spring by the present-day school house (lower right).

OFFICE OF THE OVERLAND MAIL COMPANY,
SAN FRANCSICO. Aug. 3d, 1861.

NOTICE IS HEREBY Given, that the Overland Mail Company have sold their line of stages between San Francisco and Los Angeles, and Los Angeles and San Diego, to CHARLES McGLAUGHLIN and OWEN FULLER, the sale to take effect from 1st day of July, 1861. Said McGLAUGHLIN & FULLER assume all liabilities of said line, created since that date, and the Company cease to be responsible from that date.

sept14-1m   E. S. ALVORD, Sup't. O. M. C.

FAREWELL NOTICE OF THE OVERLAND MAIL CO.
After four months of service, the Overland Mail Company
bids the Coast Route farewell.

San Francisco, Cal. as contractor in place of B. F. Mann on the due executions by the former of contracts on existing line from January 1, 1865. $24,000."

McLaughlin barely had time to harness the horses before the Department called for new bids again. William E. Lovett of Monterey submitted the winning bid of $18,000, which was accepted on March 14, 1866. At some time hereabouts the route was again re-numbered – 14,718. With Lovett in command a new day was dawning for the Coast Line of Stages, but the previous five years had been something else.

The reasons for the Overland Mail Company's sale of the San Francisco to San Diego line are anything but clear. Possibly Superintendent William Buckley could foresee the nightmare of winter coaching on a line that presented such obstacles as the Santa Clara, Ventura, Santa Ynez and Salinas rivers. Also, the company had problems enough with the transfer of the Overland Mail to the Central Route, where a one million dollar contract was involved, without dividing its attention with a 550-mile route that paid but $40,000 annually in mail contracts. Regardless of the reasons, Charlie McLaughlin was on the driver's box of the Coast Line of Stages in the fall of 1861. It is doubtful if the man's worst enemy could have picked a more inopportune moment.

The forecast of things to come appeared in the Los Angeles *Star* on October 5, 1861, with the news report that hundreds of tons of hay had been ruined by the "late rains" and grain prices were rising: "For ten days succeeding the equinoctial rain, the weather remained damp and cloudy, causing the grass on the hills to be unusually forward for this season of the year."

On November 16, the *Star* reported "abundant rains"

the past two days. On November 23, "We have had a
plentiful rain during the week. . . So now we have
mud, mud, everywhere." On November 30, "We have
had light rains during the week. . . The rains have
fallen lightly and steadily, thoroughly saturating the
earth." On December 7, "We have had during the
week, days and nights of continuous rains." It was only
the beginning, *only the beginning;* and yet after twenty-
three days and nights of almost constant rainfall those
Los Angeles newspaper editors could not understand
why the stages were having difficulty carrying out their
mail contract.

The soil of California from a submerged city of
Sacramento to the southern border was thoroughly saturated when the *real* storms commenced on December
24, 1861. It rained every day for the next forty-four days
in Santa Barbara County. Los Angeles saw the sun for a
few hours on January 23 & 24, 1862 (the *Star* maintained that several citizens had actually seen it!), but it
started raining again on the following day and continued uninterrupted through the fifth of February.
Henry Hamilton of the Los Angeles *Star* felt the unprecedented weather of enough moment to publish a
one sentence resumé of the flood as an everlasting record
for posterity:

"As a matter of record, it may be as well to state, that
from the 24th day of December to the 5th day of February, with the exception of two days, rain, more or less,
has fallen every day and night – sometimes in torrents." [6]

The intervening issues of the *Star* represent a splendid record of the most disastrous flood ever seen by
Californians. Whole towns were destroyed, livestock
perished by the thousands, mountainsides slid away, and

---

[6] Los Angeles *Star,* Feb. 8, 1862.

the roads built at such sacrifice to carry the freight wagons and stagecoaches were annihilated. Much of the destruction was wrought on January 18, when it seemed as though "the clouds had broken through and the waters over the earth and the waters under the earth were coming into conjunction." [7]

Hamilton had noted on January 4, that Los Angeles had experienced one shower since the previous issue of the newspaper, but it had lasted the entire time. Henry's real concern during this early period of the flood (it still had thirty-one days to go!) was the apparent failure of the coast road as a stage and mail route:

> For nearly two weeks no mail has arrived from the North. Our great tri-weekly mail has proved a failure. . . We suppose the contractors will be permitted to do as they please; to come or not, as suits their convenience. . . For two winters, we had the stages by the Tulare route, and a few hours was the greatest detention. Now we do not have any mail at all. . .
>
> We have been informed by a gentleman who lately traveled by the coast route, that it cannot be made available for travel during the winter months. The Salinas river is impassable for weeks at a time. In such rains as have fallen this year, it becomes dangerous, and at the crossing, quite impassable. This is not the only stream on the road which prevents wagons from crossing. And, indeed, the whole road has been denounced as unfit for travel, notwithstanding the praises showered upon it by interested parties. Then, again, the manner in which the line is stocked, is disgraceful. It is said, that but two horses are used to the wagons, and that the latter are comfortless and inconvenient in the greatest degree. On the whole, the mail arrangements are faulty in the extreme. The sooner they are reformed altogether the better for this community.[8]

It is a little difficult to understand the relevancy between the mail arrangements and stagecoach comfort; but when Hamilton's "printed mail matter" failed to arrive, almost any type of acid was apt to flow from his

[7] *Ibid.,* Jan. 25, 1862.　　　　　　　　[8] *Ibid.,* Jan. 4, 1862.

pen. As news began to seep into Los Angeles from the northern sections of the state revealing far worse conditions than those in the south, Hamilton's boiling point took a sharp rise. The State Government had abandoned Sacramento and adjourned to high ground in San Francisco. River boats were taking short cuts over farms, telegraph poles, orchards, and homes.[9] The old Tulare Valley Route of the Overland Mail was a great inland sea that no stagecoach could navigate, even though it might have managed somehow to cross the obliterated San Fernando Hill and the washed away San Francisquito Canyon road. For the one and only time Senator Merrit's bill to make the San Joaquin River navigable from Stockton to Fort Tejon appeared feasible.

On February 15, 1862, the *Star* began referring to "the late floods." If one analyzes the records from November 14, 1861, when the first lengthy rainy spell started, sixty-seven of the next eighty-three days and nights it rained.

Despite the calamitous nature of the flood, one mail stage had been able to get through from the north. On January 5, 1862, the first coach to arrive after the great storm began, mushed into Los Angeles after first floating down the Santa Clara River for a few miles and losing one mail bag. The mail that did come through was slightly saturated, much to Hamilton's disgust.

Periodic rainfall occurred for another sixty days after February 5, but the worst was over. By the end of February the *Star* could report that the stage company was busy repairing the coast road:

---

[9] For an interesting personal experience of this nature see "The Narrative of Jefferson Crane," The Ventura County Historical Society *Quarterly,* vol. I, no. 2, Feb., 1956.

> Overland Mail – Mr. Cluggie, agent for the company, arrived here this week from San Francisco. He has been employing men and setting them to work on the roads, from Monterey here. In places, as we have already said, the roads are entirely washed away, necessitating the lowering of a wagon over precipices by ropes. The Gaviota Pass is in this condition. The Supervisors of San Luis and Santa Barbara are cooperating in the repairs with the company. We have not heard if any action will be taken by the Board of this county. The road from Santa Barbara here is the worst on the line, as a greater length of road has been rendered impassable for wagons. Mr. Cluggie thinks with due exertions, the roads can be made fit for travel in about ten days; in which event, the mails would be put on the line again.[10]

On March 1, Hamilton reported the arrival of the San Francisco newspapers up to December (!) which had been transferred to the Steamship *Wright* at Santa Barbara. "They have been on the way ever since then, and considerably the worse for their journey."

It was not until March 6, that another stagecoach managed to muck its way through to Los Angeles:

> On Thursday, we received, by overland, papers from San Francisco to the 17th February, being only sixteen days on the way. Were the mails sent by steamer, they would have come to hand in forty-eight hours – a consideration of importance to those interested. For ourselves, not having the use of the institution, it makes very little difference to us, when or how it either arrives or departs.[11]

Oh no! Henry didn't care – much! On March 29, the *Star* reported that there had been no steamer and no mail in four weeks. If there had been no steamer, then there could have been no express; and if the editor of the *Star* was not using the mails, the only way he could communicate would be by express. This same issue of the *Star* reprinted an article from the Santa Cruz *Sen-*

---

[10] Los Angeles *Star,* Feb. 22, 1862.   [11] *Ibid.,* Mar. 8, 1862.

tinel in which the Salinas River was described as being a mile wide at La Soledad Mission during the floods.

These reports in the Los Angeles *Star* in late February and through March are of special interest since Postmaster General Blair in his Report of 1863, and Postmaster General Dennison in his Report of 1864, refer to contracting for a tri-monthly mail service by steamers for a period of ninety days during the floods. They did not specify the period involved, although April 14, was given as the date of the agreement. Nor was there any clear account in the *Star* of when stagecoaching resumed on a regular basis following the floods. The newspaper accounts would indicate that steamer service on a tri-monthly basis could not have begun before April. It would follow that *regular* stagecoach service did not resume until July.

After undergoing an experience such as the great floods of 1861-62, it is little wonder that McLaughlin & Fuller disposed of the line (or mail contract) to E. S. Alvord, effective October 1, 1862.

There is no more confusing aspect of the Coast Line staging story than this McLaughlin-Alvord switch, followed by a reverse switch the following summer from Alvord back to McLaughlin. This writer would not so much as attempt to make an educated guess on its significance, if any. These old stagers and mail contractors were capable of more under-the-table sleight-of-hand maneuvers than a Houdini. The point can best be illustrated by the fact that although no less than twenty-two names of "companies" were referred to in the contemporary newspapers as operating the Coast Line stages at various times, not one was ever listed with the Secretary of State as being incorporated under the laws of California. Ironically, the only incorporated stage company to operate on any portion of the Coast Line was All-man's Southern United States Mail Company. No researcher needs records to follow "Honest John" All-man; a normal sense of smell is sufficient.

There was a complete lack of staging news in the *Star* for almost two years following the floods. The first reference thereafter did not appear until November 28, 1863, when the newspaper noted that the Honorable H. Hamilton, Senator-elect, took his departure for Sacramento via the overland stage. The lack of any complaints concerning the mail service was almost sure proof that the stages had settled down to a monotonous regularity on the Coast Route road. The line had been under the management of Charlie McLaughlin, an experienced stager, since July 1, 1863; there was no reason to expect anything other than normalcy.

It is also worth noting that the two winters following 1862, were periods of excessive drought. The dust might have worn out the hubs and axles of the stages, or choked the passengers and drivers; but no one would have gotten wet staging to San Francisco. Surprisingly, the one good descriptive article on riding the Coast Line of Stages from Los Angeles northward during this period stated that the road was free of dust. The writer probably did not realize that his story would have been different if he had been traveling in the other direction, in which case the wind would have carried the dust along with the stage instead of constantly blowing it to the rear.

Hot Springs, Paso de Robles, June 13, 1864. Editor *Star:* I left the good old city of the Angels, on Friday morning, June 10th at 4 o'clock A.M. in the overland stage, taking my seat on the outside with the driver. After an hour's drive, a dense fog came up, and I got quite cold and wet, but having a bottle of cock-tails aboard, which my friend John gave me, and drinking a little of the same, made me feel all right. We jogged along, and having but few passengers, arrived at Simi pass, when I was informed that a little walk up the mountain would be healthy, and give me an appetite for breakfast. I took the hint, and started over the mountain and after walking two miles came to the house of Mr. Connor, where breakfast was waiting us. After eating a hearty meal, started off across the Simi plain, the road being in splendid condition and free of dust. Arrived at San Buenaventura at three o'clock P.M. where we had dinner.

In two hours drive, we came to the beach, and to our disappointment found the tide was in, and that we would be detained about two hours, which was really pleasant. I concluded to take a walk along the beach, to the other side, and wait for the stage, but after getting across, found it to be a tedious and tiresome trip.

The stage getting over safe, "all aboard" was sung out by the driver, and away we went, through fine rolling country, arriving at Santa Barbara at half past ten o'clock P.M., the stage stopping at the Tibbett house, and I must say, one that is well kept. Stopping there all night, I arose at 4 o'clock in the morning, and took a short trip around the burg, and found it quite a nice looking place. Having eaten breakfast, we again started with a long and tiresome drive before us. A short distance from Santa Barbara again crossed the beach and along the foot of the mountain, close to the shore, and the scene was truly a beautiful one; the broad blue Pacific stretching out, as far as the eye could reach.

A few hours drive brought us to Gaviota Pass, and for a distance all hands walked, and I must say the road through the pass, and over the mountain, was one of romance and grandeur.

In crossing the St. Inez plains in the evening, a terrific sand storm came up, continuing for some time, and it was pleasant [?] sitting out on the box getting one's eyes and face full of sand. But the boy was compelled to stand it. We arrived at San Luis Obispo on Sunday morning, at 3 o'clock . . . feeling pretty cold, but in a few minutes had a rousing fire at the hotel, which was duly appreciated.

Eating a hearty meal, left San Luis about 4 o'clock and after a beautiful drive of five hours, arrived here safe, at 9 o'clock A.M., much to my joy. The trip is not so fatiguing as might be supposed, and I will say to all my friends who wish to enjoy a pleasant and romantic trip, take the overland stage, the road being free of dust, and pleasant and agreeable drivers.[12]

With the exception of the lack of dust, a more typical description of a southern California stagecoach ride of the 1860s would be hard to imagine. The early morning departures, waiting for the ebb tide on the Rincon, a rousing fire at the hotel in San Luis Obispo in the dead of night, and walking over the steep mountain grades, were all features left on the record by various writers.

Those appetite stimulating hikes over the mountains were the source of the apocryphal cliché related by Paul Morton in the April 1901, issue of *Land of Sunshine:*

> It was during these good old days that they used to sell three classes of tickets all the same rate, the only difference in conditions of tickets being announced by the stage driver on arriving at a hill, who would then say, "First-class passengers keep your seats, second-class passengers get out and walk, third-class passengers get out and *push.*"

By the closing months of 1864, it had become obvious to the most ardent rebel that the Confederacy was a lost cause. With the end of the war in sight, newspaper talk in Los Angeles turned to the possibility of reactivating the old Butterfield Overland Mail Route. Henry Hamilton of the *Star* had suggested the idea early in the year in a long editorial pregnant with nostalgia of the good old days "when the first stage entered Los Angeles, freighted with letters and passengers, crossing the Saharas of New Mexico and Arizona and arriving here in twenty-one days from the Atlantic States." [13]

Hamilton had been *persona non grata* with Mr. Lincoln & Company, having been arrested for treason ear-

---

[12] *Ibid.,* June 18, 1864.

[13] *Ibid.,* Jan. 9, 1864. Henry Hamilton had not checked his morgue too carefully on this one. Waterman Ormsby was the only through passenger "freighted" across the southern "Saharas."

lier in the war and transported to San Francisco and
detained without his permission. Henry suspended publication of the *Star* on October 1, 1864, although financial considerations appear to have been behind the move
rather than his past political views on the war. It was
not until May 16, 1868, that the *Star* began to shine
again in Los Angeles. In the interim the Los Angeles
News, using one of its various "prefixes," was the only
newspaper published in the city.

In November 1864, the *News* picked up the torch for
the old Butterfield Overland Mail Route and carried
the dream still further:

> While such a mail line is in contemplation, it is wisdom that it
> should start from a point on the Pacific Coast, which will connect
> it with steamer facilities and travel, the telegraph, and the over-
> land mail line now running tri-weekly between Los Angeles and
> San Francisco. A line of mail-stages upon the last mentioned
> route, will be the great feeder to all future mail facilities which
> may be established to the eastward and south of this place, and
> lasting to the rich and growing mining interests which are spring-
> ing up so rapidly in the Southern portion of California and
> throughout the young Territory above mentioned [Arizona].[14]

In other words, the *News* was advocating that Los
Angeles, *not* San Francisco, should be the terminus of a
reestablished Overland Mail. By the time the war had
ended and its repercussions were dying down, San Francisco could not have cared less – the transcontinental
railroad was just over the horizon and shining brightly.

With the exception of those first two months after the
Overland Mail Company sold the Coast Route, the Los
Angeles *News* had never been the constant source of
uawarranted criticisms of the stage line that Hamilton's
Star had been. Only on rare occasions would it express

14 Los Angeles *News,* Nov. 26, 1864.

mild irritation at mail service and delays, or the poor equipment and stock of the Coast Line of Stages. Invariably, these would appear during periods of winter storms, the city editors never seeming to grasp the difficulties of coaching over muddy roads and flooding rivers. It was under such circumstances that the *News* grumbled on February 11, 1865:

> The overland stages from San Francisco have been arriving here very irregularly – or rather the mails have. We believe there are three mails now due here. Newspaper mails have not been received here for several weeks, until yesterday, and there must be paper bags yet behind on the road. Bad roads are a good excuse. The Postal Agent should "punch" the contractors a little.

It will be noted that the editor of the *News* had one thing in common with Henry Hamilton: The newspaper mails were the prime bone of contention, not the letter mail. The *News* was of the opinion, apparently, that the newspaper exchange mail was even more important than feeding the livestock responsible for its delivery:

> THE OVERLAND MAIL CONTRACTORS – We are credibly informed that the stages on the northern portion of the route, between this place and San Jose, are used for the transportation of barley and other supplies, between stations, to the exclusion of the mail-bags. If this be true it is worthy of some notice from the Postal Agent. We are now *regularly* in receipt of mails which have been on the road from six to ten days. A new contractor would just fit the occasion; let us try another.[15]

The *News* would not have long to wait until a change of contractors occurred. When new bids were called for on the San Juan to Los Angeles mail route, William E. Lovett of Monterey submitted the lowest figure – $18,000 for tri-weekly service to begin July 1, 1866. Charlie

---

15 *Ibid.,* Feb. 18, 1865.

McLaughlin had submitted a bid of $19,500 for tri-weekly service and $35,000 for six times a week delivery; but McLaughlin's bids specified San Jose as the northern terminus, not San Juan. Subsequent developments might indicate that there had been some political shenanigans involved.

State Senator William E. Lovett was a Republican representing the Monterey-Santa Cruz district in Sacramento. During the Presidential election year of 1864, Lovett had blanketed the southern end of the State in an unprecedented barnstorming tour, much of it by stagecoach, campaigning for the reelection of Abraham Lincoln. The Los Angeles *News* reported extensively from October 18, to November 15, 1864, on Lovett's strenuous efforts in behalf of the President.

Late in March 1865, the Superintendent of Indian Affairs appointed Lovett as Special Agent "to investigate any and all matters between the Indians and whites, in the Southern Counties. . ." [16] The Republicans were not so proud as to refute completely the old Jacksonian principle that to the victor belongs the spoils, or leave unscratched a deserving back.

To put the thing bluntly: because of the political situation Senator Lovett was in an excellent position to obtain inside information concerning probable future plans entertained by the Post Office Department in respect to the coast mail route and to submit his bid accordingly. Bearing in mind that the winning bidder did not take over the route until July 1, 1866, the following changes thereafter, with the increased pay involved, are of more than passing interest:

On August 26, 1866, the Post Office Department ordered the tri-weekly contract expanded to six times a

---

16 *Ibid.,* Apr. 4 & 22, 1865.

week, with an increase in pay to the contractor of $12,-
000. This brought the contract up to $30,000 per year,
still $5000 under the bid of Charlie McLaughlin for
the same service; but it must be remembered that
McLaughlin was bidding to run to San Jose, not San
Juan.

On March 26, 1867, Lovett was ordered to increase
the service to seven times a week effective April 1, with
an additional fee of $3500 allowed.

The following year, after Lovett had sold the line to
Flint, Bixby & Company, the Post Office Department
ordered the running time expedited by twenty-two
hours with a further pay increase of $7500. Llewelyn
Bixby was a brother-in-law of William Lovett, whose
original $18,000 contract had by now been fattened to
$41,000.

The unanswerable questions are: Why did Charlie
McLaughlin submit his bid to San Jose instead of San
Juan when the added distance of approximately forty
miles would have meant at least one additional station
to maintain? Would McLaughlin have entered a more
competitive bid if he had known of the expansion plans
for the route? Regardless of what the answers might
have been, the days were over when Charlie McLaughlin controlled the staging south of San Francisco.

Lovett called his line "The Coast Line, San Juan and
Los Angeles Stage Company" with the added words
"U.S. Mail" sometimes inserted between "Los Angeles"
and "Stage." As was the case with his predecessors and
successors, no incorporation papers for the "company"
were ever filed with the California Secretary of State.

If the Los Angeles *News* is to be believed, Senator
Lovett transformed the Coast Line of Stages from a
baled hay, grain hauling outfit into a line that fairly

equaled the old Butterfield Overland Mail in performance. On one occasion in 1867, the *News* went so far as to refer to Lovett's Coast Line as "The Butterfield Route," and again brought up that old dream of reactivating the "Oxbow Route" to the Mississippi:

> The great advantage that accrues to this country from the Butterfield route is a sufficient guarantee of what would accrue from the extension of the present line to some point upon the Mississippi river. Knowing, as those of us do who understand the wants of this country, that next to a Southern Pacific railroad, a daily overland mail is what we most need to attract public attention to our fertile valleys and salubrious climate, we should make it our business to foster and encourage the present line in every manner possible. . .[17]

The *News* had been hammering away since 1864 on the idea of reactivating the Butterfield Overland Mail. When service on the Coast Route was increased to six times a week in September 1866, it was suggested that Congress extend the line to the Mississippi via the Southern Route. The *News* had pointed out, with fantastic optimism, that Arizona and New Mexico were filling up rapidly with an intelligent population; and the lack of a daily mail was doing more to retard the country than all the Indians on the continent could do if transported there.[18]

Two months later the *News* was at it again. The editorial was typical of the paper in that it is difficult to tell whether the Coast Line of Stages under Lovett was as good as portrayed or whether the real purpose behind boosting the Coast Line was to encourage Congress to reactivate the trans-Mississippi Southern Mail Route:

> The stages of the Daily Overland Mail between this city and San Francisco, arrive and depart with great regularity; it has

[17] *Ibid.,* Sept. 27, 1867.   [18] *Ibid.,* Aug. 24, 1866.

already become one of the fixed institutions of the country; and
the advantages derived therefrom are duly appreciated by our business and traveling community. The old truism, that increased
facilities for travel always bring an increase in travel, has been
verified in this instance to the letter; more persons have been
booked for San Francisco from this place, than the stages could
carry, and some were forced to remain behind until such time as
seats could be secured in other stages. In proportion as our people
feel the benefits arising from a well conducted line of stages from
this city to San Francisco, they are alive to the necessity of a daily
line of stages from this city to some portion of the Mississippi
river, connecting with the San Francisco line. Congress will meet
in a short time and steps should be taken to bring the matter before that body, early in the session; the Government has been
liberal in aiding the Pacific Railroad, but the necessity of the
country demands two lines, one at the Northern extremity of the
State, and one at the Southern; and while the resources of the
country have been so freely given in aid of the Pacific Railroad,
we should certainly have a stage line through the Southern
Route.[19]

The *News* on December 18, 1866, again referred to
the subject, noting that there were no immediate plans
to extend the San Francisco & San Jose Railroad to Gilroy or beyond; and the old Butterfield Route offered the
best hope for the southern end of the State. The impossible dream of resurrecting a glorious past died an
agonizingly hard death.

There was another factor involved in the glorification
of the Coast Line of Stages by the Los Angeles *News*
after Lovett bought the line: a continuing battle with
the California Steam Navigation Company over its
accommodations, high fares and freight rates, and the
dangerous conditions existing on most of their decrepit
coastal steamers. The *News* had ample company and
solid support on this issue, there being scarcely a news-

[19] *Ibid.,* Oct. 16, 1866.

paper on the south coast that was not constantly barking at the "Steamship Monopoly." The *only* recourse to such a monopoly where passenger traffic was concerned was the stage line up the coast.

It would be an almost sure bet that if there had been adequate, comfortable, and safe transportation by sea at fair prices, the Los Angeles *News* and its contemporaries would have had little flattery for Lovett's Coast Line, San Juan and Los Angeles Stage Company. It would be an even safer bet that ninety percent of the favorable comments bestowed upon Lovett's stages were made with the idea of prodding the steamship line into putting newer and more comfortable boats on the coastal runs. The favorable editorials concerning the Coast Line stages were too frequently interspersed with the likes of the following to conclude otherwise:

CALIFORNIA STEAM NAVIGATION COMPANY – This company has had an almost continuous monopoly of the steam carrying trade upon this coast, between this city and San Francisco, for ten years, during the whole of which time, exorbitant prices have been demanded and received for freight and passengers, and although our citizens from time to time, have made some complaints about the unseaworthiness of the vessels used by the company, their want of sufficient accomodations, &c., the company have never seen fit to improve the accomodations, or heed the growing sentiment of our traveling and commercial public. . . The steamer *California,* now upon the line, is so totally wanting in all the elements of a first class passenger steamer, that *large numbers of persons prefer, even at this season of the year, when the trip from here to San Francisco is particularly disagreeable, to travel by the Overland stage,* to enduring the discomforts of a sea voyage in such vessels as the Steam Navigation Company furnish. . .[20]

The idea that a stagecoach could compete with the most decrepit of steamships in transporting any volume

[20] *Ibid.,* Mar. 16, 1866. Italics added.

SIMI VALLEY IN THE STAGECOACH DAYS

COAST LINE STAGE CO. AD
A typical ad in local papers
after Flint, Bixby and Co.
purchased the line.

COAST LINE,

Los Angeles to San Francisco.

SIXTY MILES RAILROAD TRAVEL.

TIME REDUCED, SPEED INCREASED

 THE STAGES OF THE COAST LINE, carrying the U. S. Mail, leave the Office daily at ONE, P.M., sharp time, for San Francisco,

Via San Buenaventura, Santa Barbara, San Luis Obispo, Paso Robles Hot Springs, Salinas, San Juan, Gilroy, and San Jose.

The Company having lately put on the route new Post Coaches, Passengers are assured that every attention will be paid to their comfort. Passengers are allowed the privilege of laying over at any points on the route, and resume their seats within six days.

For further information, apply at the Office, at Bella Union Hotel.

WM. BUCKLEY,
General Superintendent.

Los Angeles, Sept, 26, 1868.

of passengers was absurd on the face of it. The steamship company knew it and so did the Los Angeles *News:*

> Men and women have to travel by steamer; there are an infinitude of comforts upon a commodious steamship which are not found in a cramped and tedious stagecoach; but men and women now-a-days estimate the value of money, and will subject themselves to many discomforts to ensure a diminution of prices. . .
> We regard it the duty of our people to frown upon this corroding monopoly.[21]

The frustrations of the steamship monopoly would prevail until the day the railroad "Octopus" proved that rails could be as aggravating as salt water in the matter of services, charges, and monopolistic phenomena.

William Lovett sold his Coast Line, San Juan & Los Angeles Stage Company to Flint, Bixby & Company on January 17, 1868, for $70,000.[22] It has always been a mystery to this writer why a company whose primary interest was livestock raising on a vast scale wanted to get involved in the staging business. The Los Angeles *Star* of June 7, 1871, quoting from the Monterey *Republican,* gave a good account of the extent of this firm's operations:

> Flint, Bixby & Co., of San Juan, own about 200,000 acres of land; 19,000 in the immediate vicinity of San Juan, 140,000 in Los Angeles, 53,000 in San Luis Obispo, and over 18,000 in San Joaquin and Washington Territory, on which graze 75,000 sheep and thousands of cattle. Their wool clip this spring will realize them about $95,000 – over 300,000 pounds have been sheared.[23]

---

21 *Ibid.,* Sept. 28, 1866.

22 The author is indebted to Mr. Robert Johnston of Hartnell College for this precise date and purchase price. At a later date Miss Dorothy Flint of Hollister, California, a granddaughter of Dr. Thomas Flint of Flint, Bixby & Company, furnished the author with duplicated copies of the bill of sale, Lovett's receipt for the $70,000, and an application to the Postmaster General for relief when Lovett failed to turn over the payments for carrying the mails as per agreement.

23 This item also appeared in the Santa Barbara *Press* on June 3, 1871.

Sarah Bixby Smith in her book, *Adobe Days* (1931), thought so little of the company's stagecoaching operations that she devoted but two inaccurate sentences to the subject.

It is even more bewildering to find the advertisements for the Coast Line of Stages in the Los Angeles *Star,* the Ventura *Signal,* the Ventura *Free Press,* and other newspapers along the route, omitting the owner's name. Only on the Los Angeles to San Diego run does the name Flint, Bixby & Company appear with regularity. The advertisements for the Los Angeles to San Francisco route were usually signed by William Buckley, Superintendent. In the process of reading through forty years of newspaper files in search of items relating to staging in California, at no time has this writer ever uncovered an account wherein any partner in Flint, Bixby & Company appeared in the least interested in stagecoaching *per se.* They owned the business and expected it to show a profit, but William Buckley was the man who had the "know-how" that made profits a reality.

One possible explanation for this interesting state of affairs is that Flint, Bixby & Company became involved in stagecoaching through chance rather than by design. The theory is suggested by the wording in a legally phrased application to the Postmaster General of the United States, the accuracy of which was sworn to by Benjamin Flint and Lewellyn Bixby. In fitting the pieces of this puzzle together it is important to remember that Lovett was related by marriage to Lewellyn Bixby:

On January 18, 1868, one day after the sale of his Coast Line, San Juan & Los Angeles Stage Company, William Lovett had written and signed the following receipt: "Received of Flint, Bixby & Co., the sum of seventy thousand dollars, amount in full for the property sold to them of the Coast Line, San Juan and Los Angeles U.S.M. Stage Co. property – as per bill of sale executed to them."

The bill of sale itself had used the words: "all the property belonging or in any way appertaining to The Coast Line, San Juan and Los Angeles Stage Company of whatsoever kind or nature." Such an all-inclusive clause would certainly have included the contract to carry the United States mails, although Flint and Bixby in their application to the Postmaster General pointed out that this had also been agreed upon verbally.

Lovett himself had conceded this point by turning over to Flint, Bixby & Company the next three quarterly payments from the United States Postoffice Department for carrying the mails on the Coast Route. The following two payments Lovett put in his own coffers, for reasons unknown. With the second quarterly payment for 1869 due on July 1, Benjamin Flint and Lewellyn Bixby belatedly wrote the Postmaster General, notifying him of their purchase from Lovett of the Coast Line, San Juan and Los Angeles Stage Company – including the contract to carry the mails – and asking for "the protection of this Department in the premises that they may be paid for carrying said mails . . . and for such further relief as the Department may be able to give them. . ." [24]

The motives for Lovett's illegal actions are unknown to this writer, nor are they of any particular importance to the present subject matter. What is relevant is the

[24] From a letter or legal application addressed to the Postmaster General of the United States, dated June 26, 1869, and signed by Benjamin Flint and Lewellyn Bixby. Duplicated copy supplied by Miss Dorothy Flint.

following wording on the first page of the Flint-Bixby application to the Postmaster General: ". . . that said sale and assignment were made in consideration of Seventy thousand dollars *previously advanced to him by the undersigned.*"[25]

This wording suggests that Flint, Bixby & Company had loaned Lovett the money, either as a succession of informal loans because Lovett's wife was Lewellyn Bixby's sister, or else as a formal loan with the stage line as security. When Lovett could not meet the debt, the company took over the Coast Line, San Juan and Los Angeles Stage Company. With one of the best stagecoaching superintendents in the West in charge of the business, the firm of Flint, Bixby & Company was content to concentrate on the raising of livestock and let William Buckley run the stagecoaches.

It was Buckley who had made the Coast Line feasible for the Overland Mail Company at the outset. Charlie McLaughlin had no William Buckley to look after the operation, and the line deteriorated badly before the old San Francisco stager could bring it back to something resembling normalcy.

William Lovett was primarily a politician, so once again it was Buckley who made the wheels turn. One could hazard a guess that it was Buckley that talked Lovett into the mail contracting business in the first place, and carry the thought still further with the suggestion that the firm of Flint, Bixby & Company was only interested in the financial aspects of stagecoaching.

While this may have been true, at least the magnitude of the operation must have appealed to these livestock tycoons. The inventory appended to the bill of sale from William Lovett to Flint, Bixby & Company lists the

---

25 *Ibid.* Italics added.

Coast Line, San Juan and Los Angeles Stage Company as owning two hundred and seventy-two head of horses; twenty-two stations, with all the buildings, hay and grain, etc., necessary to care for passengers and stock; twenty-three stages, all but four of which were mud wagons; one freight wagon; forty-nine sets of four-horse harness; six sets of six-horse harness; offices and fixtures in San Francisco, San Jose, and San Juan; and a complete repair facility at Santa Barbara, with black-smith and harness shops, iron, leather, lumber, tools, etc. Yes, the size of the operation would have appealed to Flint, Bixby & Company.

A decade later when the firm sold the Coast Line of Stages, the buyers were William Buckley and his newly acquired partner, W. H. "Shotgun" Taylor, a hell-for-leather Jehu of the old school and an apt cohort for Buckley.

The corporate confusion on the Coast Line of Stages would endure for so long as the four or six-in-hand pulled the wheels with the cradle on thorough braces from Los Angeles northward, but it would seldom be so obscure as it was during those first confusing years.

5

The Heyday of Coastal Staging

There is a tendency in the human mind, not confined to the present era, most deleterious to the progress of the mental development of mankind, and which acts as a heavy clog upon the wheels of knowledge. It is that disposition to magnify the evils and ignore the virtues of the present, while the evils of the past ages are overlooked and their virtues unduly exaggerated.

J. J. Warner [1]

"Juan Largo" Warner, of Warner's Ranch fame, did not have stagecoaching in mind when he penned those all too true words to the editor of the Los Angeles *Star*. In truth, Warner was discussing the weighty subject of "Capital and Labor," but there is no more fitting theme to which the philosophy could be applied than stagecoaching. The most glamorous days of the six-in-hand were not spawned until the eighth decade of the twentieth century, and then it was on the billboards of the highways and byways and not "for real." The only contemporary-with-the-events resemblance to those unduly exaggerated displays of the virtues of stagecoaching would be the grandiloquent, colored lithographs of a bygone era which invariably portrayed six spirited steeds on the full gallop, disturbing not a spec of dust to soil the gorgeously dressed doll on the box beside the Jehu; while inside the Concord coach a full load of passengers rode as though floating on air in a 747 jetliner. Few artists ever portrayed the lowly mud wagon pulled by the prosaic and plodding mule; the Concord coach was all they felt worthy of passing on to future

---

1 Los Angeles *Star*, July 16, 1870.

generations. And when the aging whip sat rusticating in the sun on the front porch recalling those good old days for the benefit of some magazine or newspaper writer, it was only the virtues he remembered; the evils had been erased from memory as easily as the stagecoach tracks on the sands of the Rincon had faded with the rising tides.

If any period of coastal staging could be called its heyday, it would be from about 1867, after William Buckley had ironed out the kinks of the Charlie McLaughlin era, until 1882, when John Allman, alias "Little Satan," wormed his way onto a portion of the route. For the most part during this period Flint, Bixby & Company were the owners of the Coast Line of Stages, although it was Buckley that made the operation successful. During the later years the Telegraph Stage Line came into the drama on the southern portion of the route to cause considerable corporate confusion, then as well as today; while Buckley & Taylor bought out Flint, Bixby & Company and continued staging on the north end of the line. J. C. Cheney, longtime superintendent of the Telegraph Line, would preserve the "virtues" of stagecoaching for that firm as William Buckley was doing for the Coast Line.

Years after the Coast Line of Stages was but a memory, George Hugh Banning writing in the July 1934, issue of *Westways,* did a superb job of confirming J. J. Warner's philosophy. Banning described the Coast Line under William Lovett; Flint, Bixby & Company; and Buckley & Taylor, as "a model line. . . It was the exemplary line. . ." It was a stage line stocked with matched teams, "Nothing but six and always matched." Concord coaches the color of red wine and with all the

PASO DE ROBLES HOT SPRINGS
A Vischer sketch showing the arrival of the Coast Line Stage from
Los Angeles, circa 1865. Courtesy, Title Insurance and Trust Co.

SAN LUIS OBISPO

Vischer's sketch of the stage station and barns at San Luis Obispo, 1865. All the stages are mud wagons. The Concord Coach is conspicuous by its absence in most Vischer sketches of Coast Line staging. Courtesy, Title Insurance and Trust Co.

LOS BERROS STAGE STATION

Vischer's sketch of an unidentified station in San Luis Obispo Co., 1865. The Arroyo Grande Station did not open until June 1867. The primary station south of San Luis prior to that date was Los Berros. Courtesy, Title Insurance and Trust Co.

JOLON STATION

This picture of the Jolon Stage Station was taken about 1900, after completion of the railroad up the Salinas Valley. Courtesy, Title Insurance and Trust Co.

gold trimmings put on a display, according to Banning, the likes of which the old *El Camino Real* had never seen or dreamed possible. Ironically, the only mention of mud wagons was on the caption of the one stage-coach photograph taken on the Coast Line that accompanied the article. Here, indeed, was a cultural heritage, as Banning put it, "to include the finest arts and sciences of the coaching era that the world has known."

Only an idiot would criticize so glorious an era, so accommodating a mode of transportation, such glamour, color, and business genius as characterized the Coast Line of Stages described by Banning; but there were idiots in those days. They not only rode the "exemplary" stage line in the Concord coaches of the purest red wine colors, behind six prancing steeds that were always matched, the idiots were even so inconsiderate as to leave permanent impressions of that experience and thereby cast "evil" upon an otherwise "virtuous" record:

> The dust from Santa Barbara to Ventura indicates the presence of pulverized gravel of the oolite or pliocene formation, and it is possible that upheavals were of frequent occurrence here after the Chaotic Era. The last upheaval was probably my breakfast, which was shaken out of me near Carpinteria. . . The rest of the journey would have been very interesting but for the bottle of claret you gave me, and some bourbon which the driver had. The only place of note is at the foot of the mountain [Larry's Station] where we got a drink of aguardiente, and at the Eight-Mile House where the beer is good.[2]

Banning might have claimed that the correspondent for the Santa Barbara *Times* who composed the above epistle was intoxicated, possibly from looking at the

---

[2] Ventura *Signal,* June 14, 1873, reprinted from the Santa Barbara *Times.*

beautiful wine-colored Concord coach, and in no condition to report objectively. The editor of the Ventura *Signal* advised his contemporary in Santa Barbara to "lasso that correspondent as soon as possible," the reason being he had also written some uncouth remarks concerning San Buenaventura. However, it would appear that even the gentler sex was in no mood to appreciate the beauties of the "Palm City" after a stagecoach ride from Santa Barbara:

Thirty miles of stage riding over the roughest (in some places) road imaginable, when only by hanging on to the sides of the coach, literally "tooth and nail," could we avoid the involuntary game of base ball which the combined efforts of the six prancing steeds, aided and abetted by the implacable driver, caused us to play with our fellow passengers, they alternately acting as bats and we as balls, and *vice versa;* this kind of traveling is not calculated to cause one's mind to be in that condition of sweet beatitude, when the meanest things in nature have a somewhat glorified aspect, and we are inclined to call thistles roses; and the wayside stones, pillows of downy ease. Therefore, it is not surprising that the first sight of Ventura, which, by the way, one views in its worst aspect from the entrance by the way of the Santa Barbara stage road, with its *adobe* houses and rough, unpaved streets, did not impress us with that sense of admiration which its many virtues merit. However, time and a more extended acquaintance have removed, in a great measure, the unfavorable opinion which we then held of everything in general, and San Buenaventura in particular – for we are human; moreover we are a woman, and wasn't our back hair all tumbled down? Wasn't our hat knocked into as many angles as there are pieces in a bologna sausage? And as for our bruises and mangled flesh – ough! Don't mention it.[3]

---

[3] Ventura *Signal,* Sept. 27, 1873. This article is signed "Dora Darmore." Her reaction to adobe houses was almost universal among Easterners seeing them for the first time. Even the Missions were not exempt from this type of criticism.

The only resemblance between that contemporary account of coastal staging and Banning's later wine-colored dream was the six prancing steeds, and the writer obviously could see nothing about a half a dozen nags over which to get ecstatic. A later description by another author would indicate a deterioration in live-stock and coaches rather than improvement:

> The Coast Line Stage Company ought to put on better horses and stages. The ride, at this season, down the valley is bad enough, but in mud wagons behind slow teams it is simply horrible. I heard that a number of preachers enroute by stage to Los Angeles, to attend conference recently, could not sit, and that the business was all done by *standing* committees. Whether any remarks were made in the coach as they went bumping along of an unprofessional character I was not advised. The drivers on the route are all good men and careful, and we hope soon to see them in charge of better stock and coaches.[4]

The most fanatical stagecoach buff would have to concede that a difference of opinion existed between some contemporary passengers and Banning's later descriptions of the joys of coaching via San Buenaventura, Santa Barbara, *et al,* and "connecting with the cars" at Gilroy, Salinas City, or Soledad. One could carry the thought still further and note that an even greater disparity of opinion existed at the time. This was particularly true where newspaper editors and reporters were concerned.

Dr. S. P. Guiberson, Santa Paula correspondent for the Ventura papers, stated: "It is my candid opinion that a ride from Newhall to Santa Paula inside one of those Coast Line Stages will cure any case of hypochondria, measles, or hydrophobia that ever has or will

---

4 Ventura *Signal,* Nov. 25, 1876.

occur." [5] If Doc's sentiments proved nothing else, it established that he was an inveterate reader of overland narratives, from one of which he had pirated the thought.

It was more common to find the editor of those days in a flattering mood when describing long trips by stagecoach, the reason being that he was traveling on a pass from the stage company, not paying for a ticket out of his pocket as had been the case with Guiberson. A classic example of this nineteenth century mutual back scratching ceremony was written for the Santa Barbara *Press* by its editor, J. A. Johnson, in the issue of November 11, 1871:

> It is a pleasure to speak in praise of the Overland Stage Company and the unusually capable, faithful and accomodating agents and drivers on this route. On our recent trip to Los Angeles we were impressed with the superiority of the men employed by this company, and convinced that they do all in their power to make passengers enjoy the trip and secure the largest comforts the route affords. They ought to have ten times the patronage now received. [6]

Johnson had made this trip to Los Angeles soon after the infamous Chinese Massacre of October 1871. Feelings were still running high and strangers looked upon with suspicion when the Santa Barbara editor undertook the journey. Probably for this reason his staff after his departure had composed and published: "We

---

[5] *Ibid.,* Nov. 2, 1878.

[6] Editor Johnson of the Santa Barbara *Press* was praised by his friends as the most successful editor on the Pacific coast, and damned by his enemies as "Uriah the old Mormon." He carried on a vigorous style of journalism from mid-1869 until he turned the paper over to Harrison G. Otis in late 1875. Otis later became editor of the Los Angeles *Times.* For a fuller account of Johnson see Muir Dawson, *Southern California Newspapers, 1851-1876* (Los Angeles, 1950).

armed the editor-in-chief with three Henry rifles and a 32-pounder to go to Los Angeles."[7]

The Ventura *Signal,* always on the alert for dry powder with which to shoot barbs at Santa Barbara, retorted: "He had no such weapons when he passed through here. Don't you mean three pint flasks and a jug?"[8]

If Editor-in-Chief Johnson had a reply to that one, and he probably did, the *Signal* was disinclined to print it. Johnson's fellow editors had not dubbed him, "Uriah, the old Mormon" for nothing.

On October 18, 1873, the Ventura *Signal* published a long editorial on the joys and beauties attendant to traveling via Coast Line stage to San Francisco. "Six sturdy bronchos hitched to a Coast Line stage. . ; going at a rattling pace all the way. . ; away out upon the sea, the view is worth the climbing [San Marcos Pass]; we passed through the Santa Ynez country rapidly." It should be evident from such favorable expressions that the writer was traveling "on the house." In the best tradition of newspaper editors, however, he could not resist noting that the Paso Robles hot springs were as nothing compared with Matilija; the Santa Ynez Valley *might* equal the Ojai *if* it were more accessible; and if such a city as Santa Barbara could be built upon a location with so little to offer, what might be expected from "the great Santa Clara, the Ojai, the Sespe, the Santa Paula and the Ventura valleys. . ." The writer also gave an insight into one of the phenomena of the times when he observed: "The railroad as most *Signal* readers know, now runs to a place in the

---

7 Ventura *Signal,* Nov. 4, 1871. Reprinted from the Santa Barbara *Press.*
8 Ventura *Signal,* Nov. 4, 1871.

Salinas Valley called Soledad, where there is quite a town – of small pegs to denote the corners of lots. . ."

A number of years later the editor of the San Luis Obispo *Tribune* had some caustic remarks concerning the conditions of Coast Line stage travel. The tartness of the *Tribune* editor's views would indicate that he had paid for his passage:

"Again, after a three-hours ride in one of the poorest little old hacks that I ever had the misfortune to be caught in, we arrived at the little, old town known as Santa Barbara." [9]

To which Editor McLean of the Ventura *Free Press* replied: "If he made it in three hours, that is just three-and-a-half hours faster than we were ever carried over that road yet (by stage) and we travel it pretty often." [10]

All of which proves (if anything) that contemporary descriptions of stagecoach travel must be viewed with a degree of skepticism, and caution exercised in making interpretations or arriving at conclusions therefrom.

It is to be regretted that these writers more often than not omitted information that would, today, be of inestimable value to the researcher: The type of stagecoach used, names of stations and their owners or keepers, the mileages between stations, etc., were salient features that were usually omitted from these contemporary narrations concerning the Coast Line of Stages. The point is important because with each change of station ownership there was invariably a change of station name. The problem is complicated further by the fact that with changes of ownership of the stage line itself there would often be new routes used or old stations moved to new

---

[9] Ventura *Free Press*, Mar. 12, 1881. Reprinted from the San Luis Obispo *Tribune*. [10] Ventura *Free Press*, Mar. 12, 1881.

locations. The best example would have to be the famous station located at various points near the present town of Newhall. Over the years it was known as Lyon's, Hart's, Hosmer's, Fountain's, and Andrew's (Station) and eventually Newhall.[11]

Between San Buenaventura and Los Angeles no less than four different routes were followed at one time or another by the Coast Line of Stages or its predecessor, The Overland Mail Company. From the San Luis Obispo County line to Santa Barbara at least three different routes are a matter of record, and from Santa Barbara to San Buenaventura the Casitas Pass (after 1878) and the beach road were sometimes used interchangeably from week to week and even day to day depending upon weather conditions.

Confronted with circumstances of the preceding nature, it should be apparent that the problem of defining a correct itinerary on the Coast Line for any particular year is almost impossible. The possible combinations become astronomical. The task of compiling a list of stagecoach stations of *solid record* from San Francisco southward is, therefore, undertaken with the realization that there will be errors of commission, more of omission, bruised feelings of provincial pride, and scornful attitudes on the part of old-timers along the Coast Line Stage Route who are familiar with some particular station of which the author has never heard nor could reasonably be expected to uncover through diligent research.

Beginning at the time The Overland Mail Company commenced operations in September 1858, the stations as far south as Gilroy with the mileages between each

---

[11] A. B. Perkins, "Rancho San Francisco, A Study of a California Land Grant," Historical Society of Southern California *Quarterly* (June 1957).

were recorded by W. A. Buchanan, Los Angeles agent
for Wells Fargo, and published in the *Star* on August
28, 1858. "Buck" had traveled the Butterfield Route
from San Francisco to Los Angeles for the specific purpose of measuring the distances involved. Buchanan's
figures gave the distance from San Francisco to: Clark's
Ranch, 12 miles; to San Mateo, 9 miles; to Redwood
City, 9 miles; to Mountain View, 12 miles; to San Jose,
11 miles; to Seventeen-Mile House, 17 miles; to Gilroy,
13 miles.

It is interesting to compare Buchanan's figures with
those made seven years earlier by Lieutenant Warren of
the United States Topographical Engineers using a
viameter and published in the Los Angeles *Star* on
August 16, 1851. If Buchanan had continued on to San
Juan Bautista, there would have been only one and one-
quarter miles difference in the two measurements.

At Gilroy Buchanan's trip branched away from the
Coast Route to the Butterfield Route over Pacheco
Pass. The stations to Salinas, or Salinas City as it was
often called, are taken from the mail contracts numbers
5081; 12,510; 12,520; and 14,763, which were all for the
same route – San Jose to Monterey – and covered the
period beginning with Crandall & Hall in 1851,
through the California Stage Company era and followed by Charlie McLaughlin, with a few "straw bids"
thrown in for good measure. If the foregoing lacks confusion, the fact that no two Post Office Department
worksheets for this route list the same mileages between
post offices or stations should satisfy the most indiscrim-
inating reader. A mean or the most logical figures have
been accepted here. From Gilroy: to San Juan (Bautista), 12 miles; to Natividad, 12 miles; to Salinas, 10
miles.

At the time Flint, Bixby & Company took over the ownership of the Coast Line, San Juan and Los Angeles Stage Company from William Lovett in 1868, a list of the stations owned by the company was included in the inventory appended to the bill of sale. Privately-owned stations, such as Foxen's Ranch, would not have appeared on this business inventory; but others unlisted elsewhere were named. Beginning at the railhead in San Jose, the company-owned stations southward were: Seven-Mile House, Twenty-One-Mile House, Gilroy, San Juan, Lynn's, Salinas, Last Chance, Jolon, Pleito, Nacimiento, Hot Springs, Sumner's, San Luis Obispo, (Arroyo) Grande, Los Berros, Ballard's, Salvador's, Coast Station, Dos Pueblos, Santa Barbara, San Buenaventura, Mountain Station (Larry's), El (Encino?), and Los Angeles.

A careful check of records for the following five years indicates few changes in stations, with the very important exception of their discontinuance one by one as the railroad pushed southward. By late 1872, the Southern Pacific railhead was at Salinas, and on August 12, 1873, reached Soledad. Therefore, the writer has skipped to 1873, when two newspapers gave a good check list of stations and distances, together with the fares from Salinas south and Los Angeles north.[12] The United States Post Office Department's records have been used for crosschecking. From Salinas:

> to Alizal, 9 miles, fare $2.00;
> to Deep Wells, 6 miles, fare $2.00;
> to Soledad, 14 miles, fare $4.00;
> to Last Chance, 18 miles, fare $7.00;
> to Lowe's, 9 miles, fare $8.50;

---

12 Los Angeles *Star,* Jan. 17, 1873, and Ventura *Signal,* Apr. 19, 1873. Reprinted from the San Luis Obispo *Tribune.*

to Jolon, 8 miles, fare $10.00;
to Pleito, 18 miles, fare $11.00;
to Nacimiento, 15 miles, fare $12.00;
to San Miguel, 8 miles, fare $13.50;
to Hot Springs (Paso Robles) 7 miles, fare $15.00;
to Santa Margarita, 12 miles, fare $16.00;
to San Luis Obispo, 9 miles, fare $16.00;
to Arroyo Grande, 17 miles, fare $19.50;
to Suey, 16 miles, fare $20.00;
to Ballard's, 18 miles, fare $20.00; [13]
to Santa Barbara, 37 miles, fare $21.00.

(Note: At least one station has been omitted here, Pat Kinevan's at the top of the San Marcos Pass. Contemporary newspapers spelled the name "Kinnaman." Also, it should be noted that infrequent references will be found to another station at the foot of the San Marcos Pass in the Santa Ynez Valley, although this writer has never found a name for it. It was usually referred to as being near "the old San Marcos Mission." Later, there was still another station, known as "Home Station," which was located under what is now Lake Cachuma. It should not be confused with Homestead House, which was at the foot of the San Marcos Pass on the south side.)

Before the completion of the San Marcos Turnpike, the stagecoach road followed Alamo Pintado and Aliso creeks for approximately seven miles south of Ballard, then swerved on a westerly course to the summit of Gaviota Pass and Las Cruces. The stations of record south of the Las Cruces Post Office were Salvador's, Coast Station, and Dos Pueblos. There was probably

---

[13] This figure cannot possibly be correct. The distance from Suey to Ballard's via Foxen's Ranch, which has been omitted in the newspaper table, was at least thirty miles.

another at La Patera. The Santa Barbara *Press* on July 19, 1873, ran an article giving considerable information on a new mail contract from Santa Barbara to Santa Ynez via the coast and Gaviota Pass which probably would have been similar to conditions existing before the San Marcos Turnpike was constructed:

> The new line will pass from town [Santa Barbara] up to La Patera, then through the Dos Pueblos Rancho by Hollister's, Cooper's, Week's, Buck's and Arroyo Hondo and so to Gaviota, Las Cruces, Nojohui [?] and Santa Ynez Mission, where it will connect with Buckley Stages running via San Marcos.

The Coast Line of Stages, according to the above article, did not start using the San Marcos Pass until 1870, or one year after its completion. At the time they abandoned the old route via the coast and Gaviota Pass, the company was in violation of its mail contract with the Post Office Department, which specified that the post office at Las Cruces must be served. The abandonment left the postmaster at Las Cruces in a somewhat ridiculous position:

> It is amusing to see with what gravity Mr. Williams places himself at his desk to make out his quarterly report and receipt for his salary – $12 a year in postage stamps. The said report is not a very complicated document; no mail received, none dispatched; only this and nothing more.[14]

The Santa Barbara *Press* of November 27, 1873, reported that William Buckley, Superintendent for the Coast Line of Stages, was searching for a new route for the line through Guadalupe instead of via the Suey Station. This line would have run due south from Arroyo Grande through Guadalupe, curved around through the ill-fated settlement of La Graciosa (which

---

14 Santa Barbara *Press,* June 15, 1872.

Henry Newhall wiped from the face of the earth) and
continued on via the future townsite of Los Alamos to
Ballard. At the time Buckley made his reconnaissance
survey, the only settlements along the route were Guadalupe and La Graciosa. The mail station for the latter
was at Suey, a post office which the Santa Barbara *Press*
of May 11, 1873, described as being "located on a bed
and a bureau."

Suey does not appear to have been the most popular
station on the route of the Coast Line of Stages. On
March 23, 1872, J. A. Johnson's Santa Barbara *Press*
ran a long article describing conditions in the Santa
Maria Valley in which the following charge was made:

> The Suey post office is upon wheels, and the last heard from it,
> it had crossed the river into San Luis Obispo County. The people
> know not if it will continue its perambulations farther north or
> if it will make a retrograde movement and bring up in the vicinity
> of Santa Ynez. The aforesaid post office has been in motion so
> constantly for the last year or two as to cause great inconvenience
> and annoyance.

No specific date could be found for the change of the
route from the Foxen Canyon line to that through Guadalupe and La Graciosa. The Thompson & West *History of Santa Barbara and Ventura Counties, California*
(1883) stated that by 1874 Guadalupe had a post office
and Wells Fargo agency, indicating that Buckley had
made the change soon after his search for a new route.
The Post Office Department's advertisements for new
bids on Route 46,150 (Soledad to Newhall) in 1877
specifically named the post offices or settlements of
Arroyo Grande, Guadalupe, Santa Maria,[15] La Gra-

---

15 The post office named "Santa Maria" was located at this time on the
Nipomo Ranch, not on the site of the present city of that name. Santa Maria
was originally called "Central City" and was laid out in 1875.

ciosa, and Los Alamos. This route would have been slightly longer than the old Foxen Canyon line, but probably much easier for staging.

Two months prior to the Ventura *Signal's* reprinting of the information relating to stations, mileages, and fares from Salinas southward, the Los Angeles *Star* had published a similar article that defined the route from Los Angeles northward. *Specific* information in both articles stopped at Santa Barbara, although the *Signal* gave the mileage from Salinas to Los Angeles as 321 and placed the fare at $25.00. The *Star* computed the total mileage at 350 and listed the fare at $22.00. If both were correct, it was cheaper to get out of Los Angeles than it was to get in! According to the *Star* it was from Los Angeles:

> to Encino Rancho, 18 miles, fare $1.50;
> to Larry's Station (also called "Lara's," "Larey's," and "Mountain Station") 14 miles, fare $4.00;
> to Simi (Approximately at Tierra Rejada and Moorpark roads) 12 miles, fare $5.00;
> to Santa Clara (Los Angeles and Santa Clara avenues) 15 miles, no fare given;
> to Santa Coy [*sic*] 4 miles, fare $7.00;
> to San Buenaventura, 12 miles, fare $8.00;
> to Rincon, 12 miles, fare $9.00;
> to Santa Barbara, no distance or fare was given.[16]

In 1875, approximately two years after the above itineraries were published, the Coast Line of Stages moved to the Conejo Route for a period of slightly over a year. While using this route, the line south from San Buenaventura usually crossed the river at what was known as "The Lime Kiln Crossing" of the Santa Clara. The

[16] Los Angeles *Star*, Jan. 17, 1873.

location was the same as the present 101 Highway crossing below Montalvo. The first station south of Ventura was at Springville, which was located just to the east and south of the present interchange of Highway 101 and Central Avenue. The second change of horses was made at present Newbury Park where later the Grand Union Hotel was built. This was the hostelry that would be so erroneously called "The Stagecoach Inn" by a stagecoach fascinated generation in the twentieth century. The Grand Union Hotel (later it was called "The Conejo Hotel") was completed and opened for business in August 1876, two months after the Coast Line of Stages abandoned the Conejo Route.

Between Newbury Park and Encino, where the Conejo Route rejoined the old Santa Susana Pass Route, another station would have been necessary. No record of its location could be found; but an old photograph in Title Insurance & Trust Company files, in which the words "Vejar Station" can faintly be seen, places it some three miles west of Las Virgenes Canyon Road.

At the time the Butterfield Overland Mail moved to the Coast Route in 1861, that portion of the Conejo Route to as far as present day Thousand Oaks was utilized until the Santa Susana Pass road was completed in September. There is no record whatsoever in respect to stations on the route between Los Angeles and San Buenaventura at that time. The first would have been at Encino, and the second at Vejar's; but two other stations would have been needed. Their locations have been lost with time and covered with dust.

Probably no other section of the Coast Line Route possessed so many different stations in various locations and periods as the Santa Clara Valley. Even before

Flint, Bixby & Company moved onto the Santa Clara
Valley Route, two different stage lines had utilized the
valley. In April 1874, the veteran stager Sam Harper
commenced coaching operations between San Buenaventura and Lyon's Station with his Atlantic & Pacific
Stage Line. Harper's line connected the Coast Line of
Stages with that of the Telegraph Stage Line at Lyon's
Station just south of present day Newhall. The Telegraph stages were operating between Los Angeles and
the Southern Pacific railhead in the San Joaquin Valley, and continuing on to the Owens Valley and Cerro
Gordo mining district.

Harper was no neophyte at the stagecoach business,
and there was no secret about the fact that he had started
the line with the hope of obtaining a mail contract from
the United States Post Office Department. The plan,
which was a direct reversal of the usual stagecoaching
modus operandi, failed; and Harper gave up the business in July 1874.

The location of Harper's stations have been all but
obliterated with the passing of time. The first change of
horses would have been at either the Twelve-Mile
House (southwest corner of Telegraph and Cummings
roads) or the infant village of Santa Paula. One of the
few descriptive articles relating to Harper's line stated
that the party stopped for lunch at Frank Sprague's
house on the Sespe. Sprague's would have been a logical
location at this time; and, if correct, the Twelve-Mile
House would have been in the right spot distance-wise
for another station. The same article related stopping at
Camulos.[17] At a later date "hack" lines and small, locally
operated "stage" lines often used the Camulos for

17 Ventura *Signal,* June 27, 1874.

changes of horses. It is possible that Sam Harper's third station from San Buenaventura was Camulos. However, on April 2, 1881, the Ventura *Signal* published an article concerning the sighting of a grizzly bear scratching his back against a telegraph pole "near the old San Martine stage station." There is no record of any stage line using a station at San Martine Canyon. Harper may have used it for a short period, although it would have been much too close to Camulos to have used both at the same time.

The Telegraph Stage Line and Flint, Bixby & Company's Coast Line both used the Twelve-Mile House (at different periods, of course) until it was moved into Santa Paula in 1878. Sprague's ranch would have been "off limits" for a station or anything else after the More murder trials commenced in 1878, and much too close to Santa Paula in any event.

When the Telegraph Stage Line first began running the Lyon's Station Mail Route in March 1875, the Buckhorn Ranch of the Warrings was the principal change of horses and feed station. The following year the Coast Line took over the route and built stage buildings at Cienega, a site presently occupied by the California State Fish Hatchery east of Fillmore. This was the station known as "Yellow Creek Station," a name derived from the color of the water in Pole Creek. It should be obvious that a station at this location and one at Buckhorn Ranch would be incompatible because of the short distance between. It would also be too far to Lyon's Station without another change of horses. Possibly Camulos was used, or the old San Martine Station reactivated. There is simply no record to substantiate either alternative. If the Ventura *Signal's* version of the wording on the mail contract No. 46,284 was correct,

GILROY and LOS ANGELES.

COAST STAGE LINE.

W. G. ROBERTS, Agent, office 208 Montgomery street, San Francisco.
General Agent, W. BUCKLEY, San Jose, California.
Local Agents: Jos. KNOWLTON, Jr., Gilroy; WM. BALCH, San Juan; CHRIS. HAMEL, Natividad; L. C. BOCTICK, Plato Ranch; CHAS. KNOWLTON, Paso Robles Springs; J. C. ORTEGA, San Luis Obispo; ELI RUNDELL, Santa Barbara; J. WOOLFSON, San Buenaventura; GEO. M. FALL, Los Angeles.
Stage leaves Gilroy daily at 12 M. Stage leaves Los Angeles daily at 6 A. M.

From Gilroy To Los Angeles.			TOWNS May 18th, 1871.	See Page.	From Los Angeles To Gilroy.		
Fare.	Hours	Miles			Miles.	Hours	Fare.
$ 0.00	0	0	Dep..........Gilroy...........Arr.	161	366	58	
1.50	2	12	............San Juan............		354		
2.50	4	24	............Natividad............		342		
4.00	6	38	...........Uttz Station...........		328		
5.50	8	52	...........Salinas River..........		314		
8.50	11	76	...........Last Chance...........		290		
10.00	13	92	...........San Antonio...........		274		
12.00	15	107	...........Plato Ranch...........		259		
14.00	17	121	...........Nacimento...........		245		
15.00	19	136	.......Paso Robles Hot Springs.....		230		
16.00	22	150	.........San Margarita.........		216		
16.00	25	164	........San Luis Obispo.......	174	202	36	
17.50	28	180	...........Arroyo Grande.........		186		
17.50	31	196	...........Zury Station...........		170		
17.50	33	214	.............Foxens............		152		
17.50	35	228	...........Ballard's...........		138		
17.50	37	243	...........San Marcus....		123		
17.20	40	257	...........McCaffey's...........		109		
17.50	41	265	.......Santa Barbara	174	101	15	
18.00	44	280	.........Rincon............		86		
18.00	47	293	.......San Buenaventura......		73	11	
20.00	49	306	.......Santa Clara Valley.........		60		
20.00	51	320	............Sime.............		46		
20.00	53	333	.........Mountain Station........		33	5	
20.00	56	350	...........El Cino....		16	2	
20.00	58	366	Arr.........Los Angeles.....Dep.	164	0	0	

Connections.

At Gilroy, connects with cars of S. F. & S. J. R. R. for San Francisco.
At San Juan, connects with stages for Watsonville and Santa Cruz, New Idria, Castroville, Salinas City, and Monterey.
At San Luis Obispo, connects with stage for San Simeon.
At Los Angeles, connects with stages for San Diego, Fort Yuma and Tucson San Bernardino, La Paz and Clear Creek.

GILROY and SULPHUR SPRINGS.

CAVANA'S STAGE LINE.

Stages leave Gilroy daily at 12.30 P. M.; arrive at Canada de Los Assos at 2.30 P. M.; distance 8 miles; fare $1.00; arrive at Hot Sulphur Springs at 3.30 P. M.; distance 15 miles; through fare $2.00. Returning, leave Hot Springs at 8 A. M.; arrive at Gilroy at 11 A. M. Connect at Gilroy with stages for Santa Cruz, Watsonville and Monterey, and cars for San Francisco.

COAST LINE STAGE TIMETABLE, 1871
From *Bancroft's Guide for Travelers by Railway, Stage, and Steam Navigation in the Pacific States, 1872.* "Zury" should be "Suey;" "Sime," "Simi;" and "El Cino," "Encino." A comparison of this timetable with the stations listed in the text at the time of the sale of the line to Flint, Bixby and Co., and with the stations and mileages given for 1873, represents a fine example of the rapidity with which changes in stations and names occurred.
Courtesy, Wells Fargo Bank History Room, San Francisco.

VEJAR STATION

The Vejar Station, built in 1820 and apparently abandoned in this 1886 photograph, was located at the present town of Agoura. Courtesy, Title Insurance and Trust Co.

CONEJO GRADE
The remnants of the first wagon road down the present route of Highway 101
on the Conejo Grade, built in the mid-1870's, are indicated by the arrows.
The modern freeway fill is visible in the upper right corner.

GRAND UNION HOTEL
This hotel, located in present-day Newbury Park, was also called the Conejo
Hotel and "The Big Hotel." In more recent years it was affectionately, but
very inaccurately, known as "The Stagecoach Inn," having opened for business
in August 1876, two months after the Coast Line Stage Company abandoned the
Conejo Route. A Simi mail carrier sits on the cart.

"Comulos" was listed on the route and may very well have been one of the stations. It did not become a post office until October 1885. Post Office Department records for this route are among the missing at National Archives.

With only this limited knowledge of the routes and stations between San Francisco and Los Angeles, the important developments during the heyday of Coast Line staging are more easily understood. The key to the successful operation of the line was still the mail contract, but a new factor – the railroad – was coming upon the scene to complicate this financial subsidy. Even before the Overland Mail Company began through service on the Coast Route, the forewarning of this hissing monster that would push aside the stagecoach had made its appearance. The Los Angeles *Star* printed the announcement on November 3, 1860:

> It affords pleasure to announce that Messrs. Chas. McLaughlin and Alex H. Houston have been awarded the contract to build and fully equip the San Francisco and San Jose Railroad. The contract was awarded on the 24th October, and provides that the road is be fully completed and in running order, with all the necessary buildings &c., to be erected and completed, in three years from 1st October, 1860, for the sum of two million dollars. The line of the road and right of way are to be located and secured immediately, and about the 1st of April next, the contractors will commence the grading of the road.

Charlie McLaughlin, the stagecoach king south of San Francisco, had taken the contract to build the railroad that would eventually put his own stage line out of business! (If you can't beat 'em, join 'em!) The Big Four, who would later gather unto themselves this first segment of the future Coast Line of the Southern Pacific, were still eight months away from incorporating their Central Pacific Railroad; and strange though it may seem, McLaughlin was projected to start construction on the San Francisco & San Jose Railroad on April 1, 1861, the very day that the Overland Mail Company made the inaugural stagecoach run via the Coast Route. It would be forty years almost to the day (March 31, 1901) before the first *through* passenger train via the Coast Route put an end to the stagecoach era.

The contractors did not quite make the deadline as specified in the contract, but they came close. The San Francisco & San Jose Railroad was in operating condition and open for business on January 16, 1864.

The effect became apparent within a matter of months. The worksheet entry for July 20, 1864, on United States Mail Contract No. 14,753 – San Francisco to San Jose – reads: "Annual contract with Charles McLaughlin from Sept. 30, 1864, and allow one month's extra pay, and contract with San Francisco & San Jose Rail Road Co., L. Davis [?] Pres't, San Francisco, for service twice daily . . .   at $5000 per annum from October 1, 1864."

Charlie McLaughlin had performed the service tri-weekly for $1900 per annum. The great stagecoach retreat on the Coast Route had begun.

On July 19, 1866, the United States Post Office Department ordered a new contract with the San Francisco & San Jose Railroad, Henry Newhall, President, "to carry the mails on this route twice daily in Rail Road Cars at seven thousand, five hundred dollars ($7,500) per annum. . ." The company was allowed an additional $1200 on November 14, 1866, retroactive to July 1, upon the condition that it supply personnel to "assort" the mail on the cars. On January 8, 1867, the

Post Office Department raised Newhall's per mile fee by $50.00, thus adding another $2500 to the original contract. On September 11, 1869, the department ordered $6000 more added to compensate for the mails being carried to Gilroy, the railroad having been completed to that point during the summer. The San Francisco & San Jose Railroad contract of 1866 for $7500 had grown to $17,200, and the stagecoach had retreated another thirty miles on the Coast Route.

The San Francisco & San Jose Railroad was destined to play a far greater role in California history than this inevitable offensive action against staging. A group of San Francisco financeers had organized "a paper enterprise under the name Southern Pacific Railroad Company." [18] This concern was primarily interested in obtaining some of the free land grants that an overly generous United States Government had been handing out to ambitious railroad promoters. It also held a contract to purchase the San Francisco & San Jose Railroad, which by now was a going concern with an entry into San Francisco on the only available land route – the peninsula. San Francisco in its turn was "The Gateway to the Orient."

This state of affairs was not lost upon Huntington, Hopkins, Stanford, and Crocker's Central Pacific Railroad. The proper procedure was to buy the Southern Pacific Railroad Company (surreptitiously, if possible) change the name to the Southern Pacific Railroad of California, and thereby confuse everyone then and forevermore.

The intent of the original Southern Pacific Railroad had been to build south via Hollister and Tres Pinos,

---

18 Neill C. Wilson and Frank J. Taylor, *Southern Pacific* (New York, n.d.), p. 48.

through some undefined pass into the San Joaquin Valley, and thence south to about the thirty-fifth parallel and east along that fabled line through Arizona, New Mexico, etc.[19] The intent of the Southern Pacific of California under the Big Four was to corral that very important land entry into San Francisco and thereby block any opposition line. It was not destined to be a static blockade, however. On July 31, 1871, the Southern Pacific had opened the road for business to Hollister and was busy constructing a branch line to Watsonville.[20]

The following spring the branch line to Watsonville became the tail that wagged the dog. Crocker had studied the traffic potentialities of the area south and east of Tres Pinos and discovered nothing but zeros. With the aid of Congressman Cole the Southern Pacific was granted permission to change its route to the Salinas Valley.[21] Late in 1872, the railhead had reached Salinas; and on August 12, 1873, the staked-out town of Soledad, some twenty-seven miles to the south, became the terminus for the next thirteen years. Thus before the financial desperation of the Big Four was brought on by the failure of the New York banking houses in 1873, the stagecoach had been forced to retreat another sixty miles on the Coast Route.

During this period of railroad expansion and stagecoach retreat, the old problem of the mails by steamer vs. the mails by stagecoach was a constant problem – for the newspaper editors, not the contractors. When inclement weather resulted in delays on the stage line, the fourth estate clamored for more steamer mail. Con-

---

19 See the San Francisco *Alta's* report of the Annual Election of Officers of the Southern Pacific Company as reprinted in the Los Angeles *Star*, Jan. 23, 1869.   21 *Ibid.*, Apr. 24, 1872.
20 Los Angeles *Star*, July 22, 1871, and Aug. 5, 1871.

versely, when the road conditions were good and the
stages were making excellent time, the editors could see
no reason why the taxpayers' money should be wasted
sending the mail by boat. If ever there was a group of
rotten-spoiled brats in need of a sound cowhiding in the
woodshed, those nineteenth century newspaper editors
were *it*.

In an effort to placate the press, the Postmaster General in January 1871, advertised for bids for five
monthly deliveries of the mails by steamer between San
Francisco and San Diego, with stops at Santa Cruz,
Monterey, San Simeon, San Luis Obispo, Santa Barbara, and San Pedro. The contract was let for $30,000.
This was in addition to the regular Coast Line of Stages
mail contract, which fluctuated so often between six and
seven deliveries per week that any attempt to record
which was in effect at any given time would be fruitless.

Far from soothing the newspaper editors, the duel
system of mail delivery only aggravated them. Their
prime concern, as always, was with the "paper mail" or
exchanges, not the first-class or letter mail. Because of
the weight involved with newspapers, there was a tendency to hold up this class of mail for a day or two if
the regular mail boat was due to depart, rather than
overloading the stagecoaches. This resulted not only in
tardy deliveries along the route, but on "steamer day"
the towns would be blessed with two deliveries. Often
the day before and the day after would see none. The
Los Angeles *Star* explained the complaint most lucidly:

> The present mode of dispatching the mails to this place by
> steamer instead of by stage, on the day preceding and the day of
> departure of steamers from San Francisco, injuriously affects the
> service in this city. As long as there is a daily stage line leaving
> San Francisco, we should have the benefit of it in our mail service. The accident to the *Orizaba* leaves us three days without any

mails, and, by the time they arrive, the dates will be so old as to be of no essential value. . .[22]

The Los Angeles *News* was even more specific in defining the class of mail involved in the complaints: "The arrival of the steamer exonerates the Overland Stage Company from all blame in the recent delay of the *paper* mail from San Francisco. . ." [23]

The editor of the Ventura *Signal* agreed, called the $30,000 fee to the steamship line "a swindle," and added:

> This $30,000 subsidy arrangement may be of some benefit to that great and self-important city on paper, San Diego, but it evidently is to nobody else. Half the amount expended in subsidizing the Coast Line of Stages would have given the people of Southern California their mail matter a day earlier, instead of a day later as is the case now.[24]

This was not the only complaint of the hard to please editors of southern California. According to the terms of the contracts, the mail was required to be delivered before the passengers. This rather inhumane clause was more often than not overlooked by both the steamer and stage contractors. Editor Johnson of the Santa Barbara *Press* succeeded in working himself into a terrible dither in his issue of June 1, 1872, because the mail bags containing his newspaper exchanges had been allowed to remain on the wharf for a full hour while the contractor hauled the steamer passengers and express to town.

The Los Angeles *Star* was equally as merciless on this subject:

> Mail contractors are required by law to deposit the mails at

---

[22] *Ibid.*, Dec. 9, 1872. The stages connected with the railroad at Salinas at this time; they did not leave from San Francisco as the article states.

[23] Ventura *Signal*, Mar. 23, 1872. Reprinted from the Los Angeles *News*. Italics added.   [24] Ventura *Signal*, Mar. 23, 1872.

the Post Office before delivering passengers or express matter. Postmaster Bent has notified the Telegraph Stage Company's Agent to that effect, and will enforce the law on all Mail Stage Lines which run into Los Angeles. They include the Telegraph Stage Line, from Los Angeles to Sacramento, San Francisco, Stockton, Bakersfield, Lone Pine, Cerro Gordo, and Owens River; the Coast Line route to Santa Barbara, San Luis Obispo, etc.; Holladay's route to San Bernardino, and Seeley and Wright's line to San Diego. Mail Contractors will have to comply with this law. Heretofore the mails have sometimes been delayed from one hour to one hour and a half, the time being taken up by the delivering of passengers.[25]

In other words, a stagecoach full of tired and dusty passengers must remain calmly seated while Henry Hamilton's northern newspapers were unloaded at the post office!

It was this almost fanatical obsession with the newspaper mails, plus the rapid southward extension of the Southern Pacific's San Joaquin Valley line, that was responsible for major readjustments on the southern portion of the Coast Line of Stages.

Soon after the completion of the transcontinental railroad the Central Pacific had started construction on a "spur" line up the San Joaquin Valley. By November 1870, the rails had reached Modesto; on May 28, 1872, the railhead was at Fresno and continuing southward. The Los Angeles *Star* announced on February 4, 1873, that the Telegraph Stage Line carrying the mails was connecting with the rails at Tipton; and by July 17, 1873, the new town of Delano was the railroad-stagecoach connection. On November 8, 1874, the Southern Pacific reached Sumner (East Bakersfield) prepared for an assault on the Tehachapi Mountains. Twenty

---

[25] Los Angeles *Star,* Apr. 5, 1873. The wording here is confusing. At this time the railroad-stagecoach connection was at Tipton. The railroad carried the mails north from there. The stagecoaches did not run to Sacramento, Stockton, etc. as the article implies.

days later the Ventura *Signal* reported that work had already begun on the long Newhall tunnel in anticipation of the day when the rails would surmount the Tehachapis. The shape of things to come was now clear.

The effects of the rapid extension of the railroad up the San Joaquin Valley did not become apparent until the Telegraph Stage Line reopened coaching to Los Angeles in 1872, on portions of the old Butterfield Overland Mail Route. At this time a group of San Francisco business-men headed by H. M. Newhall owned the far-flung Telegraph Stage Line; while the former owner, Amos Thoms, was serving as superintendent.

The Los Angeles *Star* of June 20, 1872, noted that Thoms had left town to locate stations on the route between Los Angeles and Visalia. The company's first advertisement for the line appeared in the newspaper on July 8, 1872. The stage line did not have a mail contract at this time, the *Star* reporting on July 12, that the Telegraph Stage line was carrying the mails free to Havilah, Lone Pine, Independence, Fort Tejon, Bakersfield, and Visalia. It was not until August 21, 1872, that the *Star* announced: "H. M. Newhall, proprietor of the Telegraph Stage Line, has been awarded the contract to convey the mails from Los Angeles to Cerro Gordo, Lone Pine, Owen's River, Havilah, etc., three times a week. . ." By December 11, 1872, the Telegraph Line was advertising through fares to San Francisco and Sacramento in forty-eight hours via stagecoach and "the cars."

In April 1873, with the stagecoach connection at Tipton, a San Francisco newspaper correspondent gave the running time to Los Angeles as forty-six hours, the fare $25.00 ($1.50 extra for sleeping cars) and five meals at fifty cents each – $2.50, for a total of $29.00.

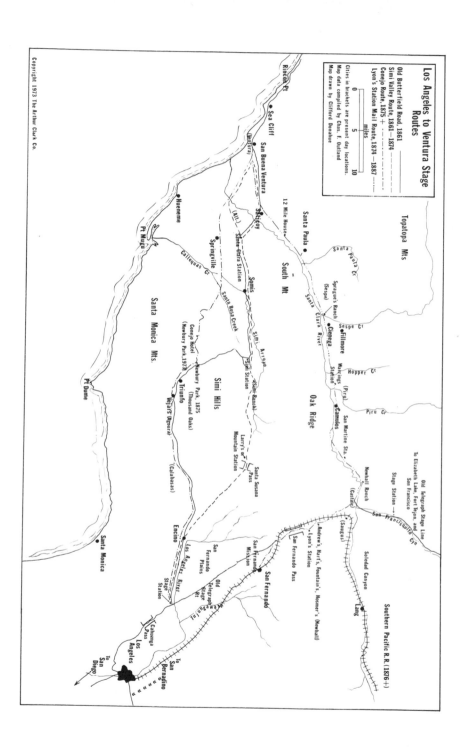

Los Angeles to Ventura Stage Routes

Old Butterfield Road, 1861 ——————
Simi Valley Route, 1861 — 1874 ——————
Conejo Route, 1875 + —·—·—·—
Lyon's Station Mail Route, 1874 — 1887 ············

```
miles
0    5    10
```

Cities in brackets are present day locations.
Map data compiled by Chas. F. Outland
Map drawn by Clifford Donahue

One year later the *Star* reprinted an article in which it was stated that the Los Angeles-San Francisco running time would be reduced to thirty-four hours when the railroad reached Bakersfield. In actual fact the first Telegraph Stage Line advertisement after the connection was made at Bakersfield announced the through running time would be thirty-six hours.[26]

Here was competition with which Flint, Bixby & Company's Coast Line of Stages could not hope to compete, nor did they try. New advertisements were inserted in the *Star* stating that after February 15, 1873, the stages on the Coast Line would avoid all night travel by leaving Los Angeles at 5 A.M. and arriving in Santa Barbara at 8 P.M. for an overnight's rest. The actual arrival time was usually nearer 11 P.M. Theoretically, the second night's stopover was to be San Luis Obispo; but contemporary accounts more often than not place the arrival of the stages at that point at about two o'clock in the morning and their departure at seven, after breakfast. It will be apparent from this state of affairs that the avoidance of all night travel was more in the advertisements than in actual practice. Even with the early departure from San Luis Obispo it required another twenty-four hours to reach Salinas and the railroad. Later, the situation was not greatly improved by connecting at Soledad.

Sam Harper was the first to grasp the significance of these developments and the importance of what was to become known as "The Lyon's Station Mail Route" in 1874. With the slowdown on the Coast Route due to the overnight layovers, and the rapid acceleration of travel

[26] *Ibid.*, Dec. 2, 1874. By far the best account of the Telegraph Stage Line was written by William Harland Boyd, Bakersfield College history teacher, and appeared in the *Pacific Historical Review*, November 1957, vol. XXVI, no. 4. Boyd did not carry his treatise past the time of Newhall's ownership.

in the San Joaquin Valley, it would be only a matter of time until Santa Barbara and San Buenaventura mails destined for the north could get to San Francisco faster by traveling east to Newhall and connecting with the Telegraph Stage Line and the railroad. What was of greater significance was the fact that the San Francisco newspaper mails could be brought into Santa Barbara twenty-four hours earlier.

Harper had conceived his Atlantic & Pacific Stage line with the idea of pioneering the route up the Santa Clara Valley and then presenting the Post Office Department and the local newspapers with a *fait accompli* and asking for a mail contract. The plan was excellent, the result a failure. Harper was a year too soon with his "brainstorm," but the idea had not gone unnoticed by the newspaper editors of Santa Barbara and San Buenaventura. Even more than their contemporaries in Los Angeles, these country editors were dependent upon their exchanges to get out a weekly newspaper.

The Ventura *Signal* started the campaign for a Lyon's Station Mail Route on September 5, 1874, with an article outlining the great advantages to be gained and maintaining that thirty hours' time could be saved between San Buenaventura and San Francisco. Editors Sheridan and Shepherd claimed the only river to be crossed would be the Santa Clara, and that would detain the stagecoaches for only a few hours after the heaviest of rains. These newly arrived boys from "The Bible Belt" overlooked the Santa Paula, Sespe, and Piru creeks for some reason (probably intentional) in their anxiety to persuade the Postmaster General of the desirability of the route.

C. A. Storke of Santa Barbara expounded on the urgency of the Lyon's Station Mail Route in the *Signal* of December 5, 1874; and when Charley Storke expounded, it was well either to listen or get out of range. The Postmaster General listened and advertised the route for bids:

> The mail route no. 46,284 from San Buenaventura by Saticoy, Santa Paula, Sespe, Comulos [sic] and San Francisco Ranch, to Lyon's Station 52 miles and back, three times a week, will be let to the lowest bidder on or before March 1, 1875. . .[27]

Unfortunately, the records for this route number are not now in existence. The winning bidder was Haskell, Nichols & Company, a concern that had only recently purchased the old established Telegraph Stage Line. The lack of official records makes it impossible to ascertain what bid, if any, Flint, Bixby & Company entered. The point was to assume importance in the staging story when the Lyon's Station Mail Route was expanded to daily service after only four months.

The Ventura *Signal* lost no time in extolling the virtues of the new route, even though it was but tri-weekly:

> Although we have but a tri-weekly mail on the route from here to Lyon's Station, we see at once the great advantage it has over the old coast line. We now get Sacramento papers within 48 hours after publication. Saturday's papers are received on Monday evening – while by the other line, even San Francisco dailies are not received until Tuesday evening. Our eastern papers are all 24 hours earlier on each alternate day than by the old line. Our mail is now all sent by the new route, although it is only taken every other day, it all reaches the city [San Francisco] sooner than by the other route. The necessity of making the Lyon's Station route a daily is urgent, and we trust that no efforts may be spared in bringing the matter promptly before the authorities.[28]

At the risk of being boringly repetitious, it should again be pointed out that the *only* reason for this acute

---

[27] Ventura *Signal,* Jan. 9, 1875.   [28] *Ibid.,* Mar. 6, 1875.

"urgency" as outlined by the *Signal* involved nothing more and nothing less than the newspaper mail! Since before the days of the Overland Mail Company, untold hundreds of thousands of dollars had been expended by the United States Government subsidizing stagecoach and steamship lines in order that newspaper editors could receive their *second-class* mail twelve to twenty-four hours sooner!

Contemporaneously with the developments on the Lyon's Station Mail Route, important changes had occurred on the Coast Line between San Buenaventura and Los Angeles. At some undetermined time prior to May 22, 1875, the Coast Line of Stages abandoned the long-used Santa Susana Pass Route and moved to the Conejo. The first intimation that the change was contemplated appeared in the Ventura *Signal* on January 10, 1874. Two months later the Hueneme correspondent for the *Signal* expressed the hope that the stages would be routed via Hueneme when the change was made.

Nothing further appeared on the subject for over a year. On May 22, 1875, the *Signal* ran an article on the Conejo in which it seems clear that the change had taken place:

> The name of the new town on the Conejo is called Newbury Park. A postoffice will soon be established there. The Coast Line stage company have changed their route through the Conejo and will run daily stages. This will give the people of the Conejo a daily mail, and easy access with the balance of the world.[29]

The following week it was announced that the Coast Line stage station of Simi had been moved to Conejo. The foregoing would indicate that the change from the Santa Susana Pass Route to the Conejo was made early

---

[29] Newbury Park at this time was located on the site of present day Thousand Oaks, not where the Grand Union Hotel was later built.

in May 1875. Less than two months later the United
States Post Office Department issued the order that
would eliminate the Conejo as a major stage route:

> The Coast Line Stage company has been ordered by the Post
> Office Department to curtail the mail route from Soledad to Los
> Angeles, leaving off Saticoy and Los Angeles. The order takes
> effect June 30. After that date the stages will only run to this
> point [San Buenaventura]. Our Lyon's Station route will soon
> be made a daily line.[30]

The effect of this order was that the Coast Line of
Stages would handle the mail between Soledad and San
Buenaventura; while the Telegraph Stage Line, contractor on the Lyon's Station Mail Route, would have
charge between San Buenaventura and Los Angeles.
More specifically, the Telegraph Line would deliver
the mails to the Southern Pacific railhead at San Fernando. Before the end of the year the rails would be
extended to Summit Station at the south portal of the
Newhall tunnel and the mail transferred at that point.

The Coast Line of Stages did not cease functioning
on the Conejo Route for another year despite the loss
of the mail contract. Undoubtedly Flint, Bixby & Company were hanging on in the hope that a new contract
would be forthcoming. The stage company continued to
deliver the way mail to Springville and Newbury Park
without compensation. E. S. Newbury, the savant of the
Conejo, wrote to the *Signal* on several occasions that the
Coast Line stages were passing through filled to capacity. However, the end was in sight. The May 20, 1876,
issue of the *Signal* reported that petitions were in circulation on the Conejo for a reissuance of the mail contract, indicating that Flint, Bixby & Company had let
its intentions be known. The same issue stated that Mr.

---

30 Ventura *Signal*, June 19, 1875.

Hammell was rapidly pushing the big hotel to completion and intended making the Conejo into a health resort.

On June 10, 1876, Flint, Bixby & Company served the final ultimatum that unless a mail contract through the Conejo was forthcoming immediately, they would discontinue the route. The company's position was quite secure; it had purchased the Lyon's Station Mail Route from the Telegraph Line in late March and could well afford to discard the Conejo.

The following week both San Buenaventura newspapers[31] ran articles on the Coast Line of Stages transferring their entire stock and equipment from the Conejo to the Santa Clara Valley. The company requested the Ventura County Board of Supervisors for road improvements and a bridge across the Sespe (there was no harm in trying) while well drillers and construction crews were busy boring wells and building stage stations along the line.

The final act in the Lyon's Station Mail Route drama took place on September 5, 1876, when the "Last Spike" ceremony took place commemorating the completion of the railroad from San Francisco to Los Angeles via the San Joaquin Valley. Henceforth the stages would pick up the mails and passengers at Newhall. No through mail to San Francisco would go via the northbound stages, only the way mail to as far north as Soledad.

Two months after the Coast Line of Stages transferred its stock and equipment to the Santa Clara Valley, an advertisement appeared in the Ventura *Free Press:* "GRAND UNION HOTEL, Halfway between Santa Barbara and Los Angeles, on 'El Conejo Rancho' is now

---

31 The Ventura *Free Press* began publication on Nov. 13, 1875. Pages one and four were misdated "November 14, 1875."

open for the reception of guests. . . Dr. Morris, Prop." [32] The "Stagecoach Inn" was completed, but the stagecoaches were running through the Santa Clara Valley, miles away.

The following February the Post Office Department once more ordered mail service to the Conejo Valley. Flint, Bixby & Company were the successful bidders for the contract; but the Coast Line of Stages had no intentions of becoming involved in the Conejo again. It immediately subleased the contract – from San Buenaventura to Hueneme, Springville, and Newbury Park to a Mr. Bouquist and his spring wagon; and from Newbury Park to Los Angeles via an unnamed horseback rider. From this time on the Conejo Route would see the most sporadic type of service – occasionally good, more frequently poor and undependable, and often none. It never again was established on anything more than a tri-weekly basis except for a short period during the mid-1880s, when it operated daily during the summer months under the John Allman regime.

Beginning in 1878, major changes of ownership occurred on the Coast Line that almost defy accurate recording and interpretation. The fact that none of the companies or "corporations" ever filed incorporation papers with the California Secretary of State in no manner aids the researcher. The indiscriminate use by the newspapers of various and sundry names to identify the stagecoach companies involved compounds the confusion, and the fact that chronologically arranged stage-coaching news items over the following four years reveal numerous discrepancies is the crowning blow.

The Ventura *Signal* announced (or attempted to) on June 29, 1878, that "The Coast Line Stage Company,

32 Ventura *Free Press,* Aug. 19, 1876.

under a new arrangement to go into effect July 1, will have the carrying of the mails from Soledad to San Luis Obispo." The remainder of the account was unintelligible due to several dropped lines of type.

The Ventura *Free Press* of July 6, 1878, did not do much better: "Messrs. Haskell & Co., the new proprietors, have commenced carrying the mail from this town [San Buenaventura] to Newhall. . . The Coast Line Company will carry the mail between San Luis Obispo and Soledad under arrangement with the present contractors." The *Free Press* failed to report who would do the honors between San Buenaventura and San Luis Obispo.

Note that the firm of Flint, Bixby & Company, long-time owners of the Coast Line of Stages, does not appear in these news reports. The name of the great stock raising company had been conspicuous by its absence since March 10, 1877, when it was named defendant in a lawsuit growing out of a stagecoach wreck on the Rincon.

The Salinas *Index* reported on August 22, 1878, that William Buckley & Company had purchased the stage line from Soledad to San Luis Obispo and would retain the name "Coast Line Stage Company." Below San Luis Obispo the "Telegraph Stage Line" would prevail.[33]

W. H. "Shotgun" Taylor was known to have been a partner of Buckley, and had been associated with the Coast Line at least a year prior to the ownership change. The Ventura *Signal* of June 23, 1877, reported that Major Taylor was in town "attending a case in court." Taylor himself placed his connections with the Coast Line as early as 1872, when he

---

[33] I am indebted to Mr. Robert Johnston of Hartnell College for this item.

was employed by Wm. Buckley, Supt. for Flint, Bixby & Co. on [the] Coast Line between Salinas City and San Diego as driver a few months and then appointed Div. Supt. of the Coast Line Stage Co. and Supt. of the Co.'s lines from Bakersfield and Caliente to Tehachapi, Mohave, Havilah, Kernville, Coyote, Borax Lake, Owens Lake, Lone Pine, Cerro Gordo, Darwin and Panamint. In 1878, Mr. Buckley and myself purchased the Coast Line and run it until 1882, at which time we were awarded a number of mail contracts and Mr. Jesse D. Carr became partner, and until 1886 the concern was Buckley, Carr and Taylor. . .[34]

Taylor's "autobiography," which appears to have been prepared for the Wells Fargo *Catalogue* at the Columbian Exposition in Chicago, is perhaps the best clue available by which to arrive at an intelligent deduction concerning ownership and interlocking stagecoaching interests from 1872 to 1886. It must be borne in mind that at the time "Shotgun" Taylor claimed the Coast Line Stage Company was involved in staging in the Bakersfield-Owens Valley region the line was owned by Flint, Bixby & Company. The area described by Taylor: Cerro Gordo, Lone Pine, Bakersfield, Kernville, etc., was predominantly Telegraph Stage Line territory. The Los Angeles *Star* of August 21, 1872, reported that H. M. Newhall, proprietor of the Telegraph Stage Line, had been awarded the contract to convey the mails from Los Angeles to Cerro Gordo, Lone Pine, Owen's River, Havilah, etc., three times a week.

In the spring of the following year the Telegraph Line came under the ownership of William "Royal Bill" Hamilton and W. G. Roberts. Hamilton was one of those fantastic, legendary characters that just naturally seemed to gravitate to Western staging. Ben Truman, who had become editor of the Los Angeles

---

[34] Letter from W. H. Taylor to James Otey Bradford, Mar. 8, 1893. Wells Fargo Bank History Room, San Francisco.

Star in the summer of 1873, described Hamilton as "A noble, generous, industrious, honest man among men; he is known as a prince among his fellows, and just as good, kind and humane to a horse or a dog as he is to a man or woman." [35] "Royal Bill" also had the reputation of being capable of drinking the entire town of Los Angeles under the table and still possess an appetite for a full course dinner washed down with goblets of *Veuve Clicquot*. What was more to the point, Truman reported that Hamilton held all the important mail contracts to Independence and Owens River. Earlier, the *Star* had reported that Hamilton & Roberts were running the largest piece of staging in the world,[36] most of the mileage being in the very area that Shotgun Taylor asserted was served by the Coast Line with himself as superintendent.

There is no corroborating evidence in the southern California newspapers up to 1875 to indicate that Flint, Bixby & Company had staging interests in this region. The Los Angeles *Star* did announce on March 10, 1871, that the Coast Line Stage Company had purchased the San Bernardino and Los Angeles stage line from Ferguson & Company, with all stock and appurtenances. Ferguson & Company had acquired the line from the estate of William Ballard.[37]

To anyone who has delved deeply into the subject, there must eventually come the realization that the so-called "Coast Line of Stages" *was* William Buckley, regardless of whether the owners were William Lovett; Flint, Bixby & Company; or anyone else. At no time has this researcher ever found a news item indicating

---

[35] Los Angeles *Star,* Dec. 14, 1873.   [36] *Ibid.,* Mar. 28, 1873.

[37] *Ibid.,* Oct. 27, 1870; advertisement Nov. 10, 1870. An earlier story described the remodeling of a stagecoach into an "ambulance" to transport the very sick Ballard from San Bernardino to his ranch in Santa Barbara County.

that Lovett, or any of the partners in Flint, Bixby &
Company, had the slightest interest in stagecoaching
per se. Always it was Buckley (and later Shotgun
Taylor) who was the driving force behind the business.

If it could be established that Buckley's interests
were confined to the Coast Line, the problem would be
simple. The exact opposite appears to have been the
case. The Los Angeles *Star* of February 19, 1874, lists
Buckley as the winning bidder for the mail contracts
from Los Angeles to San Bernardino, Los Angeles to
San Diego, and Los Angeles to Lone Pine. The first two
contracts Buckley may have signed for the Coast Line;
but on June 24, 1874, the *Star* reported that Buckley
had *purchased* the line from Bakersfield to Lone Pine.
There was nothing in the news item to suggest that
Flint, Bixby & Company was involved in the transaction.

Later in the year the *Star* of September 5, 1874,
stated: "Mr. Buckley, *proprietor* of the San Diego and
Anaheim Stage Line, and *agent* of the Coast Line is in
the city. We understand that he is going to make the
route between here and San Diego, upon completion of
the Anaheim Branch Railroad, the fastest in the State."

The questions then become: Did Flint, Bixby & Company own everything that Shotgun Taylor considered as
being part of Coast Line Stage Company, or did William Buckley own a good share in his own right? In
view of Taylor's claims to the Coast Line's operations
in the Kern-Inyo country, did Buckley have financial
involvements in the Telegraph Stage Line? The question becomes even more germane after the realignment
of 1878, which allotted everything north of San Luis
Obispo to Buckley & Taylor as owners of the Coast Line
and all south of San Luis Obispo to the Telegraph Line,

presumably owned at this time by Haskell, Nichols & Company.[38]

For six months following this rearrangement the Ventura newspapers were still referring to the stages as "Coast Line stages." During the first half of 1879 the references were to the "Telegraph stages." On June 29, 1879, Santa Paula expressman A. M. Tanner made his famous boast in the *Signal* that he would "run the new line off or bust 'em." The Telegraph Line, which presumably had been running the San Luis Obispo to Newhall portion of the Coast Route for the past year, could not have been regarded as "new."

All references from this time until the entry of "Honest John" Allman on the scene in 1882, refer to the southern portion of the route as being Telegraph Line. However, with the arrival of Allman, the Ventura *Free Press* reported on May 27, 1882, that Buckley & Taylor would run from Santa Barbara to Soledad; while the *Signal* on June 3, 1882, reported that Allman had taken over *the ownership of the line from Buckley & Taylor from Santa Barbara to Newhall.*

The Ventura *Free Press* had lamented on February 21, 1882, that the people in six counties were unhappy because the Telegraph Stage Line had lost the mail contract. Further, the Santa Barbara *Daily Press* during 1881, was running an advertisement for the Telegraph Stage Line in which it was stated that the Telegraph stages ran from Newhall to Soledad. No mention whatsoever was made of William Buckley, W. H. Taylor, or the Coast Line Stage Company and their portion of the route north of San Luis Obispo.

---

38 The announcement of the sale of the Telegraph Stage Line by Hamilton to a C. H. Cotter was made in the *Star* on June 24, 1874. Cotter appears to have been a front man for Haskell, Nichols & Company. In the 1880s Ventura newspapers made reference to the firm of Haskell, Nichols & Cotter.

It does not seem too far-fetched, when the foregoing confusion is combined with the reminiscences of W. H. Taylor, to conclude that William Buckley; later Buckley & Taylor; and still later Buckley, Carr & Taylor, were either financially involved with the Telegraph Stage Line or had a close working agreement with it.

Regardless of this corporate maze, one thing stands out clearly: The *real* stagers of the Coast Line – from neck yoke to crupper to rear boot – were William Buckley and W. H. "Shotgun" Taylor.

Buckley's name is so prominent in Western staging that it seems strange there is so little biographical information available on the man. He was originally from New York and a veteran stager at the time he became associated with the Butterfield Overland Mail as Superintendent of the Sixth Division (El Paso to Tucson).[39] For the next quarter of a century stageman Buckley had more irons in the fire than the village smithy. A master at organization and supply, his name must rank among the all time greats of coaching.

"Shotgun" Taylor was more the flamboyant type, but a genius with the ribbons as well as an experienced organizer. Taylor's career began with the Pioneer Stage Company, first as a purchaser of stock and later as a driver. Made Superintendent of the Pioneer Line in 1865, he was transferred in 1866 in the same capacity to a branch of the main Central Overland Mail Line.[40]

It was after the completion of the transcontinental railroad that Taylor moved westward and eventually became associated with the Coast Line of Stages.

There are at least two versions extant respecting the manner in which Taylor acquired his intriguing nick-

---

[39] Conkling, *op. cit.,* vol. I, pp. 126-127.
[40] Wells Fargo *Catalogue,* pp. 26-27.

name of "Shotgun." One appeared in the previously cited Wells Fargo *Catalogue* prepared for the Columbian Exposition in Chicago. The other is Taylor's own account, from which the first appears to be an "expurgated" and badly edited version. Taylor's story was given in his letter to James Otey Bradford:

> The manner in which I acquired the soubriquet [*sic*] of "Shotgun" was simply this. While driving Stage on the Washoe route in the sixties, I had a difficulty one night on the road with a man named Crosby, a freighter and a fighter of considerable notoriety. In the melee, he broke my skull. Some months later I met him on the road near Strawberry. Dr. R. R. Hammond, of San Francisco, and Mr. Fairchild, of Austin, Nev. editor of the Reese River *Reveille,* was on my coach riding outside when hostilities were renewed. Mr. Fairchild took the reins and I got my gun first; a messenger shot gun which I carried on my coach solely for the benifit [*sic*] of Mr. Crosby. He changed his mind about downing me again. (He killed two men in Va. City a few years ago in one day.) While the trouble was on with Crosby and myself, two six horse coaches appeared upon the scene driven by two famous drivers – Chas. Crowell and Chas. Watson, the latter then and there christened me "Shot Gun" and that appellation has clung to me from that day to the present.[41]

Taylor went on in his "Memoirs" to note that when he first went to Placerville half the town thought he was a preacher and the other half a Faro dealer! Shotgun would undoubtedly have been good at either or both. Of such were born the fascinations of the Old West.

A good case could be made to prove that there was never a "heyday" for the Coast Line or any other line of staging; but if there was such a time, it was during the reign of William Buckley and his pal with the "messenger shot gun" – W. H. Taylor. May their souls forever rest in that Valhalla of stagemen, where the teams are nothing but six and always matched.

[41] Taylor to Bradford, *op. cit.*

6

"Little Satan" Rides the Box

From the days of its beginnings between San Francisco and San Jose during the gold rush, the old Coast Line of Stages had seen most of the legendary figures of Western staging. There was Jared B. Crandall of the partnership of Hall & Crandall, who handled the ribbons as he raced his competitors down San Francisco Peninsula to the Capital at San Jose on the day following the news of California's admission into the Union. Seated on the box beside Crandall was none other than the Governor of California, Peter Burnett, who would leave so vivid a description of that wild stagecoach ride in his book, *Recollections Of An Old Pioneer* (1880). It was Jared Crandall, together with Warren Hall, James Birch, and Frank Stevens, who was instrumental in organizing one of the great transportation companies of the nineteenth century – The California Stage Company. Yes, it was Jared "Bob" Crandall – the man Governor Burnett compared as a whip to Clark Foss and Hank Monk – that gained fame and considerable fortune, lost the latter, and ended this life in the tragic stagecoach accident on the plains below Cahuenga Pass while driving for Flint, Bixby & Company on the Coast Line – a stager to the last.

There was Crandall's partner, Warren Hall, immortalized on the box by Waterman L. Ormsby of the New York *Herald* as that first westbound Butterfield Overland Mail stage made its anchor run into Los Angeles –

Warren Hall, who would pioneer staging from San
Bernardino to the Colorado River and meet death on
a desert mountain in one of the most bizarre homicides
in California history.

Then there were those others who had gained fame
with the Butterfield Overland Mail line: Marcus Kinyon, William Buckley, E. S. Alvord – even John Butterfield himself must be included, for he was a signatory
on the first Coast Route mail contract that would carry
the mails by stagecoach from Los Angeles to Monterey.

W. H. Taylor could call the Coast Line "Home" in
his later years – old "Shotgun" Taylor, "one of the best
known and most celebrated managers of the Stage service in the West,"[1] who began with the Pioneer Stage
Company and gained a legendary fame by his daredevil
driving while carrying Speaker of the House Schuyler
Colfax and his distinguished party between Strawberry
Station and Placerville. If any of that crowd had run
for the Presidency instead of Horace Greeley, the latter's ride with Hank Monk might long since have been
forgotten.

There were other well-known whips who had driven
the Coast Route: "One-Eyed" Charley Parkhurst, Sam
Harper, William Clift (or Cliff), Charlie Crandall,
J. C. Cheney, and Dave Green, to name but a few. With
such an illustrious "Who's Who" of staging in its history, it is ironic that one of the most sinister and evil
termites in the mail contracting business should worm
his way onto a portion of the Coast Line during its
waning years.

John Allman, alias "Honest John" Allman, alias
"Little Satan," alias a dozen or more implied but un-

---

1 Wells Fargo *Catalogue,* p. 26.

printable names, appeared on the scene in 1882. The implied aliases were to be found in the Ventura *Free Press,* and probably a dozen other newspapers if one cared to spend the time searching.

History is vague in respect to the origin of the name "Honest John." Common sense dictates that no one but Allman himself possessed so much "brass" as to bestow the title. Insofar as "Little Satan" is concerned, however, the record is clear and not a little ludicrous.

In the 1870s Allman was in the habit of dropping in on Wells, Fargo & Company's San Francisco bank. It was here that Charles Banks, suave, debonair cashier of the banking side of the great express company, took one look at Honest John Allman and applied the name "Little Satan." Eric Francis, an employee of Wells Fargo at the time, wrote that Allman "certainly looked the part," and described him as "a saturnine, dark gentleman [!] . . . and was said to have killed a man with a Bowie knife in the early days up north. . . He was one tough hombre. . ."[2]

If Allman was ever kicked by one of his stage horses, the blow unfortunately was not fatal or even serious. Honest John was still going strong enough in 1886 to be named defendant in a $50,000 seduction suit, which was a lot of seduction even by Victorian era standards.

It was in the same year of 1886, that Charley Banks proved beyond any reasonable doubt he had to be considered as something of an authority on satanic characteristics. One fine November morning the trusted cashier of Wells Fargo turned up missing; missing also were assets of a still undisclosed amount. As a matter of

---

[2] Lucius Beebe and Charles Clegg, *The Saga Of Wells Fargo* (New York, 1949), p. 211.

fact about the only assets of any importance that Banks left behind in San Francisco were a wife, three mistresses, and full equity in a seven-girl bawdy house down on the Embarcadero.

James Hume, Chief of Detectives for Wells Fargo, traced Banks to a South Sea island, where all attempts to extradite the scoundrel back to the United States proved futile. Legend has it that whenever the nose of Charley Banks began to itch, he would face toward San Francisco, scratch the offending member with his thumb while letting the gentle South Sea zephyrs waft through his fingers to create a fluttering motion. Yes, Charley Banks spoke from a position of authority when he christened John Allman "Little Satan."[3]

The subject of Allman's *modus operandi* in securing mail contracts is one of the nineteenth century's more fascinating studies – that is if the reader is fascinated by "muscle" tactics and corrupt politicians in the Post Office Department. Honest John's actions on Route No. 46,316 – Newhall to Santa Barbara – were typical. It should be noted before wading into these politically polluted waters that the records for Route No. 46,316 are among the missing at National Archives. Allman and his political cohorts may have learned a lesson or two from Charley Banks.

There was one man on that route, however, who could smell corruption miles away: H. G. McLean, editor of the Ventura *Free Press*. McLean took a quick look at the requirements demanded by the Post Office Department when the routes were advertised for bids in November 1881, and promptly exposed the racket;

[3] One of the best and most reliable accounts of this famous Charley Banks incident will be found in the Mar. 1971, issue of *The American West*, vol. VIII, no. 2.

although he obviously could not have known the details or the personalities involved at this early date:

> We fear that, notwithstanding all his care, Postmaster General James is being imposed on by some Star Route subordinates still in his employ. This is why we say so: The Department is advertising for bids to carry our mails, and this is how the proposal reads:
> "46,316 – From Newhall, by Scenega, Santa Paula, Saticoy, San Buenaventura, and Carpinteria, to Santa Barbara, 77 miles and back, seven times a week. Leave Newhall daily at 7 A.M., or on arrival of the train from Tulare; Arrive at Santa Barbara in 21 hours; Leave Santa Barbara daily at 7 P.M.; Arrive at Newhall in 21 hours."
> Seventy-Seven miles in 21 hours! About 3½ miles per hour! Just the distance the average tramp travels on foot! The same advertisement requires the mail to be carried from Soledad to Santa Barbara, over a much worse road, at a speed of 5¼ miles per hour! Mr. Covert carries the mail to Los Angeles [This refers to the tri-weekly service via the Conejo] over a still worse road, at the rate of 6 miles an hour. Why, then, is our mail to and from Newhall, over a level road, to be allowed to be carried at a snail's pace? It is our opinion there is a Star route expediting scheme on hand – unless, indeed, some expectant contractor intends to stock the road with ox-teams.[4]

At a later date McLean amended this statement to read: "Just the distance the average tramp travels *when the sheriff isn't after him.*" (There is a difference, you know.)

The winning mail route bidders were announced in the Ventura newspapers on February 18, 1882. The contract for carrying the mails from Newhall to Santa Barbara had been awarded to George Allman for $4400, approximately one-third the going rate. William Buckley and Shotgun Taylor sniffed the air, smelled an un-

---

4 Ventura *Free Press,* Nov. 19, 1881.

favorable impact on the environment, sold out their interests in the present line, and beat a strategic retreat to the north end of State Street in Santa Barbara, from whence they would carry the mails to Soledad beginning the first of June.[5] Honest John's none-too-subtle bid through his son George did not fool Buckley and Taylor for a moment.

The same cannot be said for E. M. Sheridan, *Signal* editor. Sheridan was the perfect stooge for Little Satan and fell into the web like any foolish fly. Three articles in the June 3, 1882, *Signal* tell the story and illustrate the techniques of the first act of the Allman drama:

> John Allman, the veteran stage man and contractor, has taken charge of the line between Santa Barbara and Newhall, and will hereafter run the same. Mr. Allman will have, after July, 2500 miles of staging under his control. He has succeeded in having the fare to San Francisco reduced to $34 for the round trip, or $17 each way. This will throw considerable travel overland which has heretofore gone by sea.
>
> Our friend, Charley Baker, has been retained as division superintendent of Mr. Allman's Stage line. No better selection could have been made. Mr. Baker is a popular and thorough business man, and boasts more friends than any man in the county.
>
> Al Ayers will be retained as stage agent by John Allman. There will be a change of drivers, and but two drivers, each going all the way through from Newhall to Santa Barbara. *The Taylor & Buckley company* received $11,000 for carrying the mail that Mr. Allman is getting $4400 for. There is also a reduction of the fare, hence it will be seen that Mr. Allman is contending against many odds. But he has said he will make a success of the thing,

---

5 Ventura *Signal,* June 3, 1882. The ownership of the Telegraph Stage Line at this time is quite obscure. The Ventura newspapers frequently referred to the Telegraph Line as the mail contractor and just as frequently mentioned Buckley & Taylor as owning and operating the line to Newhall. However, at a later date when the Telegraph Line outsmarted Allman – Haskell, Nichols & Company were again listed as owners.

and no doubt he will, as he is made of the right kind of stuff. He is a genial and whole-souled gentleman [!] and made many friends during his short stay in town.[6]

The picture should be clear: All the old-timers and popular figures retained on the job; fares reduced; local merchants benefiting from overland travel; and the tax-payers saved $6600 by the "whole-souled gentleman," alias Honest John Allman, alias Little Satan!

Was Ed. Sheridan actually that big a fool or had Allman bought him off? Possibly when Sheridan wrote that Allman was made of the right kind of stuff it had been after a prolonged session with Little Satan down at Hartman's Brewery Saloon. *There* was the place to find out the kind of "stuff" of which a man was made. It would take the editor many months to learn the truth, and then it was conceded in a most hesitant and reluctant manner.

With the stage set and a reliable press agent in the *Signal* editor, Honest John was in no hurry to press the issue or prematurely arouse the wrath of the populace by taking advantage of the three and one-half miles per hour clause in his contract. Allman even changed the departure time from Santa Barbara so that customers would not have to get up at three o'clock in the morning to catch the Newhall stage. It was mid-September before the *Free Press* noted the slowdown in the mails:

The mails from San Francisco and the upper part of the State, destined for San Buenaventura and Santa Barbara, arrive at Newhall at 6 A.M. Lately, that mail has arrived in this town at 9 P.M. – just 15 hours and Newhall only 50 miles away! Of course, Mr. Allman's object is plain. He intends, taking ad-

---

[6] Italics added to emphasize the Buckley-Taylor presence when the meager available records indicate that Haskell, Nichols & Company held the contract. See footnote no. 5.

vantage of his contract, to annoy the people into petitioning the government to order faster time, with, of course, vastly increased pay to Mr. Allman. But he has taken the wrong course.

We are informed that the contractor who carries the mail on the coast route to Los Angeles will agree to deliver the same here every evening at 6, three hours ahead of Allman's time, P.M., thus enabling letters to be delivered at once, instead of lying in the office all night. For this service, and daily trips, he will require additional compensation to the amount of only $1100. Let a meeting be held to consider this matter, and a committee appointed to see what can be done in regard to it.[7]

Editor McLean had called the turn exactly. The man had shown an uncanny ability all through the years of his *Free Press* editorship to foresee motives and forecast results. In the present instance public meetings, petitions, and appeals to Washington, D.C., were right in line with Allman's plans. The idea of remaking the old Coast Route through the Conejo into an actively competing daily stage line, however, was definitely *not* a part of the scheme. When that proposition became serious, Honest John would let Little Satan handle it.

It should be readily apparent to anyone who has read a United States mail contract of the period that the ideas entertained by Allman required an official in the Post Office Department collaborating with the contractor in order to make the wheels turn. The contracts were so worded that whenever the contractor failed to deliver according to terms, it could be terminated forthwith. Editor McLean had his own ideas concerning who the guilty bureaucrat in Washington was:

Mr. Allman seems to have the Second Assistant Postmaster General and the route agents in this State at his beck and nod. He has again secured a change in his schedule time, by which our

[7] Ventura *Free Press,* Sept. 16, 1882.

mails from above lie seven hours in Newhall, arriving here a little
before midnight — too late for delivery or reply. Did somebody
say the service was improved lately? We don't see it, but think
we do see that Mr. Allman won't get his route expedited by going
in for annoying our people.[8]

Even the Ventura *Signal* had to admit that the most
astute mathematician could not figure out anything
about the stages; but inasmuch as they *did* eventually
arrive with the mails, and owing to the courtesy of Post-
mistress Goodwin in keeping the office open and delivering the mails at any hour, Mr. Sheridan could not see
what all the fuss was about or why everyone should not
be perfectly satisfied.

By January 1883, Mrs. Goodwin was in trouble, ostensibly because of an oversight which returned the
outbound Santa Barbara mail pouches back to that city.
Petitions placed in circulation for her removal, however, brought out the information that she had been
approached to aid Allman in "Star-Routing" the Newhall run and had refused. At the same time other petitions were floating around town to expedite the mails
from Newhall, an indication that Allman was busy. The
Free Press exposed the plan nicely:

> The next petition we hear of is one to expedite the transmis-
> sion of the mail between Newhall and Santa Barbara through
> this city. This is the same impudent Star Route business cropping
> out again. At the time the advertisement was printed for the let-
> ting of this contract Mr. Elmer, Second Assistant Postmaster
> General, was informed (unless a thieving clerk suppressed his
> letters) that a Star Route steal was on the tapis — that in 1877
> the Department easily found a contractor who carried the mail

---

[8] *Ibid.,* Oct. 14, 1882. In the case of this particular contract the collaboration, of course, came at the time the terms were spelled out. These later incon-
veniences were, as McLean noted, purely annoyances to arouse the people to
action.

from Ventura at the rate of 7½ miles per hour. . . Mr. Elmer, nevertheless, persisted in letting the contract over a road 77 miles long, on a route as level as a billiard table, at the speed of 3½ miles per hour.[9]

Allman now played another of his annoying aces. The Southern Pacific Railroad was under no obligation to maintain a time table schedule forever, and frequent changes were being made on the schedules from Los Angeles to San Francisco. This was due in part to the completion early in 1883, of the southern transcontinental or Sunset Route of the Southern Pacific. If the connecting stage line down the Santa Clara Valley did not adjust its schedules accordingly, passengers would miss connections (a trivial item to the newspaper editors) and the mails held over for a full day, a very serious matter, indeed. Little Satan was a past master at departing Newhall just prior to mail train arrivals from the south. The *Free Press* stormed, the *Signal* protested feebly, and now the Los Angeles *Times* joined the chorus by advocating that the mails from Los Angeles northbound to San Buenaventura and Santa Barbara be sent by a daily Coast Line stage through the Conejo:

> The inefficiency of the mail service between Los Angeles and San Buenaventura is most strikingly depicted by our Ventura correspondent. . . At present it actually takes longer for the daily mail from this place to reach San Buenaventura than it requires for the San Francisco mail to reach the same point! This is not a creditable state of affairs, and the proper remedy should be applied. That consists, in our opinion, in increasing the service on the coast line, now tri-weekly, to six or seven trips a week. The stages on that line now go through in daylight, beating the mail via Newhall several hours, and carrying papers and letters a day later than by the other route, though that is combination of stage and rail.

9 *Ibid.,* Jan. 20, 1883.

We understand that a small increase of pay – less than two thousand dollars per year – will secure the desired increase, and that petitions for that object have been or will be circulated. . . We have been advised that Superintendent McKusick favors the proposed increase, and will forward to the Postoffice Department with his favorable indorsement. . .[10]

Harrison Gray Otis and his Los Angeles *Times* were foes with which Little Satan had no ambitions to lock horns or attempt to match influence in Washington, D.C. There was, however, a military maneuver known as "forming front to a flank" which seemed to fit the present need of Honest John. His foes by advocating the reactivation of the Conejo Route were, in essence, proposing to outflank Allman. The scheme had to be blocked at all costs. The very same issue of the *Signal* that reprinted the *Times* proposal carried the following news item: "There is a strong probability that the Coast Line of stages to Los Angeles will pass into the hands of John Allman, contractor for the Newhall route, as negotiations to that end are pending."[11]

Allman was forming front to a flank.

The *Signal* then reported the final success of Allman's overall plan by announcing that Honest John had received an increase in pay for the Newhall route and the old running time of twelve hours would be resumed. Allman had "Star Routed" the old Lyon's Station Mail Route. The increased figure was not mentioned, but subsequent events indicated that it was $12,500, or $1500 more than his competitors had contracted the same job for before Allman instituted his Star Route fraud. *That* was a little item which never appeared in E. M. Sheridan's *Signal*.

[10] Ventura *Signal,* Apr. 28, 1883, reprinted from the Los Angeles *Times.*
[11] *Ibid.*

Once Allman had sunk his teeth into a mail route, he could hang on with all the tenaciousness of a bulldog. The man cared nothing for the comfort or safety of his passengers, nor did he display any of the pride of owner-ship in equipment and fine horses one comes to expect of an old Western stager. The Concord coach, never a con-spicuous vehicle on the Coast Line, became almost non-existent under Allman. The celerity or mud wagon, detested by the stage passengers, was Allman's stock in trade.

> Get up at midnight and crawl into an old rickety stage without cushions, or with a few rags as an apology for cushions, inside not swept out and dusted in a month, spend twelve hours on the road, often without breakfast, and pay 10 cents a mile for the priv-ilege.[12]

Frequently the stages of Little Satan were pulled by two straining horses instead of the usual four or six; while complaints of overcrowding, piling trunks, valises, and mail pouches in with the passengers were frequent. If the creeks and rivers were near flood stage, often the mails and luggage, to say nothing of the pas-sengers, became soaked. When Little Satan held the ribbons, the stage line gave not a tinker's damn about anyone or anything – except money.

There still was the problem hanging fire of possible daily stage competition on the old Conejo Route. Ever since Flint, Bixby & Company had abandoned the Co-nejo in favor of the Santa Clara Valley Route in 1876, the Conejo at best had seen but sporadic stage and mail service. More frequently than not, the mails (when there were any) were carried to Newbury Park by spring wagon and thence to Los Angeles by horseback rider. The collapse of the Santa Barbara citizens' Co-

---

[12] Ventura *Free Press,* Apr. 26, 1887.

nejo Valley boom and their consequent bankruptcies
had left little demand for stage or mail service in the
area. For long periods there appears to have been none.

Over the years numerous individuals had contracted
to carry the mails on the Conejo Route, but usually their
efforts were ill-paid and of short duration. At the time
of the Allman trouble, G. W. Treanor held the contract
and was rendering excellent service on a tri-weekly
basis. With encouragement from the Los Angeles *Times*
and Ventura *Free Press,* Treanor had promised to increase the service to a daily basis regardless of whether
a mail contract was forthcoming or not. At the same
time, Allman was threatening to start an opposition line
of stages against Treanor, competition that the latter
was ill-prepared to meet. He had already lost his most
reliable driver when "Smoky Jim" Romaine, the Colton
Butcher, inherited a fortune from his step-mother in
New York. Treanor himself was a sick man with only
months to live. It was an ideal time for Little Satan to
move in for the kill: "Walter Knight, Allman's popular
superintendent, has purchased a half interest in the
Treanor line of stages, running between this place and
Los Angeles. The office will continue to be in the Ayers'
Hotel."[13]

Six months later Treanor was dead and before another week passed, Allman purchased from his estate
the other one-half interest in the line. The June 7, 1884,
issue of the *Signal* reported that he had purchased
Knight's one-half interest as well. Honest John now
owned the line outright and had secured himself against
any further flanking attacks between San Buenaventura
and Los Angeles.

Elsewhere in the State, however, things were differ-

---

[13] Ventura *Signal,* Sept. 15, 1883.

ent. In the northern part of California a competitor had used Honest John's own tactics to get away with a profitable mail route, forcing him to sell out Allman's Northern United States Mail Line. Little Satan was furious and sued the upstart for $100,000 for fraudulently taking away his mail route!

The Ventura *Signal,* which by now had sobered up considerably in its enthusiasm for Allman, the "whole-souled gentleman," suggested that if he won the case he might consider using some of the money for satin linings in his Newhall stages. In the meantime, Honest John's opponent up north was threatening to put opposition stages on all Allman's routes. It turned out to be a battle of words only, much to the general public's disappointment.

One week after Allman gained control of the Conejo Route, the *Signal* announced in a "hope springs eternal" vein that four-horse coaches would be run over the line. The same issue reported stage driver George Reed had been attacked on the Conejo with *cholera morbus* but was expected to recover. The illness may have been brought on by the knowledge that while four-horse coaches would roll on Reed's run, Allman would expect him to pull them with only *two* animals. Little Satan was up to his old tricks:

> Mr. Allman runs a daily stage between Ventura and Los Angeles via the Conejo. Stages start from each end of the route at 6 A.M., and reach their destination at 7 P.M. The fare is only $5 each way, the distance nearly eighty miles. As the stage does not stop for dinner, passengers should go provided with lunch. The drive from Conejo eastward is twenty-eight miles without a change of horses, which is entirely too long and too hard on the teams.[14]

14 Ventura *Free Press,* Sept. 26, 1884.

On January 31, 1885, the *Signal* reported that Allman had received an increase in pay on the Conejo line.
A long-suffering public had become so cynical of Honest
John's methods that no one expected any improvement
in the service because of the pay increase. No one was
disappointed. A description of mid-1880s Conejo staging presents a vivid picture of the conditions travelers
encountered when Little Satan rode the box:

> I left Ventura on the Allman stage line Thursday morning
> Oct. 1st. I prefer this route to Los Angeles as one escapes the sea
> sickness consequent upon steamer passage, and the night travel to
> which one is subject by the Newhall route. The scenery over the
> Conejo plateau is always impressive. At this season, however, the
> road is full of "chuckholes," and in going eastward the dust is
> carried along with the stage. But a worse drawback is the worn
> out stock upon this road. The Stages are old and disagreeable,
> and the horses are pitiable. From the Conejo to Los Angeles, a
> distance of nearly 45 miles, there is but one change of horses.
> Two poor horses are compelled to pull a heavy stage over moun-
> tain roads whether there be one passenger or nine, and the bag-
> gage, which is heavy. The fact is the proprietor ought to be
> arrested for cruelty to animals.[15]

While Allman had consolidated his position by mid-
June of 1884, the year as a whole was one he probably
would rather have skipped. January got off to a bad
start on the 17th when Honest John's eleven-passenger
westbound stage tipped over near Camulos. Investigation established that the light three-seated vehicle was
carrying seventeen passengers, all their luggage, and a
very heavy mail load.

> At this particular point in the road there is a slight sidling
> grade, around which the driver did not wish to go with his top-
> heavy load, so he made a slight detour and drove straight down
> the hill. Going down, the brake refused to act and the impetus

[15] *Ibid.,* Oct. 9, 1885.

given the coach threw it over in the soft, plowed, level ground at the foot of the hill.[16]

The driver, a man by the highly improbable name (under the circumstances) of Oliver Cropper, was a veteran whip and fortunately picked a spot where the ground was loose, thus softening the impact to some extent. All the passengers were injured to a degree, some rather seriously. Honest John found himself faced with a number of lawsuits in which the plaintiffs had every expectancy of collecting full damages. By now there wasn't a county in the State of California where Little Satan could have impaneled twelve friendly jurors; a change of venue was futile.

Nine days after the Camulos wreck the rains began. By February 2, huge piles of mail were accumulating all along the route due to flooding creeks and rivers. Every day that the mails could not get through was costing the contractor money. This was language that Little Satan understood. With the aid of Wells Fargo Agent A. O. Perkins of Santa Barbara, Allman's drivers managed to stretch a 300-foot cable across the "Ragin' Sespe" and haul the mail over two hundred pounds at a trip. San Buenaventura and Santa Barbara thus received their second mail in twelve days, but the winter had barely begun. The Ventura *Signal* of February 23, devoted one entire page to the devastation wrought by a second great storm. It was this flood that cut the huge west channel of the Sespe River which is still the main water course of the stream. Three hundred feet of cable was useless now to get the mails across.

During the second week in March a third major storm struck, again blocking the stages for days. As late

---

[16] Ventura *Signal,* Jan. 19, 1884.

as May 16, a three-inch rainstorm delayed the coaches
in Santa Paula while the boulders rolled and crashed in
the creeks. During that terrible winter thirty-six inches
of rain fell in San Buenaventura, most of it after January 26. Transporting the mails with certainty, celerity,
and security was impossible, even for Honest John
Allman.

By the time the rains had ceased and the roads had
been repaired, it was also time for new bids to be submitted on the various mail routes. The *Signal* of June
28, announced that Allman had received the Newhall
contract for $12,500, with the running time expedited.
There was one minor flaw in the story: The bids were
not supposed to be opened until July 1, in Washington,
D.C. The *Free Press* of the following week published a
letter signed "Observer," but which bore all the ear-
marks of Stephen Bowers, the man who had purchased
the *Free Press* from H. G. McLean in October, 1883:

> In last week's issue of the *Signal* the editor in a roundabout and
> doubtful way informs his readers that the contract for carrying
> the mail from Newhall to Santa Barbara has been awarded to
> Allman for the sum of $12,500 as against $4400 last year. Now
> as the bids on this line were not closed in Washington until July
> 1st, how did the *Signal* learn previous to June 28th that Allman
> was the successful competitor? It looks very much like "honest
> John Allman" and "honest" Ed. Sheridan had "pooled their is-
> sues" and tried by this little game to throw the public off the
> track and keep others from bidding. If we are correct in this the
> editor of that sheet has placed himself in an unenviable position,
> to say the least.[17]

It did, indeed, appear as though Honest John Allman
and "Honest" Ed. Sheridan had "pooled their issues."
When the winning bidders were announced, the old

17 Ventura *Free Press,* July 4, 1884.

Telegraph Stage Line had submitted the lowest figure. Haskell, Nichols & Company were returning the compliments which Little Satan had bestowed upon it two years before. The only uncertainty in the affair was whether or not William Buckley and Shotgun Taylor were associated with the Telegraph Stage Line at this time and thus involved in the fun. One would like to think that they were.

While the *Signal* may have given Allman an unsuccessful assist by "pooling issues," its account of the results was much clearer and gives the modern reader a better insight into the workings of the "straw" bid and nineteenth century chicanery, than that of the *Free Press:*

> Honest John Allman has lost his mail contract between Santa Barbara and Newhall. Messrs. Haskell, Nichols & Co., the old Telegraph Stage Company who formerly ran the route, bid $9,872 as against Honest John's $12,500 for the privilege of carrying the U.S. mail and of course "got away with the works." Allman has bid $8000 to Haskell, Nichols & Co. for a sub-contract, and in case he does not secure it says he will continue to run a daily line of stages over the road – which would be a good thing for the public in the matter of cheapening fares. If Messrs. Haskell, Nichols & Co. conclude to stock the road and run the business themselves which is likely, they will probably place the whole management of the line in the hands of Charley Baker of Santa Paula as general superintendent – which would be another thing for the public, as a more accomodating stage man than C. N. Baker does not live in all this broad state of California.[18]

In other words, Haskell, Nichols & Company had deliberately submitted a bid which, if low, could be fulfilled and still make the company money. If Allman offered to take a sub-contract, the Telegraph Stage Line could pick up a profit without so much as throwing the

18 Ventura *Signal,* Aug. 2, 1884.

LICHTENBERGER CARRIAGE FACTORY

A Concord Coach of the Telegraph Stage Line is parked in front of the factory in this 1880 photograph. On the side of the box is the name "E. A. Haskell," senior member of the firm of Haskell, Nichols, and Co. Across the top of the stage is "Telegraph Stage Line, U.S.M." Courtesy, Title Insurance and Trust Co.

STAGE BOUND FOR SAN MARCOS PASS

The six-in-hand pull a mud wagon. This is an excellent photograph to illustrate the hitching arrangement for a six-horse hookup. Note the "swing pole" or extra tongue attached to the regular pole. This avoided the use of a fifth chain and allowed all horses to be hitched to doubletrees instead of stretchers (sometimes called spreaders). If eight horses were used, still another pole was attached.

hames over the off leader or buckling the cruppers on the wheelers. With Allman offering to do the job for the Telegraph at $8000, the latter stood to gain $1872, the difference between their winning bid and Allman's offer: Uncle Sam would pay the Telegraph Stage Line $9872 as the low bid submitted, and the Telegraph would turn around and pay Allman $8000 for doing the work, and put the balance in its pocket. Clever people those old Western stagers!

A clear distinction must be made between this operation and the one that Honest John pulled off in 1882. No such thing as a sub-lease was possible in the latter case because of the very low bid submitted. Allman merely wanted to run off all competition and then secure a high fee from the government by slowing down service and operating ancient equipment and even more ancient horses until the public demanded action by the Post Office Department. As has been noted previously, this type of double-dealing required a confederate in the Postmaster-General's Office; while the Telegraph scheme was a cleverly worked out *coup d'etat* that could not fail or hurt the public.

Allman's threat to continue operations regardless of which course the Telegraph Line took was pure bluff. No one knew better than Honest John the folly of running this type of staging without a mail contract. Much to the chagrin of the general public, the Telegraph Stage Line accepted Allman's offer, pocketed their profit, and probably drank an uproarious toast to sweet revenge upon Little Satan, Ed. Sheridan's "whole-souled gentleman."

While stage lines of the magnitude of Allman's could not be operated profitably without a mail contract, the "little man" could and often did get into the act on short distance hauls. For years a line that was popularly known as "The Spanish Stage" had operated with surprising regularity between San Buenaventura and Santa Barbara. The name itself tells the story; although it should be emphasized that contemporary newspaper accounts of its operations, while sparse, were nearly always complimentary. Juan Fernandez appears to have been the originator of the Spanish Stage in 1874, after unsuccessfully inaugurating a stage line to the Ojai and Brown's Hot Springs (Matilija).[19] Fernandez solicited patronage on the basis he was "A home institution bucking the monopoly,"[20] the monopoly at this time being Flint, Bixby & Company.

Later, Pancho Ruiz took over the line, probably after several other unrecorded and long forgotten Californians had operated it. The Ventura *Signal* reported June 25, 1881, that "Pancho Ruiz, who has so long and successfully kept the opposition stage on the Santa Barbara run, is still to be found on time with his four-in-hand." No lumbering two-horse spring wagon for Pancho.

By the time the sinister Little Satan had corralled everything else in sight, the Spanish Stage was under the control of a prominent Californian, J. C. Lorenzana of San Buenaventura. Jose Lorenzana didn't give a damn for Honest John Allman or any other *Gringo,* for that matter, who tried to "muscle around" honest people.

In April 1885, E. M. Jones of the Santa Clara House had purchased a fine stagecoach and inaugurated a new line to Santa Barbara in competition with Allman. By October Jones had learned the error of his ways and withdrew from staging "in favor of John Allman."[21] Only Lorenzana and his Spanish Stage stood between

19 *Ibid.,* June 20 and July 18, 1874.   20 *Ibid.,* Aug. 1, 1874.
21 Ventura *Free Press,* Oct. 2, 1885.

Allman and a complete monopoly on the Santa Barbara to San Buenaventura route.

Little Satan set about to remedy that defect as expeditiously as possible; but if he had stood on the hill by Father Serra's Cross and shouted blasphemies for ten days, he could not have picked a worse method. Honest John began carrying Spanish and Chinese between the two cities for fifty cents a head, while at the same time charging the "Americans" one dollar! The *Free Press* howled:

> Many of our readers will regret to learn that E. M. Jones has withdrawn his stages between Ventura and Santa Barbara in favor of John Allman. Allman is now making an effort to freeze out the Spanish stage by offering to take all Spaniards at 50 cents, which we understand includes Chinamen, also, while Americans are charged one dollar each. This is an insult to every decent Spaniard in the county and we hope they will resent it by patronizing the Spanish stage. Americans will do well to patronize Lorenzana also for if he is frozen out they will most likely have to pay $3 to get to Santa Barbara instead of $1, now charged by Lorenzana.[22]

The following week the *Free Press* reported that Lorenzana was meeting with success in his duel with Allman and the latter was slowly cutting his own throat. The newspaper emphasized the point by noting a young lady had paid her dollar fare to Santa Barbara and then had been forced to ride sandwiched in between six "Chinamen" deadheading at fifty cents apiece.

The *Free Press* also revealed, probably inadvertantly, how E. M. Jones had been induced to withdraw from staging in favor of Allman: "We are informed that Allman caused it to be reported in Santa Barbara that the Palace Hotel was closed, in order to turn trade from that house."

---

[22] *Ibid.*

The Palace Hotel being the chief competitor of E. M. Jones' Santa Clara House, it should take the most naive reader but a moment to untangle the threads.

Unfortunately for history, the outcome of this interesting little stagecoach war never appeared in the newspaper. Much like Tom Bard's Hueneme & Newhall Railroad Company, it "vanished like dew before the sunlight, casting no shadows before nor behind." [23]

It should be noted, however, that long after the Southern Pacific Railroad had forced Allman to retreat with his tail between his legs, J. C. Lorenzana was running a four-horse rockaway and a spring wagon between the railhead at Carpinteria and Santa Barbara. Like Jared Crandall and the others, Lorenzana could be considered a stager to the end.

The Allman-Lorenzana affair, however, did bring to light another of Little Satan's shenanigans that might otherwise have been lost to the narrator. While Lorenzana was wrestling with Honest John on the Santa Barbara route, an H. D. Stamler, who ran a livery stable in Santa Paula, had been quietly operating an accommodation hack line to Camulos and Newhall on a somewhat irregular basis, or whenever the demand warranted. Even this modest competition was too much for Allman's pride, however, and he approached Mr. del Valle with the suggestion that it might be prudent for the latter to discontinue furnishing Stamler with a change of horses when needed. Del Valle informed Honest John that the Camulos Rancho would furnish horses to whomever it pleased and, although not specifically stated in the newspaper, there was a much more appropriate place than Ventura County for Sa-

---

23 Ventura *Signal,* Apr. 2, 1881.

tans, be they Little or large; and that was where Honest John could go.

For the second time John Allman had picked on the wrong Californian, although he still did not realize the fact so far as del Valle was concerned. When the next stagecoach came along, it pranced merrily past the Camulos without stopping to drop off the mail as was customary. Little Satan had given orders to his drivers they were not to go in by the ranch house, accommodate Mr. del Valle in any manner, or carry the mail matter for Camulos.

Del Valle knew the answer to that nonsense and possessed enough influence to see it through. He promptly petitioned the United States Government for a post office at Camulos, was successful in getting it approved, and received the postmastership for Juventino del Valle in the bargain. Little Satan could either deliver the mail to Camulos or explain the reason why to Uncle Sam; del Valle would tolerate no more funny business from Honest John Allman.[24]

From this time on Allman dropped from the newspaper columns except on rare occasions. On January 1, 1886, it was reported that he had been named defendant in the aforementioned seduction suit. On another occasion the *Free Press* reported a runaway Allman stagecoach had nearly run over a child. That was all. Little Satan appeared to have vanished.

On June 25, 1886, an article in the *Free Press* seemed to indicate that Allman was no longer connected with the Santa Barbara to Newhall route:

---

24 Ventura *Free Press,* Oct. 16, 1885. It is interesting to note that while the confirmation of the establishment of a post office at Camulos was published in the *Free Press* on Oct. 16, the records at National Archives show it was established on Oct. 29, 1885.

N. Wines, of the Utah, Nevada & California Stage Company, has been in Ventura several days arranging for the stage route between Santa Barbara and Newhall. He informs us that he has ordered new wagons, and has already purchased good horses, and aims to be prepared to carry the mail promptly and passengers comfortably. Mr. Wines is a man of sobriety, and we miss our guess if he is not a gentleman of strict integrity. He will take up his residence in Ventura, we are glad to learn.[25]

Mr. Wines was a scholar and a gentleman without the remotest question of a doubt. He was also the most myopic businessman that ever landed in Ventura County – or possibly the man had been afflicted with "sun grins" while associated with the Utah, Nevada & California Stage Company. It would be interesting to know if and when he bought out Allman, particularly if Little Satan unloaded prior to April 16, 1886. That was the date the Southern Pacific Railroad announced it was beginning construction from Newhall down the Santa Clara Valley, and from Soledad up the Salinas Valley. In the face of the inevitable, Mr. Wines had purchased a stage line and bought new equipment and stock. A few months after the railroad reached Ventura, a notice appeared in the *Free Press* announcing the insolvency of Mr. N. Wines. A news article stated he was returning to Chicago.

As for Little Satan, alias Honest John Allman – *quien sabe*. On August 31, 1889, the Ventura *Vidette* reported a John Allman had been arrested in Los Angeles, but the editor doubted that it was "the old stager." This writer, for one, would not care to bet on it.

---

[25] Ventura *Free Press*, June 25, 1886.

7

Those Tall, Slim Boot Pads

boot – a receptacle or place for baggage
at either end of a vehicle.
pad – a highwayman.
The American College Dictionary

"The regular stage robbery in Santa Barbara County occurred on Saturday evening. Nothing particular in the box or the event."[1]

Not that Editor McLean had anything against a nice exciting stagecoach robbery to report in his Ventura *Free Press;* he simply could not resist digging the ribs of his Santa Barbara neighbors (or the Democrats either, for that matter) whenever the opportunity presented itself. The week before, he had been able to report that a "tall, slim boot pad" had robbed the Coast Line stage near Graciosa. Two weeks later McLean noted with an obvious yawn, "The usual weekly stage robbery in Santa Barbara County" without giving any details. The thing really was getting too repetitious to be classified as news anymore; and with Dick Fellows behind bars, it was hard to work up much enthusiasm over these thirty-cent, "throw-down-the-box" Santa Barbara affairs.

It was this latter point that puzzled McLean and even today appears somewhat ridiculous. As the *Free Press* pointed out, Wells Fargo did not ship any substantial sums of money via the Coast Line stages (McLean always added, "particularly in Santa Barbara

---

[1] Ventura *Free Press*, Apr. 7, 1877.

County"). However, the express company was getting a little bored with the nuisance of the holdups; and Flint, Bixby & Company had become so tired of highway robberies they had built strongboxes secured to the undersides of the coaches in such a way that it required time and powder to open them. The "tall, slim boot pads" paid no attention to such precautions; if they could not get the box, they could and did "go through the passengers." Even in this respect there was some question as to how profitable their operations were. Editor J. A. Johnson of the Santa Barbara *Press* noted that, "the road agent is a fool who thinks a man has any money in this part of the country." [2]

It had begun in the early days of western staging and would continue until the only remaining segments of the Coast Line of Stages were from Santa Barbara to Los Olivos, and San Luis Obispo to the railhead in the upper Salinas Valley.

Tiburcio Vasquez may have been the first "tall, slim boot pad" to rob a stagecoach on a portion of the Coast Line, long before the Overland Mail Company opened up staging south of Monterey. Joseph A. Sullivan described Tiburcio as "a wily rascal of medium height," [3] but so far as newspaper editors were concerned, all highwaymen were "tall, slim boot pads." Vasquez himself was claimed to have made the statement to Ben Truman of the Los Angeles *Star,* while being interviewed soon after his capture, that holding up a stagecoach had been his second venture into crime:

> My first exploit consisted in robbing some peddlers of money and clothes in Monterey County. My next was the capture and

2 Santa Barbara *Press,* Aug. 13, 1870.

3 Eugene Sawyer, *The Life and Career of Tiburcio Vasquez, The California Stage Robber,* ed. Joseph A. Sullivan (Oakland, 1944), p. VII.

robbery of a stagecoach in the same county. I had confederates
with me from the first, and was always recognized as leader.
Robbery after robbery followed each other as rapidly as circumstances allowed until, in 1857, or '58, I was arrested in Los Angeles for horse stealing, convicted of grand larceny, sentenced to
the penitentiary, and was taken to San Quentin and remained
there until my term of imprisonment expired in 1863. Up to the
time of my conviction and imprisonment I had robbed stagecoaches, wagons, houses, etc., indiscriminately, carrying on my
operations for the most part in daylight, sometimes, however,
visiting houses after dark. . .[4]

Neither Eugene Sawyer nor George Beers in their
biographies of Vasquez appears to have noticed this
interview, or if they did they put no credence in Tiburcio's memory or veracity at the time the *Star* editor
interviewed him. It is possible that Sawyer and Beers
were afraid to use the material, as Truman's very rare
pamphlet on Vasquez which resulted from the interview was dated a year prior to the works of the other
two biographers. Further, Sawyer and Beers were probably aware that Vasquez had omitted a few germane
items when he talked to Ben Truman, not the least of
which was his escape from San Quentin, followed by
more illegal escapades, recapture, and a year appended
to his sentence. So far as San Quentin was concerned,
Tiburcio had *not* remained until his sentence expired;
the scoundrel had been A.W.O.L. for some little time.

It was Sullivan who wrote that Vasquez "was surely
the cleverest, if not the greatest, stage robber of all
time." [5] The statement is argumentative at best when
one considers the likes of Black Bart and Dick Fellows.
Most highway robberies of the Vasquez era are a matter

[4] Los Angeles *Star,* May 16, 1874. The *Star* of July 25, 1857, reported that
the Los Angeles County Sheriff had arrested Vasquez for stealing horses in the
San Buenaventura area.   [5] Sawyer, *op. cit.,* p. III.

of record, although a number were never solved. How many were the work of Tiburcio is only a guess; he may or may not have been the cleverest and/or the greatest stage robber of all time, but one thing is certain: for pure, unadulterated audaciousness the likes of *Señor* Vasquez have never been equaled. Here was an *hombre* who had by his own admission robbed stagecoaches, broken into homes, waylaid peddlers and innumerable travelers, stolen horses; and while Tiburcio claimed innocence insofar as murder was concerned, the jury disagreed and sent him to the gallows. Despite this unprecedented record of anti-social behavior, Tiburcio Vasquez had the unmitigated "brass" to bring suit to recover the loot taken from him at the time of his arrest:

> Vasquez, the notorious bandit, is about to bring suit against Sheriff Rowland, of Los Angeles county; Albert Johnston, Under-Sheriff; George Beers, of Alameda, and H. M. Mitchell, W. E. Rogers, D. K. Smith, Frank Hartley, Sam Bryant, and E. Harris, of Los Angeles, for the recovery of sundry rifles, revolvers, saddles, bowieknives, riatas, saddleblankets, etc., which those gentlemen took from him "by force of arms" [!] at the time of his capture in May last. The bandit claims that these articles were purchased by him, or by his agents in Los Angeles, and paid for with coin; that he can prove his lawful ownership, and that the capturing party had no right to divide the "booty" or dispose of any portion of it. The robber doubtless has some ulterior object in view in bringing the suit.[6] – [Doubtless!]

Tiburcio Vasquez had taken the wrong turn somewhere in his youth. The fellow was a superb actor and if he had followed the legitimate stage instead of those of the Coast Line, he would have gone far. At the time he was being transported north on the Steamship *Senator* to his trial and execution, large crowds came down to

---

[6] Los Angeles *Star,* Nov. 21, 1874. Reprinted from the San Francisco *Chronicle.*

the wharf at San Buenaventura to catch a glimpse of
the highwayman. The Ventura *Signal* reported: "He
plays the genteel, and would have it believed he is of the
high toned class of thieves, and that he only murders in
extreme cases. He finds some poor dupes to lionize
him.   ." [7]

The *Signal* editor was so impressed with Tiburcio's
ability to play upon the heartstrings of humanity that
he predicted no jury would go further than giving him
life imprisonment. The editor was wrong. The records
state that Vasquez dropped eight feet before the rope
around his neck checked his fall. It couldn't have happened to a finer paranoiac.

Ben Truman was not the best man in California to
interview Vasquez, the reason being that five years
earlier the *Star* editor had been on the receiving end of
one of the most famous of all Coast Line stagecoach
holdups. The affair occurred on the moonlight night of
October 20, 1869, as the Coast Line stage was leaving
Los Angeles. William Cliff (or Clift, as Truman spelled
it) a veteran and popular whip was handling the reins;
and by his side sat the Special Correspondent for the
San Francisco *Times,* and Special Agent for the United
States Post Office Department, Benjamin Cummings
Truman, later to be editor of the Los Angeles *Star*. The
coach had left the Bella Union Hotel at six-fifteen with
eight passengers and the usual mail and express shipments:

> The stage had proceeded to a point just one mile beyond the
> Hebrew Cemetery, and down a gentle slope, when two masked
> men, who were seated upon the side of a parallel road, a few feet
> off, sprung [*sic*] up and ran toward the team, and attempted to
> take the nigh leader by the check, shouting at the same time,

[7] Ventura *Signal,* May 30, 1874.

"Hold up, there! Put down that brake!" Quick as thought the team was reined in, when one of the men, the captain of the gang, rushed up to the wheel horse, and, addressing himself to the driver, demanded the treasure boxes, saying, "You keep your horses quiet, and let that gentleman beside you throw out the express, and there will be no trouble." With a revolver pointed at Mr. Truman, the robber remarked, "Now, hurry up that express matter," at which the former immediately threw out one of the boxes and then halted in the performance of the disagreeable job. "The other box – and be d—d quick about it, too!" coolly ejaculated the captain; and away went the other box, turning flip-flaps in the soft moonlight, as though it had been ejected from the premises by an experienced baggage-smasher.[8]

Up to this point the highway robbery had followed archetypal lines – with one notable exception: It was being committed within two miles of the Los Angeles County Courthouse, the last place anyone would be looking for bandits. Major Truman, "thinking that no further outrage would be committed at so unreasonable an hour and at such a place,"[9] was resuming his seat when ordered by the leader of the banditti to get down from the box and proceed to the rear of the stage, which, to use his own words, he did "with considerable grace." The robbers apparently felt that this man seated beside the driver must be riding shotgun and therefore had to be disarmed before matters could safely proceed. The Major actually had only a small pistol, of which he was promptly relieved, along with his money bag containing $180.

The robbers, four in number, now proceeded with the fun of "going through them," and in the process made a first class liar out of Editor Johnson of the Santa Barbara *Press,* who would later remark that no one in these parts had any money. From eight passengers the follow-

---

8 Los Angeles *Star,* Oct. 23, 1869.   9 *Ibid.*

ing loot was confiscated: One gold watch, a beautiful crystal oval, some fine gold specimens, one derringer pistol, one fine revolver, one Spencer rifle, and $1371 in cash. The express loss was set at $1000. By various subterfuges the passengers had managed to hide no less than $855. The total loss was computed at $2500.

Major Truman, as Special Agent for the Post Office Department, returned to Los Angeles to report the robbery and start pursuit of the highwaymen. The Major must have laid the story before his listeners in wild-eyed fashion to cause his friend Hamilton of the *Star* to report: "While we regret to be called upon to chronicle such an event, serious at all times, in all communities, we could not check a smile as we listened to the adventure as described by the pocket-depleted but not heart-broken Major." [10]

Hamilton should have lived to read what Truman wrote about that affair some twenty-nine years later in a story for the *Overland Monthly*. In the original account Truman said he had returned to town on the down stage; in the *Overland Monthly* story the Major claimed that he had continued on for five miles with the robbed passengers and then walked back to Los Angeles on the "lower road," which ran out Sixth Street.

Twenty-nine years after the holdup, Truman wrote that when he returned the robbers were engaged in gambling at the Bella Union Hotel, but he could not identify them. The Major failed to explain this paradoxical statement. At the time, almost a month passed before any further word appeared on the highwaymen – when

---

[10] *Ibid.* It is clear from the tenor of this lengthy account that Hamilton was getting a fiendish "kick" out of Truman's plight. The next issue of the *Star* carried a flattering account of Los Angeles signed B.C.T., which Truman had been preparing for Hamilton during his Los Angeles visit.

they tried unsuccessfully to rob a stagecoach between San Diego and Yuma and were captured as a result.

In 1869, the total loss in the robbery was given as $2500. By 1898, when Truman wrote his story for the *Overland Monthly,* it had increased to "nearly eight thousand dollars."[11] Perhaps the Major was computing and compounding the interest on $2500 for the twenty-nine years.

What is of more historical interest in this most fascinating piece of "highwaymanship" was the fast action taken by the courts to convict the robbers after their capture. To be very blunt about the thing, it was a simple matter of sheer expediency. Either the courts acted and acted fast or else:

VIGILANCE – During the week the atmosphere of our locality was thick with rumors of vigilance committee – that a body was organized, which would take in hand the cases of many gentry hanging around town without any visible means of support, and who would make very short work of all such, saving the county much expense, and effectually preventing any further attempts at highway robbery. Such reports prevailed for some days; and it was rumored that investigation would be made of the allegation that certain parties in town had conspired against the peace and welfare of the citizens and in favor of the highway robbers, by subscribing money, and making up a purse to defend and save the stage robbers from the legal effects of their villainous conduct. Such were the rumors about town, and many considered that prompt and summary punishment should be visited on those who living among us, were ready to take sides with the highwaymen against the honest citizen, the banded ruffian against the peaceful and confiding traveler. Fortunately, the breeze of temporary excitement passed over, without producing any breach of the peace. An honest jury did their duty, and the majesty of the law was vindicated in the punishment of the principals, though their aiders

---

[11] Ben C. Truman, "The Knights of the Lash," *Overland Monthly* (Apr. 1898), p. 312.

and abettors escaped unwhipped of justice. It is better so. We do not like vigilance committees. The exhibition of a row of dead bodies hanging in front of the jail, was a ghastly – a horrid sight. We would dread its repetition. But if men are found who will protect robbers and murderers, as against the interest of the citizens, and the law be found powerless to interpose in defense of society and to punish the aggressors, then, in that case, the people will, must protect themselves.[12]

What Henry Hamilton was saying was: "I believe in law and order, *but* ——." At the time of the robbery Hamilton had offered a very sound piece of advice to travelers: If you travel by stagecoach, leave your gold watches, double eagles, diamonds, etc. at home. On the other hand keep your powder dry:

Let our citizens, then, who travel by stage coaches upon long and unfrequented highways, be always prepared to meet these fellows of the road and give up nothing. Should an opportunity offer of getting a drop on any of these gangs, we advise a hearty scattering of cold lead. Should any of the desperadoes be captured, hemp is cheap. *Sabe?* [13]

Well, as Hamilton said, "We do not like Vigilance Committees." Obviously, Henry preferred the informal type of "non-committee" action!

The great Los Angeles stagecoach robbery had a final bit of humor. As one of the highwaymen, Charles G. Ames, was being led away from sentencing (fifteen years in San Quentin) he requested the officer in charge to go back and challenge the Judge to a game of old sledge, the stakes to be thirty years or nothing.

Henry Hamilton of the Los Angeles *Star* had reminded his readers that hemp was cheap, the inference being it represented an excellent remedial measure

---

[12] Los Angeles *Star,* Dec. 4, 1869. It is unclear in respect to which of numerous lynchings Hamilton was referring.   [13] *Ibid.,* Oct. 23, 1869.

where highwaymen were concerned. H. G. McLean of the Ventura *Free Press* was a staunch advocate of extra-legal corrective procedures, particularly in the case of horse thieves. McLean had the dubious distinction of being the only newspaper editor on record to deplore that a stagecoach was *not* "held up." The story is of special interest in view of a crime previously committed and the legends associated with it.

In the summer of 1878, a thief had disappeared with a fine piece of horse flesh owned by William O'Hara of Santa Paula. A few weeks later Hugh O'Hara and Charles Tompkins traced the villain to San Francis-quito Canyon, captured him with the stolen property, and returned him in irons to Santa Paula. Here a stop was made for breakfast before continuing on to the county seat at San Buenaventura. The thief was taken upstairs in the hotel and the shackles removed so that he might wash before eating. The prisoner was left alone and promptly climbed through an open window onto the low roof over the porch, dropped to the ground and disappeared. The Ventura *Signal* reported that he was last seen in the willows east of town.[14] No further mention of the incident was ever made in either Ventura newspaper, a most singular fact considering the circumstances of the case.

The old-timers of the town, however, were quite fond of telling the rest of the story – of how the prisoner had been left alone intentionally and allowed to escape. They admitted the part of the story respecting his last being seen in the willows east of town was correct, but those who saw him swore he was suspended from a cottonwood tree with a rope around his neck. Those old-

14 Ventura *Signal*, Aug. 10, 1878.

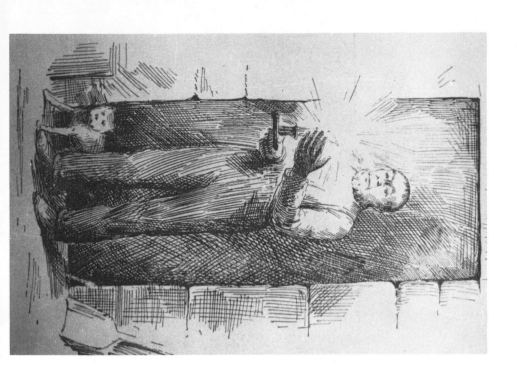

$1,000 REWARD!

THE UNDERSIGNED will pay the sum of TWO HUNDRED AND FIFTY DOLLARS each, for the arrest and conviction of the robbers who stopped the Overland Stage, on the night of August 10th, about fifty miles North of Los Angeles, and took therefrom the Company's Express box.

WELLS, FARGO & CO.,

Per Wm. PRIDHAM, Agent.

aug11w1.

WELLS FARGO REWARD ADVERTISEMENT
Wells Fargo offers $1,000 reward for the capture of the banditti who robbed the Coast Line Stage on the Los Posas Rancho in August 1870.

LAWRENCE HOWARD
The host at Larry's Station in the Simi Valley at the foot of Santa Susana Pass was a familiar figure to stagers on the Coast Line. From a drawing in *Overland Monthly*, Jan. 1890.

timers could never present proof of the tale, and it was usually passed off as highly exaggerated. Thanks to H. G. McLean and his *Free Press,* however, a different interpretation is possible.

Some sixteen months after the above episode occurred, a Ventura County deputy-sheriff was returning a horse thief from Los Angeles via train to Newhall and stagecoach to San Buenaventura. Here is McLean's classic "giveaway" respecting what had happened in the Santa Paula Hotel incident of 1878:

> As there was no possible doubt as to this fellow's guilt [the one the deputy was returning in 1879] we would have been delighted to chronicle the fact that fifty ranchers stopped the stage, taken the prisoner and allowed him to "escape." Horse thieving must stop.[15]

Sabe?

The success, albeit temporary, of the Los Angeles holdup within two miles of the County Courthouse apparently stimulated some of the knights of the road to serious thoughts concerning these easy pickings. If four highwaymen could get away with $2500 only a mile from the city limits of Los Angeles, the job should be easy out in the sparsely settled countryside.

Early on the morning of August 11, 1870, as the Coast Line stage was coming down through the Las Posas Rancho some twenty miles south of San Buenaventura and fifty miles north of Los Angeles, four men held up the driver with the usual demand for the Wells Fargo treasure box. There were no passengers aboard, and the driver was at a distinct disadvantage. The robbers were presumed to have been the same four men who had been hanging around Larry's Station on the west side of the

---

[15] Ventura *Free Press,* Dec. 13, 1879.

Santa Susana Pass. The superintendent of the line, Andy Horn, happened to be at the Las Posas Rancho at the time and started an immediate pursuit.

William Pridham, Wells Fargo agent in Los Angeles, expressed the opinion that there was very little money in the box, but nevertheless promptly posted a one thousand dollar reward for the arrest and conviction of the villains. Wells Fargo was always reticent to announce their loss in any specific robbery, and the amount of the reward offered in this case would not necessarily indicate a substantial sum of loot had been taken. It would also seem to suggest that something in addition to an empty box was involved. The Santa Barbara *Press* agreed with Wells Fargo – probably in an attempt to discourage similar future incidents in the county – noting in its issue of August 13, 1870:

> On Thursday evening last the stage bound for Los Angeles was stopped about twenty miles below San Buenaventura by the self-appointed road agents, and a call made for the treasure box. It would seem that these robbers have acquired such a habit of overhauling stages that they pounce upon one without any regard as to the probabilities that it may contain money; otherwise we cannot account for the fact that they would molest a down stage. Of course they only got the box and a few letters. . .

Precisely why a down bound stage would have less money aboard than one bound for the north is somewhat vague. At this point Johnson of the *Press* appeared to be indulging in a bit of promotionalism: People leaving southern California went with their britches full of money; those coming down were poverty stricken.

The four men presumed to have committed the crime were captured in Santa Barbara shortly afterwards; but the driver being unable to identify them positively, they were turned loose. It was thought they were ex-soldiers still unsettled from those trying days of the Civil War. The point is worth noting, as many holdups and robberies being committed as late as the early seventies could be traced to those men, both Union and Confederate, who found normal life impossible after the strain of battle.

There was nothing unique about the four suspects having been seen hanging around Larry's Station. Those boulders of the Santa Susanas were as attractive to murderers, bandits, renegades, and other anti-social personalities as the rocks north of Soledad Canyon and east of the Agua Dulce were to Señor Vasquez. On one occasion a German disappeared – permanently – after leaving Larry's in company with two known banditti. On another occasion the genial "Host" of Mountain Station, Lawrence "Larry" Howard, was the victim of a burglary, the Los Angeles *Star* of December 19, 1871, reporting the station had lost a horse, saddle, bridle, and two "six-shooters." The Ventura *Signal* of December 16, also reported the robbery, and noted that "three gentlemen of leisure" who strongly resembled the suspects were prowling around San Buenaventura. Nothing further came of the matter.

Many decades later those same crags and boulders would be used by Hollywood to protect the villains in black hats from the bullets of the sharpshooting posses in white. Those occasions must have felt like "Old Home Week" to the Santa Susanas.

The real action by "those tall, slim boot pads," however, was taking place farther north, where the aristocrats of the highwaymen had always held forth. There were three prime areas of danger on the Coast Line

Stage Route: from the north side of the Santa Ynez range of mountains in Santa Barbara County to the Santa Maria River; from the point where the route diverged from the upper Salinas Valley at the Nacimiento River to Soledad; and from Natividad to San Juan. Probably ninety percent of the successful robberies occurred in one of these three regions. As late as the early 1880s, the description by J. Ross Browne of the Nacimiento, Pleito, Jolon section of the route as they existed in 1849, would still have been valid.

During the summer of 1870, a gang composed of four or five road agents made life thoroughly miserable for whips, passengers, and Wells, Fargo & Company on a hundred-mile section of the Coast Line south of San Juan. The known members were Benjamin Claughton, who appears to have been the leader; Thomas E. Selby; James L. Burns; and a man with the surname of Barry, who would later turn state's evidence to convict the other three.

Their first robbery was committed eight miles north of the stage station of Pleito on the fourth of June. Two men stopped the northbound coach, demanded the Wells Fargo box, and then permitted the driver to continue. The highwaymen carried their loot a short distance up a creek, smashed it open and confiscated the letters and one hundred dollars in cash. Five passengers, all unarmed, were not molested.

On July 1, the banditti struck again, this time within a mile and one-half of the site of the previous robbery. Again two men on horseback halted the stage and captured the treasure box, although no report was ever made respecting the contents.

By this time Wells Fargo had become concerned

enough to send down Detective Noyes, who immediately offered a $500 reward for the arrest and conviction of the robbers. Noyes trailed the gang south through San Luis Obispo County and over to Cambria, where he found the citizens up in arms over an organized gang of hoodlums who had been running off stock and committing "other atrocities." The Cambrians had organized a strong vigilante group which gave every indication of possessing a keener interest in capturing the renegades than in convictions and/or rewards.

The gang in the meantime had displayed a bit of discretion and doubled back to the north before robbing another stagecoach, this time forty miles nearer to San Juan. The driver of the Los Angeles bound coach, a man by the name of Tilford, secured a relief driver and pursued the robbers into Natividad and obtained their capture.

The contemporary description of the region in question indicated beyond any doubt that little social progress had been made since the days of J. Ross Browne's "A Dangerous Journey":

> The detectives state that the country where the robberies occurred, is infested by gangs of desperate men, who invade farms and carry off cattle, and commit all kinds of atrocities, making the organization of a Vigilance Committee necessary, for the protection of life and property.[16]

Ever since the early days of Tiburcio Vasquez, the area had been a source of annoyance to stagers. The following might well have been one of Tiburcio's escapades since no solution to the crime ever appeared:

> San Jose, July 7, 1864. The Los Angeles stage from here yesterday morning was stopped by robbers between San Juan and

---

[16] Los Angeles *Star,* Aug. 6, 1870. Reprinted from the *Alta.*

Natividad, last night. Passengers cleaned out and express box taken. It did not contain much treasure.

Reed, Ag. W. F. & Co.

Thus read the telegram to Los Angeles. The *Star* concluded: "The stage thus cleaned out will arrive, in due course today, if not detained by the operations." [17]

Not content with robbing the down stage, the same highwaymen repeated the performance a few days later on the up stage within one hundred yards of where the first outrage had been committed. This second holdup appears to have been a somewhat good-natured and sociable affair if one is to believe the lengthy description given of it in the Los Angeles *Star*. After looting the passengers of all they had, about $65, and obtaining the express box, the bandits got into a conversation with the roadmaster for the stage line, who was riding the box with the whip:

> The stage agent told the robber that he would be obliged to him if he would give up the letters in the express, when the robber politely replied, "Certainly, we will accomodate you at once." The robber went off about fifty yards and broke the box open with a hatchet, and on his return he presented the box to the driver, who asked the robber if he got any money out of the express, and he said, "Not a d—d cent!" The driver then asked if they got as much money this time as they did when they robbed the passengers on Wednesday night, and the robber replied that they did not; did not get much either time; damn poor crowd both times. After this the agent invited the robbers to take a drink out of his flask, which they did, and then said, while pointing their guns towards the stage, "Boys, you can go ahead now; we will not trouble you any more; it don't pay us to come here – you carry too poor a crowd. [18]

The highwaymen apparently meant what they said.

[17] *Ibid.,* July 9, 1864.   [18] *Ibid.,* July 23, 1864.

The next robbery three weeks later was on the Visalia to Gilroy line, the results – unrecorded.

There are times when fate works in strange ways. If the threatened vigilante action had superceded the law at the time of the Los Angeles stage robbers' convictions in 1869, California history would probably have been deprived of one of its more colorful outlaws; and Chief of Detectives James Hume of Wells, Fargo & Company might have had a few extra years added to his life. Among the ne'er-do-wells with no visible means of support was a young man of some twenty-five summers who had spent the previous three or four years in the San Buenaventura area. His name was George Bret Lytle, alias Richard Perkins, alias Dick Fellows.

According to the Ventura *Free Press* of a much later date (February 11, 1882) Fellows, when he did anything at all, was engaged in farming. The young man decided (and quite correctly, too) that there must be easier ways to earn a living than tilling the soil. Unfortunately, Fellows picked the wrong occupation, highway robbery, and the most inauspicious time imaginable to inaugurate his new career. It was a trait, or the luck of the man if you will, that would mark his outlaw fortunes. When Wells Fargo shipped a reputed $100,000 by stage from Caliente to Los Angeles, Fellows picked the wrong stagecoach to rob; when hiding from the law in a haystack, Fellows burrowed into the one spot that the owner would stick his pitchfork; and when stealing horses for robberies or escapes, Fellows invariably chose the most cantankerous broncos available – to heave him in the dust for easy capture or a broken leg. It was only natural, therefore, that the outlaw chose a time to hold

up a man on the Cahuenga Pass road when the Los
Angeles vigilantes were threatening to stretch the necks
of every renegade for miles around.

This crime has often been referred to as a stagecoach holdup, probably because one of the two charges
brought against Fellows was highway robbery. Another
version has Fellows holding up his first stage on the
outskirts of Santa Barbara *after* successfully waylaying
the victim in Cahuenga Pass.[19] There is no record of
such a robbery nor did the author cite any source for the
statement. The point is of more than passing importance
because of subsequent events. The contemporary newspaper version appears to be correct and is more or less
corroborated by the record at the time of Fellows'
sentencing.

> Dick Fellows was examined before Justice Grey, and held on
> two charges – one, highway robbery, in stopping a man near
> Cahuenga and robbing him of his pistol and money; and the
> other, an assault with intent to kill. His bail was placed at $2000,
> and, in default, he was remanded to jail to await the action of the
> Grand Jury.[20]

The dates in this case are important. It will be noted
that Fellows failed to post bond, as reported in the *Star*
of December 11, 1869. The Los Angeles Grand Jury
returned a true bill against him soon after the first of
the year; and the *Star* concluded the case on January
22, 1870, by noting that he had been sentenced to eight
years in the State penitentiary. The logical conclusion
must be that Dick Fellows could not possibly have rob-

[19] Eugene Block, *Great Stagecoach Robberies of the West* (New York,
1962), p. 129. Joseph Henry Jackson in *Tintypes in Gold* (New York, 1939),
p. 125, stated: "So far no one has discovered what was behind the charge of
robbery with assault to murder for which Dick was sent to San Quentin
Prison on the 31st of January 1870." Jackson's overall account of Fellows appears more reliable than that of Block.

[20] Los Angeles *Star*, Dec. 11, 1869.

bed a stagecoach outside of Santa Barbara, or anywhere else, *after* the assault and highway robbery in Cahuenga Pass.

In San Quentin, Fellows became a paragon of virtue and clean living, an advocate of honesty and integrity, and was reported to have organized a Bible class. If it was legal, moral, ethical, and non-fattening, that was where Dick Fellows stood – foursquare. And it worked! Governor Booth pardoned the highwayman on April 4, 1874, after he had served but half of his eight-year sentence.

Fellows' activities for the following twenty months are not a matter of record. He next entered the stage-coach drama in the town of Caliente, railhead for the Southern Pacific Railroad building south over the Tehachapi Mountains. It is at this point that the question of whether or not Fellows had robbed a stagecoach in late 1869 (or any other prior time) assumes importance. The usual stories are that Chief of Detectives Hume of Wells Fargo had heard of Fellows' presence in Caliente, and "having a keen eye fixed for discharged stage robbers" [21] was somewhat uneasy, the cause of the uneasiness being that Hume was expecting a large gold shipment which was to be transferred from train to stagecoach at Caliente and for which Hume and two other men were to ride shotgun protection into Los Angeles.

After the affair was over, the contemporary newspapers said the sum involved was $100,000. The previously cited source claimed it was $240,000. The exact

21 Block, *op. cit.,* p. 130. There were two holdups on the Coast Line of Stages in which Fellows *might* have participated after his release but prior to the Caliente episode. One occurred about ten miles north of San Miguel on July 15, 1875. The other was in San Luis Obispo County and reported in the Ventura *Signal* of June 5, 1875.

amount is unimportant. If Fellows had *not* been involved in any prior stagecoach robberies, as the record would seem to indicate, his presence in Caliente at the time of the gold shipment was purely fortuitous; and his shrewdness in observing the transfer of the three heavy chests from train to stage was the true beginning of his career as a stagecoach robber.

Hume himself would have had no reason for undue uneasiness over the presence of a man who had been convicted of a stupid assault and two-bit robbery of a lone victim in Cahuenga Pass six years previous to the events in question. The fact that Hume had not become associated with Wells Fargo until March 1872, should be cause in itself for skepticism concerning stories of this nature. There were undoubtedly far more dangerous characters hanging around the booming railhead of Caliente than Dick Fellows. The record in this case is far from clear, but there must be a strong suspicion that many "pot-boiling" stagecoach authors were influenced by the much later throw-down-the-box antics of Fellows when they wrote of the famous events at Caliente.

There are several versions of what happened after Fellows decided to turn stage robber in the Tehachapi Mountains. The only person who was ever in a position to know the truth was Dick Fellows himself, and it is quite possible the variations in the yarn stem from the highwayman's own variable accounts. Before the comedy was over, he had been thrown from two horses – one rented, the other stolen – missed a chance at the big loot and robbed the up stage instead, getting somewhere between $1300 and $2000; ended up with a broken leg, recapture, escape from the Bakersfield jail, again recapture and finally back to San Quentin.

If ever there was a time in the life of Dick Fellows when it could truthfully be said that he was lucky, it was when he missed the "opportunity" of holding up that stagecoach carrying those three chests of treasure. With enough gold ballast aboard to stretch the strongest thorough brace out of shape, Detective Hume and his companions were as trigger happy as a neophyte Los Angeles hunter in a face to face encounter with a bull moose.

Back at San Quentin, Fellows again became the paragon of virtue – the model prisoner and Bible teacher. He even wrote to Hume that he had reformed and would never, never bother a stagecoach again. By May 1881, he was once more a free man. By July 1881, the Coast Line of Stages was having trouble with a "tall, slim boot pad."

As in the Caliente case, the problem for the historical writer interested in accuracy reverts back to 1870, when Fellows was first sentenced for the 1869 Cahuenga Pass assault and holdup. Did he somehow manage to get to Santa Barbara and commit highway robbery upon a stagecoach before his arrest, or was the Los Angeles incident the only highway robbery involved? The reason for the question is that later writers invariably ascribe the new Coast Line stage holdups to Fellows from the beginning because of the *modus operandi* and the fact that he was at large again. However, it should be plain that one stagecoach robbery, the Caliente affair, could not possibly have established a *modus operandi* for Fellows which Chief of Detectives Hume could recognize.

A close examination of the newspaper accounts of all the robberies from July 1881, until Fellows was recaptured, indicates that the perpetrator of the crimes was a complete mystery to everyone involved. Hume may have suspected Fellows, but only because of his recent release from prison.

The newspaper reports of one robbery shred the oft-repeated legend that Fellows always operated alone. On January 3, 1882, the Santa Barbara *Press* reported the successful escape of the stagecoach driven by George Richmond from unknown banditti two miles north of Los Alamos. On January 9, the *Press* reported the aftermath of the incident:

> Three robbers stopped the stage last night near the unoccupied adobe house a couple of miles above Los Alamos. Twice last week ineffectual attempts were made near this same place to stop the stage, but both were thwarted by the driver's presence of mind in driving away from the robbers. This time they made a sure thing, one being on horseback, and *the other two* planting themselves squarely in front of the stage. After calling for the Wells Fargo & Co.'s box, which was promptly handed over, one of the highwaymen demanded the driver's watch. George Richmond, the driver, had been presented with a very fine gold watch by the stage company, and with this fact the robbers seemed familiar. As the driver delivered up the watch, the man who did the talking informed him that it would pay him for running away from *them*, and that *they* would keep it to remember him by. A lady passenger who was in the stage, was not molested. She reports that *three men on horseback* passed the stage about two miles beyond the place where the robbery was committed. It is supposed these were the robbers, and that having passed the stage and observed that it was not protected by a guard, they made a detour and reached the place of robbery in time to prepare for its arrival.[22]

When Fellows was captured some three weeks later, he had in his possession Richmond's watch, rather sound proof that on at least two occasions he had worked with confederates.

---

[22] Santa Barbara *Press,* Jan. 9, 1882. The italics are added.

The Santa Barbara *Press* on January 30, 1882, printed a recapitulation of Fellow's robberies, or those attributed to him, after his release from San Quentin in May 1881:

July 29, 1881: San Luis Obispo stage robbed.

December 12, 1881: Stage robbed near Soledad.

December 29, 1881: Stage robbed five miles north of Arroyo Grande by one man.

January 2, 1882: Unsuccessful attempt to rob the stage north of Los Alamos.

January 8, 1882: Stage robbed north of Los Alamos; Richmond's watch stolen.[23]

January 14, 1882: Down stage robbed near Pleito Station by one man.

On the night that driver Richmond lost his watch, a bay mare, saddle, and bridle were also stolen. When the January 14, robbery was committed, the highwayman told the driver that the stolen horse would be found hitched down below San Luis Obispo – the old bay mare "was no account or he would have kept her."

The Santa Barbara *Press* could never quite get over the fact that so little money was being lost in these continuing escapades. After the capture of Fellows, the *Press* stated in its recapitulation of January 30, that "the aggregate losses of the company [Wells Fargo] amounted to no considerable sum." During the height of the holdups the *Press* in an editorial demanded that Wells Fargo "do something" about the robberies even though little financial damage was occurring. It was the position of the *Press* that only the presence of the express box was responsible for the outrages, and therefore it was up to Wells Fargo to catch the villains.

---

[23] This account is at wide variance with the contemporary report in the same newspaper at the time of the holdup. The latter specifically involved three robbers; the recapitulation has only a single bandit. The Jan. 9, 1882, version appears the more accurate.

The average value of Wells, Fargo & Co.'s box between here and San Luis does not exceed ten dollars per trip. Any moderately expert thief could make more money stealing chickens than he could stopping these stages, but now that the highwaymen have taken to firing guns at the driver and endangering the lives of passengers, it is about time to check their career. It is not probable that any very shrewd or noted characters would be engaged in the petty business of stopping stages in this part of the country.   .   .[24]

If the above quotation proved nothing else, it should establish that less than a month prior to the capture of the robber, no one in Santa Barbara County had the remotest conception that Dick Fellows was involved; or if they did, they were unwilling to concede the point.

It would be too much to expect that H. G. McLean of the Ventura *Free Press* could remain silent while his Santa Barbara contemporaries growled about inconsiderate road agents. "Mac" came up with a superlative suggestion on how to stop the stage holdups: Take all the money out of the box and insert original poetry in its place. If the robbers read it, they would be bored to death and nevermore annoy Wells Fargo.

McLean's idea was no more asinine than the real life farce that followed. From the time the holdups had started in July 1881, Wells Fargo had assigned Detective Aull to the case. Aull had formerly occupied a position in San Quentin which brought him into constant contact with the prisoners; and it was Aull, not Hume, who first began to suspect that Fellows might be their man.

The detective had been close on the trail of Fellows and was in Santa Barbara when the robbery took place near Pleito Station on January 14, 1882. Aull took the

---

[24] Santa Barbara *Press,* Jan. 3, 1882.

next boat to San Francisco and from there went to San Jose, where he learned that Fellows was in Santa Cruz. The highwayman in the meantime had left Santa Cruz and "hitch-hiked" a ride on a wagon with two men. The latter recognized the fugitive, overpowered him, and turned him over to the authorities, with Fellows ending up in the custody of Constable Burke of Santa Clara.

Burke entrained for San Jose with his captive in handcuffs. Upon arrival, Fellows suggested that before going to jail it would be nice to have one final drink in the saloon under the Arguello House, as it would be a long time before he would have another chance. Outrageous though it may seem, Burke agreed. Fellows ordered a large horn of brandy and gulped it down, unimpeded by the awkward handcuffs.

After finishing their drinks, the men left the saloon, when much to Burke's dismay Fellows suddenly bolted on the dead run down St. John Street. The constable pulled his gun and fired, but the bullet missed the high-flying Fellows.

> The bar-keeper had heard the noise, and at once came out and gave pursuit, bareheaded. He instinctively pulled his revolver as he ran, but not knowing who the prisoner was, he did not fire. When running by the Minnesota House, Fellows stumbled and fell, but he immediately sprang up, leaving his hat and shawl behind him. The bar-keeper placed the hat on his own head [!] and followed, pursuing the fugitive down San Augustin street. . . Had he known the prisoner was a stage robber he would have stopped him with a bullet, being at one time almost within reach of him. . .[25]

After the most ridiculous pre-Laurel and Hardy era comedy imaginable, Fellows was on the loose again, but not for long. If the irrepressible highwayman had

[25] *Ibid.,* Jan. 30, 1882. Reprinted from the San Jose *Mercury.*

picked a nice patch of clover in which to sleep instead of Dr. Gunckel's haystack, he might have eluded the law for an indefinite period. The doctor, upon feeding his horse in the morning, rammed the pitchfork squarely into Fellows. Thinking his uninvited guest to be but a hatless tramp, although skeptical of his hidden hands, the doctor and a neighbor sent him on his way after graciously securing him another hat. It was several hours later that the doctor suddenly realized his error and notified the authorities.

Fellows had fled in the direction of Los Gatos, where pursuing officers captured him while eating breakfast in a farm house.[26]

It was decided that the now legendary highwayman should stand trial in Santa Barbara County, where so many of his holdups had been committed. The proceedings were held late in March with the verdict of guilty a foregone conclusion. On April 1, 1882, the Ventura *Signal* informed its readers that Dick Fellows had been sentenced to life imprisonment. Every Jehu from Soledad to Los Angeles breathed a premature sigh of relief.

> In Santa Barbara, on Sunday morning, Dick Fellows, the noted stage robber, knocked down Deputy Sheriff George Sherman, took his pistol and left. On the street he mounted a horse which bucked him off [!] and he was recaptured. He did not shoot nor attempt to. Had the horse not thrown him, he would probably have reached the brush and escaped.[27]

[26] The news accounts of Fellows' final capture are so varied it would be impossible to be positive of the precise sequence of events. There are several versions of how he removed his handcuffs. A San Jose dispatch dated February 4, stated he was eating supper, not breakfast, when captured. The newsmen could not even agree upon the spelling of the pitchfork-wielding doctor's name. The only unanimity appears to have been that Fellows was "the boss stagecoach robber" on the coast. Detective Hume agreed.

[27] Ventura *Free Press,* Apr. 5, 1882.

Dick Fellows had been born fifty years too soon; the Keystone Cops could have used that man.

In Folsom Prison, Fellows again started the righteous act by announcing he was preparing a lecture to be given to the public. That scheme had worked for the last time, however. It would be many years before he again saw the outside of a prison – a strange world where Pullman cars and automobiles had preempted the old Coast Line of Stages. The stagecoach was an antique and but a memory by the time Fellows breathed the fresh air of freedom again.

Of course Fellows was but one of many who would attempt to gain an illegal dollar by highway robbery. There were the two road agents who robbed the stage near Lyon's Station in June 1876, and then brazenly rode into Santa Paula for a Sunday dinner. Dr. Guiberson, the Ventura *Free Press* correspondent for the valley, wrote that "they partook of the sumptuous fare at Snuffins Hotel. They remained sometime in town." [28] In an era when every man went armed, there was probably enough "artillery" in the little wild west town to start a third battle of Bull Run; but no one took the trouble to molest the robbers or notify the sheriff in Ventura.

Again on January 20, 1877, the stage was robbed near Newhall, the road agents getting away with about $300 in loot, including the $150 gold watch of the driver, Dave Green. One robber was caught in a few days near Elizabeth Lake, and the other was captured later in the year. As in the previous case, however, the Santa Clara Valley citizens appear to have expressed little concern for the crime. The correspondent for the Sespe wrote: "The stage robbers receive little attention here, I sup-

---

[28] *Ibid.,* June 17, 1876.

pose not having stolen enough to establish their reputation as first class thieves." [29]

This news item is possibly deceptive. The bulk of the dispatch had been concerned with a meeting of the Sespe Grange, a close perusal of which leaves little doubt that a far more sinister crime than stagecoach robbery was discussed that night, one which would rock California and become a *cause celebre* across the nation – the murder of T. Wallace More. By comparison, a $300 stagecoach robbery was as nothing.

It was not until after the railroad had been completed to Santa Barbara that anyone surpassed the audaciousness of Dick Fellows. The scene was on the San Marcos Pass Toll Road, and the highwayman was a character possessed of enough pure "gall" to hold up a grain wagon and two stagecoaches at the same time. Fellows in his palmiest days would never have attempted such a feat.

The first indication of trouble was when the Santa Barbara bound stage from Los Olivos, W. J. Wheelis, driver, reached a sharp turn in the road three miles beyond Home Station. A few yards ahead was a grain wagon with a man and a boy seated on top and both wearing white masks over their faces. The horses had been unhitched and tied to a tree. As the stage pulled up a third masked man stepped from behind a tree and pointing a revolver at the driver ordered the stage to stop. The usual demand for the box was complied with, but at this juncture the *modus operandi* of the highwayman took a unique twist. Masks of the same type that were blinding the man and boy on the grain wagon were produced and the stagecoach passengers and driver

[29] *Ibid.,* Jan. 27, 1877.

forced to put them on. The whip was allowed to remain on the box holding his six-in-hand under control, but the passengers were ordered to be seated beside the road. With his victims completely blinded by the masks and helpless, the road agent proceeded to loot purses, baggage, and express boxes at leisure. It must be remembered that during this process the man and boy on the grain wagon, as well as the driver and passengers of the stage, were unable to see anything that was occurring because of the masks that fell below their shoulders.

After completing his task, the robber inquired of the driver what time the north bound stage would arrive, and was told in about an hour. The group must have been dumbfounded to hear the highwayman reply, "We'll wait."

One of the women passengers, unable to remain silent any longer, asked the robber how he was going to vote in the Presidential election. The man replied politely that he intended to vote for Cleveland. The lady snorted and said she knew it; no Republican would stoop to robbing stages!

When the Los Olivos bound coach arrived, George Heller on the box, the robber repeated the same process as outlined for the first stage holdup, after which he departed in haste leaving about a dozen substantial Santa Barbara County citizens seated by the road and on the stagecoaches and grain wagon, blinded with masks that fell to their shoulders. A more ludicrous scene would be hard to imagine.[30]

If Black Bart or Dick Fellows ever read the account of that 1888 San Marcos Pass robbery, their reaction must have been: "Now why didn't I think of that!"

---

[30] *Ibid.*, Nov. 9, 1888. Reprinted from the Santa Barbara *Press News* [?] Nov. 4.

It would be interesting to know the total losses sustained from stagecoach holdups on the Coast Line during its existence. Wells Fargo was always reluctant to give out figures for specific robberies; but at the time of the 1893 World's Columbian Exposition in Chicago, the company listed a total of their losses from all types of robberies between 1870 and 1884 – $927,726.55. So far as the losses from the 313 stagecoach holdups were concerned, the vast majority would have been in the mining areas of the West. In 1893, Wells Fargo appeared to take a certain sentimental pride in the attention it had been given by the Western road agents, probably because of the promptness with which it could boast that all losses were settled by the company.

> No general report on the subject has since been made [since 1884] which has not been due to a dearth of material. *The years subsequent to 1884 have been as rich in similar events as those proceeding;* and the history of them would be quite as startling and impressive.[31]

Even "the great express wigwam" looked upon highway robbery of its box as "impressive" and rich in historical significance.

---

31 Wells Fargo *Catalogue,* p. 32. Italics added.

8

Wild, Woolly, and Wet

On and after November 23rd, coaches of the Coast Line Stage Co. will leave Los Angeles daily at 6 p.m. via San Buenaventura, Santa Barbara, San Luis Obispo and Paso Robles Hot Springs, connecting at Salinas, with the cars of the Southern Pacific Railroad for San Francisco.[1]

Thus read the "death warrant" of one of the greatest stagers of all time, although no one could foresee the tragedy of the following night. November 24, 1872, was moonless, starless, and dark as the inside pocket of a black suit, when the Coast Line stage pulled away from the Bella Union Hotel. Only the candle lanterns on the sides of the coach gave off a faint flicker of light with all the lustre of a cigarette in a fog bank. Seated on the box with the ribbons was Jared B. Crandall, co-founder with Warren Hall, James Birch, and Frank Stevens of the famed California Stage Company of an earlier day.

A good case could be made for the firm of Hall & Crandall having started the Coast Line of Stages, if one wants to consider the word "stagecoach" in its real sense. True, a John Whistman had inaugurated a "transportation service" of sorts between San Francisco and San Jose in the autumn of 1849, with a French omnibus and long-eared Missouri motive power of very ancient vintage. It is also true that a firm calling itself Ackley & Maurison started a competing line the following spring, "furnished with the best stages and horses the country

---

[1] Los Angeles *Star*, Nov. 21, 1872.

can produce,"[2] which was not saying too much, but enough to force Whistman to sell out to the experienced stagers Warren Hall and Jared B. Crandall. It was Hall & Crandall who made the thing go, extended the line to Monterey, and secured the all-important mail contract on October 16, 1851, to insure financial success.

Some seven years later it was Jared Crandall who staked out and pioneered that legendary road from Placerville through Strawberry Flat and over the Sierra summit and along the shores of Lake Bigler to Genoa on the Nevada side. Crandall had taken the Pioneer Line, which formerly ran only to Placerville, and proved the feasibility of the "Central Route" over the Sierra, only to become discouraged and sell out to Louis McLane on the eve of the big strike on the Comstock.

It was this same Jared "Bob" Crandall (at one time a wealthy man but forced through business reverses back to the whip end of the staging game) that drove off into the darkness and headed for Cahuenga Pass on the second night of the Coast Line's new evening departure schedule. It was Crandall's first trip over the road at night. At his side sat another veteran stager whom the newspapers called Mr. Legget, or Leggitt (William Liggett?). Before taking this Los Angeles run for Flint, Bixby & Company, Crandall had driven relief from Ballard to Foxen's Station in Santa Barbara County.

As the coach rolled through the darkness and neared the Seven-Mile House on the plains below Cahuenga Pass,

the leaders stepped off the road down a small embankment, and as Crandall endeavored to pull them, they jerked him completely

---

[2] Oscar Osburn Winther, *Via Western Express & Stagecoach* (Stanford, 1947), p. 5.

out of his seat, throwing him head foremost between the wheel horses. In his fall he is supposed to have struck his forehead against the pole, or else to have been kicked by one of the horses. . .[3]

Crandall's companion on the box jumped to the ground, grabbed the lines, and managed to halt the horses, but not before they had dragged Crandall some distance and overturned the coach. The old stager did not appear to be badly hurt; and after helping to unhitch the horses, he walked to the Seven-Mile House. Here, while cleaning and dressing his wounds, he fainted. A courier was immediately dispatched to Los Angeles for medical help; but Jared Crandall, "the prince of drivers," died within three hours.

> Mr. Crandall was one of the most careful drivers on the road between here and San Francisco. He was also one of the most genial and pleasant drivers to ride with employed in the service of the company. Those that have ridden with him will remember the animated manner in which he recounted his early experience, which was always full of thrilling adventure. His whip also attracted attention of all passengers that rode his coach, the handle being ornamented from butt to tip with gold and silver rings. This whip was a record of the number of years he had been in the State, each ring representing a year. It now bears upon it twenty-three of these rings, such being the number of years that have come and gone since his arrival. . .[4]

The Los Angeles *Star* of November 26, 1872, re-

---

[3] Ventura *Signal,* Nov. 30, 1872, reprinted from the Los Angeles *News.* The account of the accident in the Los Angeles *Star* stated that Crandall had been pitched off when the stage hit a rut caused by recent rains. The Santa Barbara *Press'* version reported Crandall became lost in the darkness and drove into a corral near the road and tipped over in a gully. All agreed on the approximate location as being near the Seven-Mile House on the plains below Cahuenga Pass. The real puzzle is how an authority of the caliber of Professor Winther could have placed this accident eight miles south of San Francisco on the peninsula at a time when the Southern Pacific railhead-stage line connection was far to the south at Salinas. Winther, *op. cit.,* p. 25.

[4] Ventura *Signal,* Nov. 30, 1872.

ported: "The funeral was quite large and respectable, and two stagecoaches draped in mourning, were in the procession."

Thus passed from the scene the third member of the original group that founded the California Stage Company who had met death through violence. The famed James Birch had been lost at sea with the sinking of the side-wheeler *Central America* four hundred miles south of Cape Hatteras in 1857. Birch did not live to see his thirtieth birthday. Warren Hall, Crandall's partner for so many years, had met violent death in 1862 in one of the most bizarre and weird homicides in California history.

After the formation of the California Stage Company, Hall and Crandall became somewhat difficult for the researcher to follow. Early in 1855, Warren Hall had arrived in Los Angeles with a large band of horses, which the editor of the *Star* interpreted as meaning that the California Stage Company was preparing an overland route to the States, either by way of El Paso or Salt Lake City. Nothing further ever appeared in the newspaper on the subject; Hall and the horses simply vanished so far as the *Star* was concerned.

Hall next came into prominence with the laying out of routes and stations for the Overland Mail Company in 1858. His was the torrid responsibility of finding a line with water from Fort Yuma to San Bernardino (later changed to Los Angeles) across the forbidding Colorado Desert. After bringing in the first Overland Mail coach over his division and winning the plaudits of correspondent Ormsby, Warren Hall again faded from clear view. His name did not appear again in the *Star* until April 19, 1862, when the paper reported his return from a hunting expedition in which two grizzlies were killed. "One of the bears was an old stager weighing about 400 pounds; another was a cub."

Banning and Banning [5] refer to Hall as being responsible for keeping one end of the Central Overland Mail tied together in 1863; but if this was correct, the Los Angeles *Star* and the Los Angeles Semi-Weekly *Southern News* were guilty of the most grievous *faux pas* in journalistic history when they reported the wrong man killed in late October 1862. Because of Hall's prominent position in Western staging, the entire article as it originally appeared in the *Star* is given here:

> On Saturday last the citizens of Los Angeles were astounded by the report that on the previous evening, Mr. Warren F. Hall and Henry Wilkinson, of the California Stage Line, had been murdered by a man named Gordon, near Smith's rancho, about ninety miles east of this, on the Colorado road, and that the murderer had escaped. Much excitement, of course, prevailed upon receipt of such news, and of the bloody death of two persons so well known to the public. Subsequent arrivals from the scene of the tragic occurrence, confirmed the report of the killing, with the particulars substantially as follows:
>
> In coming in on the trip proceeding the last, about ten or twelve hundred dollars had been stolen from the stage, and Gordon had been suspected of the crime, was arrested and confined at Smith's rancho for about ten days, till the return of the stage from the next trip. Then, with the intention of extorting a confession of the robbery and a discovery of the money, Messrs. Hall and Wilkinson threatened Gordon with death, taking him at eight o'clock in the evening of Friday, into a canyon a short distance from the house, forcing him to carry a pick and shovel for the purpose of digging his grave. Arriving at the spot selected for his burial, Wilkinson directed him to dig his grave (so Gordon reports) when Gordon asked Wilkinson if he really meant to kill him – his reply was that he should. Mr. Hall had not yet come up, when Gordon drew a knife that he had concealed, and stabbed

[5] Captain William Banning and George Hugh Banning, *Six Horses* (New York, 1930), p. 291.

Wilkinson, killing him almost instantly. Hall ran up and caught Gordon, who immediately stabbed him with fatal effect. Gordon then fled, and on the following day came into San Bernardino and surrendered himself to the authorities. He declared his innocence of the robbery, and justified the killing on the plea of self defense, and that he would do so again if he were placed in the same situation. There is no doubt that Messrs. Hall and Wilkinson really believed that Gordon took the money, and their threats were only to frighten him into a confession, and produce the money. In any event, it was a mistaken policy, and the result most unfortunate.

It is sad to contemplate that thus should terminate the career of a man with the energy, enterprise and public spirit of Warren Hall, or so promising a young man as Mr. Wilkinson. Mr. Hall was well known throughout the State as a prominent and pioneer stage man. He, with Crandall, established the first line of stages from San Francisco to San Jose, and afterwards the then most extensive line in the State, from Sacramento to Shasta, which they run [sic] with extraordinary speed and style, until the formation of the California Stage Company, of which Warren Hall was one of the chief men.

The bodies of the unfortunate victims were brought to this city and interred on Monday, followed to the grave by a large concourse of citizens.

Since writing the above, we learn that Gordon was examined at San Bernardino, before Justice Clark, and after hearing the testimony of three witnesses the prisoner was discharged.[6]

Thus those two great pioneer stagers, Jared Crandall and Warren Hall, each in his own way and each in the best and worst traditions of a West that was wild in every sense of the word, came to the end of the run – the last station – where only the setting sun marked the road into the unknown.

---

[6] Los Angeles *Star,* Nov. 1, 1862. The Los Angeles *Semi-Weekly News* of Oct. 29, 1862, reported the murder but did not give any of the details that appeared in the *Star.* The *News* reported that Hall and Wilkinson were "of the Colorado Stage & Express Company," *not* the California Stage Company. The *News* of Oct. 31, gave a short notice of the acquittal of Gordon, but still did not reveal any details.

Stagecoaching accidents were, of course, of no great rarity. The Ventura *Free Press* of July 8, 1876, felt obligated to call the attention of Flint, Bixby & Company to the fact that accidents were altogether too frequent on the Coast Line:

> On Monday, about two miles west of town, the coach went over the grade and rolled over, injuring two or more of the passengers severely. The next day, just above Santa Barbara, a collision with a rock threw the driver off, whereupon a passenger named Charles Sutton, seated on the roof, undertook to jump off, but fell between the wheels, one of which crushed his head so that he died. We hear that the first accident was caused by the dangerous condition of the road. Whose fault is that?

This was probably intended as a back-handed slap at the Ventura County Board of Supervisors. Hardly a year passed in which mention was not made in some of the newspapers of the sums expended by the stage companies to repair the various counties' roads. William Buckley claimed in 1872 that Flint, Bixby & Company had spent over two thousand dollars repairing the roads in Santa Barbara County alone.[7] Frequently the stage companies would submit a claim for county road repair work; sometimes their requests were honored, but more frequently the county bureaucrats could find excuses for rejecting these legitimate claims.

If road conditions became too dangerous, the newspaper editors would sound alarms until some official action was taken; but it required a "rip-snortin" Jehu riding herd on the Ventura County Board of Supervisors to show how these matters should be handled:

> Our friend Cheney, who swings the buckskin and jerks the ribbons between this place and Santa Barbara, has been after our Supervisors to fix up the beach road, a much traveled one, and

---

[7] Santa Barbara *Press*, Mar. 30, 1872. This figure would not include any portion of the San Marcos Pass Toll Road.

last week Supervisor Brown took a trip over it to give it his personal attention. Men are now at work on it, and a new bridge will be put in and the road straightened where the barranca is crossed at Los Pitos, and other improvements will be added. Our Supervisors mean business and so does Cheney, and it won't be long before the road will be a credit to us.   . .[8]

It is not hard to visualize Supervisor Brown's personal attention trip if J. C. Cheney acted as driver and guide. By the time the effervescent whip returned Brown to San Buenaventura, the latter would have been in a frame of mind to give the stage company the Rincon, its road, and throw in the Pacific Ocean with the bargain. This was not the first time that Cheney had wrestled results from the politicians where dangerous road conditions were concerned. A month or so prior to the Ventura County action, Cheney had reminded the Santa Barbara County Board of Supervisors of an antiquated bridge some six miles south of town, adding that it was cheaper to build a new bridge than it was to pay damages for broken passengers if the stagecoach fell through into the barranca.

Oddly enough, the one permanently treacherous portion of the San Buenaventura to Santa Barbara road, the quarter-mile section south of Rincon Point, does not appear to have been the scene of a serious stagecoach wreck. It was here that the currents washed away the sands, leaving the rocks and boulders exposed much of the year. At low tide the stages could thread their way through, but at high tide all danger was covered with water. Frequently two and three-hour delays occurred waiting for the ebb tide.

---

[8] Ventura *Signal,* May 7, 1881. J. C. Cheney had long been associated with the Telegraph Stage Line, at one time being General Agent of the Newhall to San Buenaventura run when the Lyon's Station Route was inaugurated.

On one or two occasions serious efforts were made to overcome the problem by cutting a road into the bank. The editor of the Santa Barbara *Press* noted in his issue of November 12, 1870, after returning from a trip to Los Angeles, that the beach road could now be avoided for part of the way "by means of a dug road which cuts into the face of the bank just above high water mark." From the description given, it was made clear that this "dug road" was only used when the surf was heavy and the tide was high. It should also be clear that any road would have to be built much higher than "just above high water mark" to have successfully avoided rapid erosion by the sea.

On less frequent occasions the problem of the tide prevailed at Punta Gorda and Sea Cliff. No solution to the dilemma was ever found during staging days, and it was not until the fall of 1912 that the completion of the causeways insured that any type of vehicle could pass through in safety regardless of the tide.

There was a stagecoach station at Rincon Point for changes of horses, and meals for the passengers. It was just beyond Rincon Station that one of the more serious accidents of the Flint, Bixby & Company era occurred. Early United States Geological Survey maps show the stage road running north did not turn up the canyon and swing around the mountain in the manner of the first paved road of World War I vintage. Rather, the route more nearly paralleled the present freeway alignment. From the station it descended slightly for about two hundred yards and then commenced a very steep pull. Usually six horses were used from Rincon Point to Santa Barbara, but on the occasion in question only four had been attached. At the foot of the steep climb the horses balked, and the passengers got out and walked. Halfway up the hill, the horses appearing to have settled down, the driver stopped and the passengers again boarded the coach. At this time the leaders on the swing pole suddenly swerved around, cramping the wheels and overturning the stage. One passenger was injured to the extent of a jaw broken in two places, three teeth missing, one broken rib, and "three more other bruises upon his person," [9] location unspecified.

The stage company claimed that "the stage was well appointed, the horses gentle [!] and well driven and that the accident arose from circumstances which no human foresight could have averted." [10] The jury disagreed by exactly $5000, a significant sum in 1877.

While Punta Gorda and Sea Cliff were not the constant hazards that Rincon Point represented, there were more accidents, probably because the drivers were not so cautious as at the Point.

> The down stage from Santa Barbara upset at Punta Gorda last night, throwing passengers, baggage, mail, etc., into the surf. Everything was thoroughly drenched, and the waybill lost and one man was thrown clear over the driver's head into the breakers, but luckily no one was injured. [11]

Next to fording flooding streams and high tides, roads were probably the greatest hazard faced by the various companies that operated over the Coast Line, particularly at night. An unseen chuckhole, or a wash that was not there on the last trip, could easily overturn the stage or, as in the case of Jared Crandall, throw the driver from the box with a consequent runaway.

[9] Ventura *Free Press,* Mar. 10, 1877. This information was taken from the testimony of the suit for damages trial. The wreck does not appear to have been reported in either Ventura paper at the time of its occurrence.

[10] *Ibid.*   [11] *Ibid.,* Aug. 6, 1886.

Not infrequently land owners adjacent to or through which previously declared public roads ran would barricade or place obstacles in the road to impede or stop traffic. Usually such action was taken in lieu of nonpayment for land acquired for road purposes. Such a situation arose in Carpinteria soon after the Overland Mail Company inaugurated coastal staging in 1861. The Santa Barbara County Board of Supervisors was forced to order obstacles removed from the public road and appoint appraisers to fix land damages.[12]

The Ventura Supervisors were forced to take similar action against G. B. Taylor west of San Buenaventura in 1876. The road through the ranch was a headache at best to stagers and teamsters without the addition of any artificial barriers constructed by the owner. The natural source of still more natural Jehu verbiage was a huge three-quarters of a mile long sand dune that neither Taylor, the Supervisors, nor nature was inclined to remove. The *Free Press* failed to define the nature of the obstruction put up by Taylor, but it was obviously intended as a deterrent to the Coast Line stages, as the company had filed the complaint with the Supervisors.

Even smooth and unobstructed roads constituted a hazard in the sense that the driver could be lulled into letting his horses go all out for a time with the consequent danger of the top-heavy coach capsizing on a curve. Once the whip was unseated, the horses were free to drag an overturned coach with the passengers trapped inside. Two such incidents north of San Luis Obispo are worthy of note:

It was during July 1871, when the southbound, or "down" stage, met with a serious accident near Pleito

---

12 Santa Barbara County Board Of Supervisors, Minutes, Book A, p. 302.

Station. The details of what caused the mishap were not reported, partly because they could not have been known under the circumstances, but mostly because the heroism of an eighteen-year-old girl overshadowed other considerations.

It would appear that the driver had been thrown from the box and run over – unnoticed by the lone passenger, the girl. The uncontrolled team continued on for another two miles, at which point the stagecoach struck a stump and capsized. The horses still continued on, dragging the overturned coach at a greatly reduced speed, while the girl inside broke out the glass windows with her bare hands and managed to crawl out, shredding her dress and body in the process.[13]

Once free of the capsized coach, the girl ran her fastest, caught up with the leaders and brought them to a halt. She then unhitched the horses and tied them to the wheels of the stage.

The next problem was to find the driver, the girl not knowing whether he was under the wreck or miles back on the road. Ascertaining that he was not under the wreckage, she started backtracking in the darkness expecting to find his body at any moment. After walking for three miles, the girl came upon the unconscious driver, his leg broken and obviously suffering from severe internal injuries after being run over by the wheels of the coach.

The girl straightened and bound the broken leg with pieces of her own clothing and then, seeing a light in the

---

[13] For a detailed description of glass windows in stagecoaches see *Wagons, Mules And Men*, by Nick Eggenhofer (New York, 1961), p. 168. This superlative book is unsurpassed for details of this nature. It is highly recommended reading for all academic interpreters of Western history who know not the difference between a whiffletree and a flowering peach, or who think the hounds are something one follows on a fox hunt.

distance, walked another two miles for help. Securing a jug of water, she returned to the injured man and remained at his side for the rest of the night and part of the next day until help arrived.

> Miss Plunkett is from Oakland, and was on her way to take charge of the public school at San Miguel. . . She is about eighteen years old, handsome, smart, and able, has a good disposition and deserves the commendations and kindly assistance of the people wherever she may go. We are in favor of such young ladies always to be in charge of our public schools.[14]

The idea of the *Standard* was excellent, but the Santa Barbara *Press* had a finer one. It felt that the girl was entitled to a handsomer reward than teaching in the San Miguel country school.

Ten years later the San Luis Obispo *Tribune* was called upon to report "one of the most frightful accidents" ever to occur on the Coast Line. The scene was on the north side and near the foot of the Cuesta Grade. As in the earlier wreck, it was dark; but this time five passengers rode the coach – four inside and one on the box with the driver, Dave Green.

Green, whose wife was a daughter of the prominent San Buenaventuran, A. G. Escandon, had long been a popular whip for the Coast Line under Flint, Bixby & Company. After the Telegraph Stage Line took over the lower portion of the route in July 1878, Green continued to drive on this section until April of the following year, when he went to San Luis Obispo and drove north for the successors of his old employers. It was, therefore, an able and experienced driver that drove the stage at a rapid rate on the down grade of the Cuesta's north slope.

---

[14] Los Angeles *Star,* July 9, 1871, reprinted from the San Luis Obispo *Standard.*

There was a sharp curve and a short bridge near the foot of the grade; and the driver, although having his team well in hand, was allowing them to set a brisk pace. The momentum was too great for the top-heavy coach, which upset just after crossing the bridge. Green and his passenger on the box were catapulted head first into the brush, while the horses continued on with the unfortunate passengers still inside the capsized coach. With a free rein now, the animals broke into a run and gathered speed on the downhill pull.

> Three or four hundred yards down the road the wagon struck against two large hitching posts set in the ground in front of Borondo's house. This checked the horses long enough to allow the passengers to get out, which they had no sooner done than away went the frightened animals again, dragging out the posts and stringing the running gear of the coach in all directions.   .[15]

None of the passengers was seriously injured, but Green was still unconscious and obviously critically hurt. The occupants of a nearby farmhouse were aroused, a fire built, coffee made, and a conveyance sent for to transport the unfortunate driver back to San Luis Obispo. It was felt that he could not survive due to the serious nature of his head injuries, but five weeks later Green was back in San Buenaventura and looking well. However, there was never any further reference in either Ventura paper to his driving stagecoaches again.

During the staging era along the coast there had been little serious competition between the mail contractor of the moment and opposition lines. At the time of contract bidding, however, spirited rivalry could be expected and a possible change of contractors or ownership

---

[15] Ventura *Signal,* Sept. 10, 1881, reprinted from the San Luis Obispo *Tribune.*

occur. There were, however, numerous individuals who ran short haul express and passenger services along the same routes as the prime stage line; and occasionally a first-class stagecoach race would result. One such rivalry existed between Nephi Jones, a regular whip on the Telegraph Stage Line's run between Newhall and San Buenaventura, and A. M. Tanner, owner of Tanner's Express in Santa Paula.

Albert Miles Tanner had come to California with the Mormon Battalion at the time of the war with Mexico, and later opened the first hotel in Sacramento in partnership with Sam Brannan. At one time he was quite wealthy but lost most of his fortune in one of Sacramento's periodic floods. It is not known when he came to the Santa Paula area, but he had settled on a preemptive land claim east of that town by the early 1870s.[16]

Tanner's chief claim to fame after coming to Ventura County was his nickname, "Six-bits," acquired by reason of the fact he would haul passengers between San Buenaventura and Santa Paula for seventy-five cents. It was probably more than coincidental that Tanner would arrange his express schedule so he left either town ahead of the regular mail stage driven by Nephi Jones. Loafing along the road and conserving his horses, Tanner dawdled until the rapidly closing Telegraph stage was almost at hand; and then he would put the whip to his horses and the race was on.

To say that this type of racing on roads scarcely wide

---

[16] *Ibid.,* July 19, 1879. Tanner's obituary stated that he was a native of Bolton, Warren County, New York. It is interesting that no mention was made of the Mormon Battalion in the obituary. Rather it stated that Tanner came West with Kearny. The Mormon Battalion was nominally under Kearny's command, so the obituary could be construed as technically correct. The trial of John Doyle Lee concerning the Mountain Meadows Massacre was still too fresh in most minds to mention the word "Mormon" in Ventura County.

enough for passing was good clean fun, and safe, would
be a rank travesty of the truth. On one occasion in 1878,
the boys came tearing into town at night in a howling
Santa Ana windstorm (Camulos swells) with near disastrous results. Dr. Guiberson, the ever facetious reporter for the Ventura newspapers, described the action
as it developed on the town's principal thoroughfare,
Mupu Street:

> There will be a petition before Congress asking for an appro-
> priation to erect a lighthouse near Tanner's so that Capt. Nephi
> may be able to land at our wharf without first double-reefing his
> jib in crossing the Mupu reef. Owing to the heavy Camulos
> swells the other evening, the schooner "Six-bits" came very near
> colliding with the stern-wheeler "Manzanita Shark." Fortu-
> nately, however, Capt. A. M. heaved his vessel to, and the pro-
> peller taking a lack [?] on her rudder, landed safely at the dry
> docks with a fair cargo of asphaltum and gypsum from the Sespe.[17]

Guiberson might have curbed his inherent wit if he
could have foreseen the tragedy of the following summer. There is something of the mysterious about the
episode's background. On June 28, 1879, the Ventura
Signal inserted a one-sentence "warning": "A. M. Tanner says he will run the new stage line off or bust 'em."
Precisely what was meant by "the new stage line" is not
known. The Telegraph Stage Line had held the mail
contract from Newhall to San Luis Obispo since July 1,
of the previous year. No notice of any change ever appeared until John Allman swindled his way into the
picture in 1882. However, a compilation of all news
items concerning coastal staging indicates some change
of management, or policy, beginning about the middle
of April 1879. It is possible that this was the time
Taylor & Buckley entered the south coastal staging

17 *Ibid.,* Dec. 7, 1878.

scene, either as part owners or as representatives of the Telegraph Stage Line.

Regardless of the corporate intricacies involved, the Ventura *Signal's* news item of the following week told the tragic story in brief:

> A. M. Tanner, the Santa Paula express driver, had a severe accident happen to him while driving to Santa Paula Wednesday last. When about four miles from town he was overtaken by the regular stage, and a race ensued, when Tanner's wagon ran into a chuckhole, throwing him out and he received a bad fracture of his right leg.[18]

Dr. Bard was immediately called into the case and was forced to amputate the crushed limb. Two weeks later Albert Miles Tanner died of lockjaw.

The regular stage driver was not named in the news account. It is significant, perhaps, that less than a year later Nephi Jones accepted a position in Folsom Prison and no further reference to his driving stagecoaches ever appeared.

Regardless of causes, the overturning of stagecoaches was the most common type of accident; although contemporary writers and editors much preferred to use the synonym "capsized." When Albert Bierstadt, the famous painter of Rocky Mountain scenes, was en route to the Cerro Gordo mining district from Bakersfield, the coach he was riding "capsized" three times before reaching Havilah, which must be a record of some kind. The *Star* reported that Bierstadt was hobbling around on one leg, while a fellow passenger "got off with a representation of the map of Mexico on his frontispiece."[19]

The other common type of mishap – sinking, capsiz-

---

[18] *Ibid.*, July 5, 1879.   [19] Los Angeles *Star*, Apr. 15, 1873.

ing, torn to shreds, or just plain drowning while attempting to cross flooding California coastal streams – does not come under the category of "accidents" in this writer's book. This was plain damned stupidity, nothing more, nothing less. If there be those who would argue the point (usually on a sunny day during a dry year) let them go down to the banks of the Santa Clara, Sespe, Santa Ynez, Ventura, Santa Maria, or Salinas rivers when any of those streams are approaching flood stage, or even "half-flood" stage, and try to visualize crossing in a stagecoach with six scared mustangs straining on their doubletrees. To complete the picture, put eight or ten passengers aboard, plus trunks, valises, and mail pouches, then plunge into the muddy torrent. In midstream the horses start swimming, the coach floats up and swings around with the swift current; harness, coach, and horses become entangled; passengers panic as the coach capsizes; the mail bags are lost, horses drown, but luckily the passengers *usually* reach shore. That was the miracle.

It did not require so critical a situation as described to turn a commonplace river crossing into sudden disaster. The following account reprinted from the San Luis Obispo *Standard* could be used as a textbook example of the dangers of wet weather staging:

> On the night of December 28th, at about ten o'clock, when the coach of the Coast Line Stage Company coming from Santa Barbara to this place, reached the Corral de Piedra creek, five miles south of this town, the driver found the creek much swollen from the effect of the recent rains, but not so much so as to render the crossing dangerous. Unfortunately, however, in crossing, when the lead horses had reached the steep bank on this side of the creek, one of them slipped and fell, caused the coach to stop

in the bed of the stream. Mr. Andy Horne, the agent of the Stage Company, who was riding with the driver, immediately jumped down, and found the lead horses so entangled that it became necessary to unhook them, in order to extricate them.

He at once called to the driver, and passengers, of whom there were three in the coach, to come to his assistance. The driver and one of the passengers got down to assist him, leaving another passenger holding the reins. In the meantime the creek was rising very rapidly, and before the lead horses could be rehitched, the current swept the coach and wheel horses down the stream. At this time, Mr. T. H. Mitchell, one of the passengers, having been warned of the danger, had gotten out of the coach and was standing on the rear boot; before he could get off, was carried down with the coach. Every effort was made to save him, but without avail. . .

The next day his body was found, on a sand bar a mile and a half below the crossing, where he had been deposited by the flood. . .[20]

During periods of protracted rains and excessively high waters, staging came to a halt for weeks on end. The great floods of 1861-62 had so disrupted communications that the Postmaster General was forced to make arrangements for a tri-monthly steamer mail between San Francisco and the south coast towns. This agreement did not come about, however, until April 14, 1862, a salutary piece of practical wisdom on how bureaucracy could close the barn door after the horse had been stolen.[21]

Even so the steamers had carried the mails for a period of ninety days, giving some indication of the terrible destruction wrought upon the roads by the floods. Two years later the steamship company still had not been reimbursed by the government for this temporary service, the United States Auditor claiming that

[20] *Ibid.,* Jan. 10, 1872.
[21] *Report Of The Postmaster General, 1863* (Blair).

the Postmaster General had not acted legally in authorizing it.[22] It is little wonder that for years there would be almost constant friction between the coastal steamers and the Post Office Department over the carrying of mails during periods of winter floods.

Beginning in December 1866, and continuing through the next two and one-half winters, the rains and floods were of such an excessive nature that interruptions of stagecoach and mail services for a month or more at a time were not uncommon. In an effort to overcome the impossibility of stagecoaches crossing the Salinas and other raging streams, Superintendent William Buckley of the Coast Line of Stages conceived the idea of carrying the mails across in boats. The Los Angeles *News* of January 4, 1867, reported the construction of the boats and the fact that the mails were again arriving daily, adding: "The thoughtful industry of the Overland Stage Company in supplying our citizens with the mail under the disadvantages of unprecedented storms and wind and rain should entitle them to the prompt support of the business and traveling public."

Buckley's idea appears to have been operative for only a short time before real trouble developed. The *News* of March 12, 1867, reported no mail had arrived for two weeks. Three days later it stated:

A mail coach arrived here yesterday, from San Luis Obispo,

---

[22] *Report Of The Postmaster General, 1864* (Dennison). The postal records for mail contract No. 12,507 clearly indicate the friction between the California Steam Navigation Company and the Post Office Department. The entry dated "1861, Jan. 10" noted that the contractors had declined to execute the modified terms of the government and service was to be discontinued Apr. 1, 1861. However, the Auditor was authorized to pay the California Steam Navigation Company only to July 1, 1860. Subsequent carrying of the mails by boat appears to have been more a matter of service to California businesses and the people for public relations rather than from any monetary considerations.

bringing the mail of the 25th ult., which had been delayed at that point. No communication overland with San Francisco had been had later than the above date. We understand that one of the employees of the company was drowned in one of the streams this side of San Luis Obispo, by the capsizing of a boat.[23]

There is far too little information available on this interesting idea of the stageline using boats for expediting overland communications during flood periods. It is apparent, however, from an item in the Los Angeles *Star* on January 3, 1872, that five years later Buckley was still utilizing the system during extreme emergencies:

> Intercourse with San Francisco by mail has been interrupted since the 26th ultimo, occasioned by the high stage of water in the streams, and the impassable conditions of the roads. The mails and a large number of passengers including women and children, have been for several days water bound on the north side of the Nacimiento, near San Luis Obispo. Also passengers from the south are on this side of that stream waiting for the water to abate, and at present have to be fed from San Luis Obispo – provisions being brought to them in a skiff hauled from one side of the stream to the other by means of a rope; passengers, however, are unwilling to risk their lives in this frail and dangerous transportation craft. . .

In may have been that this Buckley brain storm of using boats was responsible for his own near loss of life in 1876. One of the newspapers of the State, identified only as the *Chronicle,* had reported the Coast Line's superintendent as drowned in the Salinas River. The Ventura *Free Press* made the correction on March 25, 1876, but again with an exasperating lack of details:

> The statement in the *Chronicle* that William Buckley, general superintendent of the Coast Line of Stages, had been drowned in the Salinas River, is incorrect. We are informed, however, that

---

23 Los Angeles *News,* Mar. 15, 1867.

he was only saved by a Spaniard lassoing him and drawing him ashore.

When one was in the middle of a raging torrent of California flood waters, it made little difference whether he was riding a stagecoach or a boat. He was a simpleton and a damned fool for not being somewhere else! No further reference was ever found by this writer to William Buckley using boats to expedite the United States Mails during high water.

The great floods of 1867-68, equaled in most instances and surpassed in others the better recorded and remembered winter of 1861-62. The Los Angeles *News* of January 14, 1868, reported no mail had been received for a month and that the agent for the stage company (Buckley) was sending out a "pony mail daily, and hopes are entertained that a connection may be made in a few days." However, it was not until February 21, that the newspaper reported the arrival of all back mails.

Some conception of what these tremendous storms did to the stage roads can be gained from a description of Cahuenga Pass in March 1868. The stage drivers reported the Pass was full of mud holes and ruts; and in one location, with the stagecoach hugging the canyon wall, there was exactly three inches clearance between the outside wheels and the precipice. One Jehu even went so far as to suggest it was dangerous![24]

The following year the Los Angeles *Star* reported that the Gaviota Pass road had been obliterated:

> The late rains have washed away the roadway in the Gaviota Pass, so that the mails have to be packed on men's shoulders to connect with the stages at each side. Mr. Ballard arrived here on

[24] *Ibid.,* Mar. 27, 1868.

Wednesday, having had to pack the mail on his back for five or six miles. . . It will be some time before the road is in passable order.[25]

Two other types of hazards during wet weather river crossings should be noted: quicksands, and boulders that had been rolled into the normal crossing zones by the flooding but were invisible after the muddy or murky water had receded to a safe level. The Santa Clara at what was known as "The Lime Kiln Crossing" (the present Highway 101 crossing at Montalvo) was notorious for its quicksands, and untold numbers of horses were trapped and lost at this point by stagecoaches and private rigs attempting to cross in high water. It became standard practice during winter months to move up river to what was called "The Middle Crossing," which was located a mile or two west of the present Saticoy Bridge, or to "The Upper Crossing" just to the west of Punta de la Loma at the Sanchez Rancho.

The Ventura River was a fine example of where danger could be anticipated from unseen boulders. Later, when the Coast Line of Stages moved to the Santa Clara Valley route, the Sespe, Santa Paula, and Piru creeks were equally as dangerous.

During the floods of 1884, the Spanish Stage had been held overnight on the west bank of the Ventura River because the water was too high to make the attempt at crossing. In the morning the river had receded to a level where Jose Lorenzana considered it safe to cross, and the horses plunged in.

The water bubbled into the bed of the vehicle, a covered wagon, but the driver kept on bravely. When near the centre of the stream, and in the most dangerous part, one of the hind

25 Los Angeles *Star*, Feb. 20, 1869.

wheels gave way, being literally smashed among the tumbling
boulders, and the water poured in, thoroughly drenching the
passengers. Mrs. Loveland climbed forward to the driver's seat,
which was somewhat elevated and of course dryer than the back
part of the wagon. The regular stage had driven in soon after the
first stage started, and was now close behind the broken-down
vehicle. A brawny Spaniard from the shore, seeing the danger the
party was in, waded in, and, taking Mrs. Loveland upon his
shoulders, started with her for the other stage, probably 20 yards
back. He would not have made the distance in safety had not a
horseman come to his aid, but, catching hold of the horse's tail the
strong current was successfully breasted and the lady placed in
the stage. Horsemen then made fast *riatas* to the tongue of the
broken stage and it was dragged to the bank, where a pole was
slipped under the hind axle and the stage came on into town.[26]

That was how it was done: poles replacing broken
wheels, *riatas* tied to the tongues for power, brave Californians carrying the girls on their shoulders in the
floodwaters, and horsemen placing a mustang's convenient tail where the swimmer could grab hold. The
story could be repeated and documented dozens of
times during the staging era, but that one short account
provides the typical example.

The natural question that arises in the modern
reader's mind is – why? Why were these stagers of a
long gone generation so willing to risk life and limb of
passengers, as well as their own, in such daredevil
antics? There were probably as many reasons or excuses
as there were incidents, but in the main the answers
usually added up to one word – mail. For every mention

---

[26] Ventura *Signal,* Mar. 15, 1884. The term "covered wagon" as used here
did not denote a "prairie schooner" or Conestoga wagon. The expression was
commonly used to describe a mud wagon, celerity wagon, or even a spring
wagon with a top and used as a stage. Properly used, the word "coach" meant
only the familiar Concord Coach, the finest made.

in the newspapers of a passenger's life in danger, a hundred can be found concerning the mails – its non-arrival, its arrival two weeks late, its arrival in a wet and soggy condition – the absence of the paper mail in particular receiving attention from the critical newspaper editors. In addition to some very sarcastic remarks from the fourth estate upon the delay of their precious exchanges, there was the further consideration from the stage line's viewpoint of financial penalties imposed for non-delivery of the mails as per contract.

The myopic reactions of some of the newspaper editors of the day are worthy of preservation. The San Luis Obispo *Pioneer* had been in business less than two weeks when it "lowered the boom" on the Coast Line, San Juan and Los Angeles Stage Company because no mail had arrived for over two weeks. This was in January 1868, at a time when the stage company might have navigated the Salinas River with a Coast Guard cutter, but certainly not in a stagecoach. The Los Angeles *News,* one of the few newspapers with a slight understanding of California rivers and floods, reminded the *Pioneer* that it had been the experience of every traveling editor since the beginning of time that San Luis Obispo County had contributed less to keeping the roads in passable condition than any other county on the Coast Route and, "We think the *Pioneer* a little fast in thus charging neglect and indifference upon a stage company that has put forward such exertions to deliver the mails on schedule time." [27]

The *News* could not resist reminding the San Luis Obispo newspaper of the occasion when the stagecoach

[27] Los Angeles *News,* Jan. 21, 1868.

from the south arrived in town two hours ahead of schedule and the postmaster had refused to get out of bed to receive the mail until the scheduled time of arrival.[28]

Henry Hamilton of the Los Angeles *Star* could probably castigate the Post Office Department and stage lines with more vitriolic verbal venom than any of his contemporaries. Appended are a few samples from Henry's pen:

[January 15, 1871:] The overland mail to San Francisco, and way offices, closes at 9 o'clock P.M. . . The mail for Northern Arizona is weekly, and closes every Friday morning at 7 o'clock. . . The mail for San Bernardino leaves daily, and closes at half past six A.M.

We would like to add a few lines complimentary to the great efficiency displayed by the postoffice officials of California, but after a lengthy acquaintance with the department, and diligent divings into its operations, we are reluctantly compelled to express the opinion that no such "efficiency" exists. . .

[March 7, 1871:] Yesterday we received from Messrs. Blake, Robbins & Co., San Francisco, two letters, postmarked February 8th and 15th respectively. We hope the Department will not be crippled in its resources by this ruinously prompt dispatch of business.

[December 23, 1871:] The mails have been delayed because the stages could not cross the flooded streams to the north; the express, for the same reason. The steamer has not arrived, for the Lord knows why! And the rotten wires of the telegraph line have no doubt snapped in a dozen places "north of Visalia" . . .

It is likely that some great event has transpired, which it is our

---

[28] The account of this incident appeared in the Los Angeles *News* of May 31, 1867, in a long article apparently written by the editor, who was a passenger on the stage and a witness to the humorous affair. It is of interest in that the Coast Line, San Juan & Los Angeles Stage Company was still being referred to as "The Overland Mail Company," which had not been involved in coastal staging since July 1861. Further, The Overland Mail Company no longer existed as a corporate entity, having been absorbed by Wells Fargo in November 1866.

luck to hear nothing about for a long time after its occurrence. Perhaps the whole world north of Visalia has sunk or burned up, or been drowned, or perhaps the great day of judgment has commenced up there, and it takes a longer time to sentence the wicked than was expected.

[January 8, 1872:] About ten tons of papers and letters [note that the papers still come first!] due in this city sometime between now and next spring, but which were started from San Francisco by the overland stage company some two weeks ago, have failed to arrive. . .

It may not have been Henry Hamilton who first used the old cliché about "The mails must go through," but the chances are excellent it was a newspaper editor who did. One wonders if possibly the United States Post Office Department did not subsidize Special Agent Ben Truman when he bought out Hamilton shortly after the fiery editor penned the above quotes.

All in all, however, it was a dangerous era in a dangerous country, where dangerous conditions were the norm. Crossing the Santa Clara River when, as one very scared Damned Yankee from Way Down East put it, it looked "like the rapids above Niagara Falls,"[29] was only in keeping with the spirit of the times.

[29] Ventura *Signal,* May 15, 1880.

(Bakersfield)

Gaviota Pass
Las Cruces
Los Olivos
Nojoqui
Baron (Gaviota)
Dos Pueblos
San Marcos Pass
Santa Barbara
Carpinteria
Rincon Pt.
Ventura
Ojai
Santa Paula
Saugus
Santa Clara River
Simi
Calabasas
San Fernando
San Susana Pass
(Newhall)
Soledad
Elizabeth Lake
Cahuenga Pass
Los Angeles
San Pedro
San Diego

San Francisco

Clark's Point

San Mateo

Redwood City

Mountain View

Santa Clara

San Jose

17 Mile House

Gilroy

Pacheco Pass

San Juan Bautista

Monterey

Salinas

Alizal or Gabilan

Natividad or Tynn's

Deep Wells (Gonzales)

Los Banos

San Joaquin River

0   10   20   30   40   50

Twentieth century cities are
included for reference and are
shown in circles.

Map based on C. Hart Merriam

Channel Islands

9

Never a Dull Moment

*It was the stage-driver's story, as he stood with his back to the
  wheelers,
Quietly flecking his whip and turning his quid of tobacco,
While on the dusty road, and blent with the rays of the moonlight,
We saw the lash of his whip and the juice of tobacco descending.*
                                                        Bret Harte

The modest hero of Bret Hart's "The Stage-Driver's
Story" would have fared well in the liars' contest at a
barbecue of any Westerners Corral. The hilarious description of that wild ride down the famous old Geiger
Grade, with the Pioneer stagecoach losing first one
wheel, then another, and still another, but remaining
upright because of "the fearful momentum" until it
"sank in a heap" at the next station, is probably un-
equaled in Western literature. Before composing that
twenty-four-karat gem of stagecoach lore, Bret Harte
had undoubtedly heard the tale in some variation from
a Jehu with an uncommonly keen ability for "drawing
the long bow." Mark Twain or J. Ross Browne may
have equaled or surpassed "The Stage-Driver's Story"
somewhere along their infinite trails of Western jot-
tings; if so, this writer has yet a treat in store.

However, it is to the devotees of the schools of
thought that "Truth Is Stranger Than Fiction" and
"History Is But A Lie Agreed Upon" that the contents
of this chapter are dedicated. All the tales and news
accounts were published in various magazines and California newspapers between 1851 and 1890 – the heyday
of Western staging. If their retelling here serves no

other purpose, it should illustrate the origins and reconstruction techniques of the likes of "The Stage-Driver's Story."

It would take little imagination, for example, to garnish the following news item from the Los Angeles *Star* of October 5, 1871, into a yarn worthy of Bret Harte, J. Ross Browne, or Mark Twain: "We understand that the gentleman whose rattlesnakes were decapitated at the stage office in this city recently has still on hand about twenty boxes of snakes."

Three days earlier the *Star* had reported: "The shipper of those snakes which arrived in this city via the overland stage, last week, and fell victim to the dislike of the passengers to travel in their company, reached town yesterday in search of his property."

The brief news accounts did not distinguish between the United States mails and Wells Fargo Express in respect to which had accepted the reptiles for shipment; but it is a sound assumption that postal regulations would have prohibited the putting of snakes, night crawlers, lizards, etc., into the mail pouches. It is also reasonable to assume that Flint, Bixby & Company, and/or any of their drivers, would have wanted no part of the responsibility for a couple of dozen crates of rattlesnakes. That leaves Wells Fargo in command.

The writer makes no pretense to being an authority on the rules and regulations governing Wells Fargo shipments, with the exception of those which were published in the Los Angeles *Star* on February 10, 1873:

> Among other things that Wells & Fargo's firm is not responsible for as carriers is couched in the following language in their regulations: "Not for any loss or damages by fire, the acts of God, or of Indians, or any other public enemies of the government."

"Any other public enemies of the government" undoubtedly referred to the Democrats, what with Ulysses S. Grant in the White House and the air still fouled with Civil War gunpowder. But rattlesnakes? No, there was nothing in the regulations forbidding the shipping of rattlesnakes by Wells Fargo. After all, had not the express company hauled a gross of nitroglycerine from the San Francisco docks to the corner of California and Montgomery streets in 1866? Of course, a goodly portion of the town had to be repaired after an employee tried to open the case with a hammer; but Wells Fargo would still ship anything.

In the spring of '71 :

> The express business being a little dull at present, the enterprising and well-known firm of Wells, Fargo & Co., "determined to keep up with the times" have commenced expressing vegetables East on their own account. Yesterday the first shipment was made, consisting of three baskets and two boxes of "garden sass," consigned to Henry Wells, the old head chief of the great express wigwam.[1]

Two months later the express company shipped to Los Angeles from San Francisco a consignment of cabbage, cauliflower, celery, and asparagus. For the one and only time during his editorship of the *Star,* Henry Hamilton did *not* have a good word for Wells Fargo; any damnfool knew that Los Angeles could raise the stuff better than San Francisco!

Yes, Wells Fargo would ship anything, sometimes to its own astonishment. In November 1870, the Los Angeles agent for the express company was dumbfounded to find listed on his waybill of incoming express an eight-year-old girl that had been shipped from Mokelumne Hill via Wells Fargo Express. The lass an-

[1] Los Angeles *Star,* Apr. 14, 1871.

swered only to the name of "Dear"; and to complicate matters further, the agent had never heard of the consignee. A frantic notice inserted in the *Star* located Dear's father, resulting in a happy reunion and one very relieved express agent.[2]

Is it any wonder that "the great express wigwam" would forever become synonymous with Western tradition and stagecoaching? You could not only trust the company with your money, you could ship the children by their messengers as well; and there was the further consideration that more than money for services rendered was involved. How could it be otherwise when George Pridham, Los Angeles agent for Wells Fargo, would take the trouble to insert a notice in the *Star* urging parents to leave the names of their children with the company so that no child would be overlooked at the Episcopal Church Christmas party.[3]

And when carpetbaggers were running rampant following the Civil War and most Northern "Public Be Damned" corporations were rubbing the South's nose in the mess, what was Wells Fargo up to out West? The great express wigwam was raising money and collecting food to send to the relief of defeated Americans who were on the brink of starvation.

The West began where a man's word was as good as his bond and any disparaging words about Wells Fargo had better be spoken with a smile, stranger.

Many newspapers in the east had not the remotest conception of where the West began and cared even less. (In Boston it was thought that a north-south line drawn through Worcester ought to be about right.) It *was* an excellent source of humor, however, what with

[2] *Ibid.*, Nov. 23 & 24, 1870.   [3] *Ibid.*, Dec. 15, 1874.

Mark Twain, Bret Harte, and J. Ross Browne roaming the land; so it was probably only natural that there would be those who would attempt to imitate the famed trio. Consider this effort by a member of the New York fourth estate:

> A San Francisco stage driver made his brags that he could drive over a hilly place of road just as well when drunk as when sober. The coach spilled over a precipice, and when the passengers crawled out from under the wreck, they begged to differ with him, with a piece of rope. The stage company buried him.[4]

The *Star* thought it was not very funny, possibly because there had been too much hemp stretching in Angeltown for far less offenses. It was a subject matter much too delicate for eastern newspapers to comprehend, and one with which the Western editor did not appreciate interference from his colleagues "back in the States." Furthermore, no California editor would have dared to hint that the famed Western Jehu even so much as sniffed a cork, let alone sampled the contents of the bottle. In the process of searching through forty years of newspaper files, this writer never found one instance wherein a stagecoach driver was accused of drinking; while such authorities as Professor Winther, H. H. Bancroft, and Ben Truman went out of their way to impress their readers with the sobriety, albeit eccentricities, of the Western whip. In fact, one becomes so suspicious of this preponderance of one-sided literary evidence on the subject of Jehu sobriety, that J. Ross Brown's observations are a welcome diversion:

> Everybody is aware that the climate of California is peculiarly dry, but it is not generally known that the effect of this exceeding drought is to evaporate all the juices out of the physical sys-

---

4 *Ibid.,* July 9, 1870.

tem. Hence it becomes necessary constantly to renew the supply, in order to keep from withering up. Water is not always to be had; and, consequently, many very temperate people are obliged to drink whiskey, of which there is never any scarcity. I am acquainted with several excellent stage-drivers on the Sacramento, Mud Springs, Hangtown, Murderer's Bar, Grizzly Flat, and Devil's Gulch routes, who, by reason of constantly riding in the sun, evaporate so rapidly that they are compelled to stop for a drink every half hour. During the intervals they become highly irritated lest any unforeseen circumstance should have occurred to cut off the supply at the next tavern, and begin to swear horribly in about ten minutes after the last drink, and keep on swearing at a frightful rate of progression till it becomes absolutely shocking to hear them. Stages filled with passengers are often turned over during these intervals of raging thirst, and legs and arms broken without regard to the owners. These drivers are very clever fellows in their way, but not proverbial for their civility, unless you furnish them with an extra treat, which immediately operates upon their organs of benevolence, and, in extreme cases, secures a top-seat, when they will be pleased to entertain you for many hours during the day with an elaborate account of each team, and of every driver, and every pretty girl, and every fight, and every frolic, that ever was seen or heard of on the route.[5]

One thing must be conceded: The psychoneurotic behavior patterns of the Western stage driver, as described by all contemporary observers, bore a striking resemblance to an exuberant Irishman who had overindulged in "a drap o' the crathur" on St. Patrick's Day. Horace Greeley may not have said or written anything disrespectful concerning Hank Monk's driving, but the famous editor must have thought some mighty powerful, unprintable thoughts. Strangely enough, the drawing entitled "California Stage-Driver" which accompanied the article of J. Ross Browne cited above, is

[5] J. Ross Browne, "The Coast Rangers," *Harper's New Monthly Magazine* (Feb. 1862), pp. 297-298.

often reprinted with the caption, "Hank Monk." Browne never mentioned Monk in the original story, and it requires some imagination to recognize the famous driver in the caricature.

While the newspapers may have been guilty of a lack of candor in respect to stage driver behavior, no such qualms ever manifested themselves where passengers were concerned, particularly if the inebriate or oddball happened to be a tergiservated female of the species.

In the days when William Buckley and "Shotgun" Taylor owned the Coast Line, an elderly lady alighted from the Santa Barbara stage in San Buenaventura in a somewhat "woozy" condition. The Ventura *Signal* reported her as "an unfortunate old woman" who was intoxicated, and added that she was placed upon the north bound stage to be returned to Santa Barbara. (Nothing was too good for San Buenaventurans to send to Santa Barbara in those days.) The Santa Barbara *Press* welcomed her back in the following style:

> It is with mingled feelings of pleasure and regret that we record the fact that the Italian Countess, Madam Bridget Meany, of whose doing the *Press* the other day made mention, has returned to her chateau in this lovely nook, and is determined to enjoy the climate – so superior to that of the scenes of her childhood – Nice and Mentone. The Countess started out the other morning on the stage for Ventura, armed with a bottle of *eau de vie* from a neighboring province. By the time she reached Carpinteria the bottle was gone, but the Countess was only then well prepared for another. With all the fervor of her Italian blood she bounced brother Anderson down there for some native grape, and Mr. Anderson, in a moment of weakness, looking down into her melting eyes, filled up her flagon. By the time the Countess reached Ventura she was very much in the condition of one of Father O'Keefe's owls, should the latter be immersed in boiling water. We grieve to relate that the Countess descended from the stage only with the assistance of several postillions.

Arrived in the provincial hamlet of Ventura, Madame took a ten minute's snooze and started out to see all the sights of the town. She ran into a gendarme almost before she had left her apartments. The gendarme, who saw that she was a lady of rank – he judged of this from a close observation of her respiration – called in the prefect of the town to know what should be done. It was finally resolved that a lady of such conspicuous position should be returned to her chateau at Mentone – that is to say Santa Barbara – in hope that our lovely Italian skies, and soft balmy air, might abate the excitement under which she was evidently laboring. They therefore placed the Countess on the return stage, and the lady arrived here this morning.[6]

On another occasion the northbound stagecoach came upon a most pathetic woman, or possibly a superb actress. She had started from San Buenaventura carrying a washtub filled with clothes. The woman would carry the tub a short distance and then go back and get the clothes. In this manner she had traveled possibly ten miles when overtaken by the stage. The driver stopped, picked up the hitch-hiking laundress, and brought her into Santa Barbara, where she identified herself as Lucrezia Borgia. The good citizens of the Channel City decided the woman must be crazy (a not too far-fetched conclusion) and took up a subscription to pay her fare to San Francisco, where she claimed she had a brother and son, presumably members of the Borgia family, also. The Santa Barbara *Post* observed that she was undoubtedly a fit patient for the Stockton Asylum. It probably never occurred to the *Barbarenos,* but it was also a fine method to secure free fare to San Francisco if one is flat broke.[7]

The feminine role in staging should not be left, even temporarily, in so morbid a condition. In 1881, San Buenaventura witnessed a scene that must have recalled

6 Ventura *Signal,* July 10, 1880. From the Santa Barbara *Press.*

7 Los Angeles *Star,* Aug. 1, 1868.

to the well-read citizens of the town the amazing saga of "One-Eyed" Charley Parkhurst, who, in her earlier years, had driven over portions of the Coast Line south of San Jose and would always be remembered as one of the truly great Western whips and the greatest of male impersonators.

The heroine of the 1881 episode was a wealthy lady vacationing in the Ojai, and one who had been well trained in the philosophy that while a horse or mule can be considered in a good many ways, the worst place to consider him is directly from behind. Unlike Charley Parkhurst, this high society matron had always been discreet enough to allow ample space between her face and the horses' hind feet and therefore still possessed *both* eyes. When the Ojai stage rumbled into town on February 7, 1881, it was she alone who adorned the box, handled the ribbons, and rolled the coach neatly up to Uncle Sam's post office. The Ventura *Signal* was unable to report whether the feminine whip had driven the stage on a dare or was merely trying to vary the general ennui of the Nordhoff Hotel life. Everyone agreed when departure time came, however, that she "mounted the box and went gaily out of town with a sharp crack of the whip" in regular Hank Monk style. "Staging is not pleasant, but we venture to say that very few travelers would have hesitated to take a trip in the Nordhoff stage last Monday. At least we would not." [8]

The droll antics on the stagecoach of an inebriated "Countess" from Santa Barbara was one thing, but a mean male drunk on board was simething else. In a period when every man from the itinerant preacher on down carried a hand gun, it took very little booze mixed with gunpowder to generate quite an explosive situa-

[8] Ventura *Signal*, Feb. 12, 1881.

tion. Many such incidents can be found in the newspapers of the times; the following is typical:

> Wednesday night a drunken fellow got aboard the Newhall stage at Santa Paula, after traveling a few miles toward Ventura, drew a revolver threatening to kill the passengers. There were five others in the coach, including a lady. The revolver was taken from him by a passenger, and he was with difficulty restrained during the remainder of the trip to this place. Why are such characters permitted to travel inside a coach? It seems to us that somebody is responsible for this and ought to be held to account.[9]

As a matter of fact, such characters were not always "permitted" to ride inside the coach, or outside either. One very "soused" passenger was put off the southbound stage at Carpinteria in 1883. Sobering up, the man became even more obnoxious and wrote a whining letter of complaint to the Ventura *Free Press,* knowing that the editor thereof had been engaged in an undeclared war with the stage line. However, Editor McLean disliked drunks even more than he disliked "Honest John" Allman and refused to print the letter, stating that the writer had only gotten his just deserts by being forcibly disembarked in Carpinteria.

A drunk with a gun holding five passengers in terror, a pseudo-Countess with an inclination to over imbibe on *eau de vie,* and "Lucrezia Borgia" with a washtub full of clothes – all were a part of the never monotonous life of stagecoaching; but imagine a crazy man on the coach roof holding a raised hatchet over the Jehu's head for mile after mile and yelling: "There they come! Drive for your life! If you let them overtake us I'll split your head open!" Well, as someone said, there was never a dull moment.

---

9 Ventura *Free Press,* Nov. 14, 1884.

The episode had its beginnings in front of the Ayers Hotel in San Buenaventura on the evening of June 15, 1880, as the east bound stage for Newhall prepared to depart. The veteran conductor, Charley Baker, was on the box and would drive through to the end of the run. Two passengers were booked for the trip: a traveling salesman from San Francisco named Lester, and an E. S. Mills, nephew of the prominent A. A. Low of California. Mr. Lester rode the box with Baker, while Mills had the coach to himself with only a near-full moon for company.

Baker and Mills had exchanged a few unfriendly words over the whereabouts of the latter's trunk while the coach was still in San Buenaventura. At Saticoy, Mills was still insisting that his trunk was not on board; so Charley Baker, to quiet him, uncovered the rear boot and displayed the trunk to its owner. This appeared to satisfy the man on the subject of the luggage, but now Mills wanted to ride on top with Baker and Lester. The driver refused with the excuse that there was no room, and the stage proceeded on its moonlight trip toward Newhall.

At this period the stage road up the Santa Clara Valley did not follow the present alignment of Highway 126 east of Camulos. Soon after passing the ranch house, the road continued on a straight line, crossed the river, rolled over a short stretch of the mesa on the southeast bank (still on a straight line) and then ran in the river bottom through Blue Cut and continued on. At varying points up to San Martine Canyon the road climbed the steep embankment on the north side of the river and continued eastward on approximately the same alignment as the present State Highway. The point at which the road climbed out of the river bottom depended upon the conditions in which the embankment had been left by the last flood.

The fireworks began just as Charley Baker's stagecoach pulled up the San Martine Grade. Without warning, Mills suddenly appeared on the top of the coach behind Baker and Lester and, of course, above them. The driver warned the man to get back, that there was danger of the stage turning over with so much weight forward. Instead of obeying, Mills broke out into song. Even Baker conceded that the "nut" could sing! After a few choruses of some long forgotten tune, Mills turned sullen and morose and then suddenly burst forth with his cry of "There they come! Drive for your life!", etc.

Looking around Baker saw the maniac sitting above him, brandishing a new hatchet in dangerous proximity to his (Baker's) head. Baker saw immediately how completely Mr. Lester and himself were in the power of the madman, and there was no other way but to humor him. Baker put the whip to the team, and they dashed on at a break-neck speed. The wild-man sat above them, and would allow no stoppage or swerving from the road. Those two men sat on the seat like sphinxes, knowing that a single movement would send the gleaming blade crashing through the skull of the driver. The maniac entirely ignored the passenger, Mr. Lester, and when, to find a way out of the difficulty, Mr. Lester proposed that Baker stop while he got some cigars out of his valise, the maniac yelled, "Don't stop or I'll kill you." There was nothing to do but drive for life. At times the man could hear the supposed pursuers on his track. And there, in the light of the fast sinking moon and the shadows of the over-hanging mountains sat those three men, the one with the deadly instrument raised over the head of the driver, and the devil in his gleaming eye, and the other two silent but cool and nervy. It was their coolness that carried them through; but Baker said it was a wild night ride, and one never to be forgotten. He has been shot at by Indians and lost his break [sic] on the steep mountain grades, but he said that during his life he has never had so wild a drive. Every device was tried to get out of the scrape, but the madman was determined that no stop should be made. Baker finally thought of a sandy piece of road where he could upset the coach without harm. He tried it on a full run, and suddenly threw his horses around, but the stage only spun around on the two wheels. The madman saw the trick immediately and threateningly raised his deadly hatchet. Baker swung into the road and drove for it. He thought he might stop at the Newhall's ranch house, ostensibly to change horses. The madman insisted that they should go through with the horses they had. Baker told him it would kill the horses, but he said no. Baker, however, drove up to the barn very suddenly and the man very quickly jumped down. Baker then went to the house for help, and when they returned the man had disappeared. The next day he walked into Newhall – a distance of six miles – where he was, with difficulty, secured. On his person was found the hatchet stuck down into his waist band. He is now in the hands of friends. He is a graduate of an eastern college and a man of much intelligence.[10]

Charley Baker and traveling salesman Lester were more of the opinion that Mills was operating a hair trigger mouth with a flintlock brain, but Mills was undoubtedly intelligent in an academic sort of a way. The affair could have been much worse. Imagine the same scene but with "Lucrezia Borgia" and "Countess Bridget Meany" aboard, plus two dozen crates of rattlesnakes in the rear boot.

It was not necessary, of course, that a hatchetman be on board in order to have a hair-raising ride via western express and stagecoach. All too frequently the horses themselves could think of good and sufficient reasons to take the bit in their teeth and go.

It will come as no surprise to old-timers with some experience in these matters that the horses (or mules, as the case might be) did not need a good and sufficient

---

10 Ventura *Signal*, June 19, 1880.

excuse, or even a reasonable facsimile thereof, to display their running capabilities. These critters are possessed of the courage to stand with perfect docility in close proximity to the most awesome sounds or fearful spectacles that the human mind can imagine and show no more reaction than a flip of the ears from aft to fore. But let a mere paper bag flutter across their path, a lone quail take flight fifty feet from the nigh leader, or an old hat blow off the noggin of the scarecrow in the adjoining field, and those ears will then go from fore to aft and lay flat, feet will start flying; and if one does not have a tight hold on the reins, there is nothing ahead but unadulterated trouble for so long as the team can run. A case reported in the Ventura *Signal* on July 8, 1876, is a perfect example:

> On Monday the down stage from Santa Barbara with four passengers upset in a grove near Escandon's place. The horses were scared by the falling dirt from above the grade and shied, taking the stage off the embankment. Mr. P. V. McCarty and wife, Frank White of Philadelphia, Mr. Dunn and two Chinamen were the passengers. Mr. McCarty was severely but not seriously injured. Mr. White received several painful bruises and cuts about the head and shoulders. Mr. W. is now in Ojai and doing as well as possible. Mrs. McCarthy was uninjured. Mr. McCarty informed us that the stage turned over three times. It is marvelous that more serious injuries were not inflicted.

It will be seen that just a bit of falling dirt was the cause of what could have been a fearful accident. It will also be noted that there is an apparent discrepancy in the *Signal's* arithmetic in respect to the number of passengers on board – those identified adding to six, not four, by the new as well as the old mathematics. It may come as a shock to some readers in this more tolerant age, but "Chinamen" simply were not counted in 1876.

So far as the editor of the *Signal* was concerned, the Orientals could have been killed and left for the condors and the details would be of no moment.

The contemporary descriptions of some of these early stagecoach runaways would put to shame the modern TV script writer's efforts. The following true story taken from the San Luis Obispo *Standard* and reprinted in the Los Angeles *Star* would fit nicely into a Laurel and Hardy comedy, but it would probably be hooted at in derision by the modern "Cut 'Em Off At the Pass" Western buff:

> Overland Stages – For the first time since we have been in San Luis Obispo, are we called upon to record an accident on this line. On last Sunday night the team hitched to the stage coach which had just arrived from below, started from the Postoffice at a fearful rate down Monterey street and on making the turn at the Mission building the stage tipped over. At this juncture the leaders became detached and went pell-mell towards the Overland stage stable. The wheelers followed with the two front wheels which had been uncoupled, and when passing Mr. Esquer's residence something turned them and they ran into his back yard, they ran around the yard several times, knocking out-houses, chicken coops, pigpens, etc., into pi; finally they made their exit, and brought up at the stable. No particular damage was done to the stage. The next morning Dick Bayer repaired the injuries in very short time.[11]

A similar incident but *sans* outhouses, pigpens, etc., occurred in Los Angeles at the post office:

> While Mr. W. D. Addington, driver of the overland stage, was unloading the mail at the Post Office, yesterday morning, the horses took fright and ran off down Spring street, colliding with and carrying away the sign of Stevens' livery stable, the porch and awning of Mr. Brodie's grocery store, and damaging fences

[11] Los Angeles *Star,* Mar. 3, 1871. Reprinted from the San Luis Obispo *Standard.*

generally. Mr. Addington had his leg injured in endeavoring to stop the horses. Strange to say, neither the coach nor the horses sustained injury. No blame can be attached to the driver, as he should have assistance in unloading the mail, and not be under the necessity of leaving his box.[12]

While the driver may have needed assistance at the post office, it was also true that there were commonly accepted practices for preventing such episodes when the whip was required to leave his team unattended. Any uneducated farm boy would have dropped the inside traces from the double tree and taken a tight tie on the reins if driving a single team. With four or six he would have tied the leaders securely or never have left his team unattended under any circumstances, even for the United States Mails. In instances of this nature the conclusion must be that the drivers had become careless and/or complacent and too lazy to spend a few moments for safety's sake. One such circumstance just prior to the coming of the railroad down the Santa Clara Valley was nearly disastrous:

> Tuesday morning's stage met with a mishap at Cienega. The driver was assisting the passengers to alight for breakfast, when the horses became frightened and ran away, with Miss Annie Wagner and two children inside. The team dashed down the grade and up the next hill, when the occupants found an opportunity to jump out. The horses ran about a mile further and stopped after overturning the stage, which was slightly damaged.[13]

The very natural inclination to "bail out" of a runaway stagecoach more often than not resulted in serious injuries or instant death. Too frequently the jumper would fall back under the rear wheels and be crushed. Seldom did the passenger that remained inside suffer

---

[12] Los Angeles *Star*, Dec. 18, 1869.

[13] Ventura *Free Press*, Feb. 3, 1887. Cienega was located east of Fillmore in the approximate vicinity of the present State Fish Hatchery.

STAGE CROSSING SLIPPERY ROCK, 1880

The northbound stage climbing the San Marcos Pass at Slippery Rock, 1880. Note the grooves for the wheels, and the "washboarding" of the road which enables the horses to get better footing. Courtesy, Title Insurance and Trust Co.

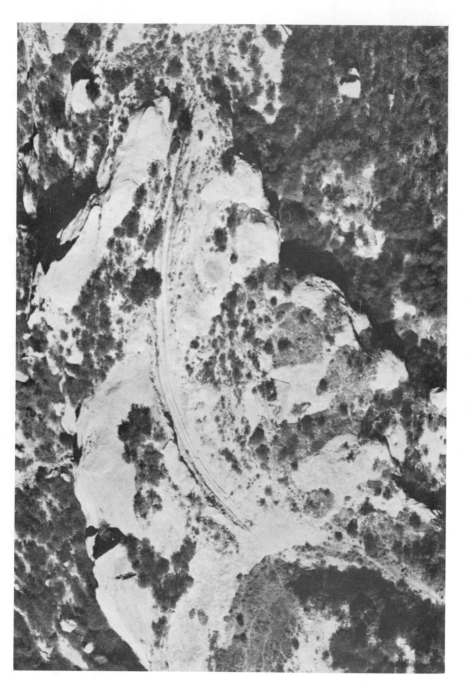

AERIAL VIEW OF SLIPPERY ROCK, 1971

The grooves for the wheels of the mud wagons measured five feet, four inches wide and are still clearly visible. Photograph taken December 16, 1971. Courtesy of Ynez D. Haase.

seriously, even though the coach may have rolled over several times; but the urge to jump was overwhelming. Even Judge Sepulveda could not remain calm and seated when caught up in a runaway stage on the Conejo. The Santa Barbara *Independent* reported that "Hizzoner" was badly bruised; the Ventura *Signal* scoffed at the very thought that such a high ranking dignitary as the Judge could be injured in Ventura County and stated Sepulveda's injuries were "trivial." [14] It was probably fortunate that Editor Sheridan of the *Signal* was never called upon to appear before Judge Sepulveda.

One of the more important exceptions to the "remain calm and seated" rule was when trouble developed on the San Marcos Pass. From the historian's point of view, it is an unfortunate fact that the Santa Barbara newspapers were inclined to omit the more illuminating details of stagecoach mishaps. It was bad enough to have the stage upset, without upsetting the ecology and capsizing the tourism plans of the local Board of Trade. For example, no great damage to the Santa Barbara "image" could result from this mild account by the Santa Barbara *Press* on May 11, 1872: "The down stage overturned, Thursday, just above Pat's Station. A Mr. Conway had his ear cut in trying to protect a little girl from injury. No other damage done."

The Ventura *Signal* was more accommodating, but barely, with this report in its issue of January 23, 1875:

> Sheriff Stone had some lively experience crossing Santa Barbara Mountain Sunday in the stage. The lead horses were precipitated down an embankment 150 feet and killed, and the passengers and coach had a very narrow escape.

It remained for Editor H. G. McLean in the Ventura

---

[14] Ventura *Signal*, Aug. 4, 1883.

Free Press of July 28, 1883, to portray in three sentences why it was prudent to be prepared to jump on the San Marcos Pass:

> Whilst the stage going south from Los Alamos, Santa Barbara county, was descending the side of the mountain Wednesday the horses became unmanageable and the stage went over the bank down to the bottom of the canyon, a distance of 200 feet. The driver and three passengers jumped off uninjured. Two horses were killed.

Special attention should be called to the fact that McLean very carefully placed the scene in Santa Barbara County. It would never do for eastern readers to be confused on this point.

Even when one of the most incredible stagecoach runaways on record occurred in Ventura County along the beach between San Buenaventura and Santa Barbara, the Ventura newspapers did not mention the old home town; it was the "Santa Barbara stage":

> Last Sunday, about 4 P.M., the horses attached to the Santa Barbara stage took fright, at Rincon Point. They dashed down the beach for three miles then started for the ocean. They succeeded in passing beyond the breakers; then tried to return, but became entangled in the traces. They would have been drowned but for the aid of some men, who swam out and rescued them. The passengers, being all out, were not hurt.[15]

The rule that says one should never jump out of a runaway stagecoach is never valid when the horses get beyond the line of the breakers. In this contingency it is best to remain inside *only* if one cannot swim.

Runaways through the surf were not the only sources of excitement on the Rincon during the heyday of Coast Line staging. A short distance below Rincon Point is a natural phenomenon known to science as a "solfatara,"

---

[15] Ventura *Free Press,* Aug. 23, 1879.

but more familiarly called a "volcano" by the *hoi pol-loi*. For a decade and a half during the 1870s and '80s the "Rincon Volcano" was quite active at intervals. It became the not unwilling duty of the stagecoach drivers to investigate and submit impromptu reports upon the current status of the hot vent when arriving in San Buenaventura or Santa Barbara. The Ventura *Free Press* of July 2, 1881, reported that J. C. Cheney, a regular whip on the Santa Barbara run, had brought cinders from the volcano into town and placed them on display in Cody's Drug Store. Cheney related that the surrounding rocks were getting hotter each day and were already untouchable. *Free Press* Editor McLean went on to state that "if the heat keeps increasing, there will be a veritable volcano there shortly, and then the Santa Barbara papers will swear it was gotten up expressly as an attraction to summer tourists."

By October 27, 1883, the stage drivers could report that flames ten feet high were issuing from the volcano, and rocks were being hurled into the air. The situation was not quite so funny by then, but it was probably sheer coincidence that McLean sold the *Free Press* at the same time.

The disturbances on the Rincon soon subsided into an occasional flareup of smoke, a situation that would continue long after the demise of the stagecoach. It was possibly the sighting of those flames, however, that resulted in a Santa Barbara lawyer remarking to fellow passengers on the stage that he would rather live in hell than in Ventura. The Ventura newspapers agreed that hell was a much more suitable place for Santa Barbara lawyers than San Buenaventura.

It was not always necessary to ride the coaches in order to participate in the thrills and chills of nineteenth century staging. The Santa Barbara *Press* of June 24, 1871, reported the case of one Mr. P. Varnum, keeper of the tollgate and stagecoach station at the top of the San Marcos Pass. It seems that Mr. Varnum and a companion were disturbed one evening by the lowing of a cow in the nearby corral. The reporter's use of the word "lowing" appears rather novel in view of the fact that the cow was being consumed by "a huge grizzly bear," but let it pass. The grizzly took one look at Varnum and his companion, dropped the cow and started in pursuit of the toll collector. Mr. Varnum, to use the words of the *Press,* "proved himself a good runner," and managed his escape by dodging through the herd of cattle. No explanation was given in respect to why the critters themselves had not long since stampeded, or how it was possible for Varnum to hide behind the tails of the innocent bovines while alluding the angry grizzly – all were still in the same corral! The reporter simply noted that, "We would not give much for this bear's chances for life with Mr. Varnum on his tracks." (This author hereby takes a solemn pledge to reread that article at the first opportunity to verify who was on whose tracks!)

Never a dull moment? There were undoubtedly more than enough dull moments for the average stagecoach traveler, although the man named Joe who asked the driver to stop near Paso Robles and then calmly stepped to the ground, drew a revolver and blasted out his brains was probably psychotic rather than bored.[16]

In an age when gun-toting was an acceptable social custom, it is not surprising to find many accidental shootings mixed up with staging and mail carrying. The Los Angeles *News* on August 12, 1865, reported such

---

16 Los Angeles *Star,* June 13, 1871.

an affair when the San Diego mail carrier met a friend on the road who offered some "refreshments." As both parties sat "refreshing" themselves, the mail carrier's gun fell, struck the wheel of the coach, and discharged the ball through his side. The friend brought the mail into Los Angeles, while the carrier laid over to recuperate.

This type of accident was not confined to stagecoaching. After the Southern Pacific started running passenger trains to San Fernando, the *Star* reported a case where one of the passengers noticed a coyote racing the cars. Calling the conductor's attention to the animal, a Californian offered his gun to the ticket puncher and suggested he shoot the varmint. The railroad official thought it a superlative idea and blazed away – *hitting the gun's owner in the leg!* The *Star* stated that no blame could be placed upon the conductor as he was one of the most careful attaches of the Espee. It failed to add, however, that he was also the worst shot west of the Pecos River.[17]

Another common phenomenon of the times was the horse thief. For almost four decades after the Mexican War, California had more horse thieves than a new shirt has pins. Stage stations were lucrative targets for these criminals, particularly on the original line of the Overland Mail Company. Long after the demise of the Butterfield line, however, the depredations of the horse thieves continued. In 1874, Tiburcio Vasquez and his gang borrowed six of Sam Harper's horses right at the time the veteran stager was inaugurating his Atlantic & Pacific Stage Line from Newhall to San Buenaventura.

It was rather ironic that after a horse thief had been caught, convicted, and sentenced (if he happened to be

---

17 *Ibid.,* Sept. 11, 1874.

so fortunate) he was usually transported to San Quentin by boat rather than behind horses on a stagecoach. One case where a horse thief was to be transported by stage ended with a missing criminal still wearing the handcuffs of a red-faced deputy sheriff, who had returned to San Luis Obispo empty-handed.

The scene was the same area described by J. Ross Browne so many years earlier – the region around the Pleito stage station on the Nacimiento River-Jolon-San Antonio route. There were undoubtedly many of the same old renegades described by Browne still hanging around and calling the locale "home," for the method used by the thief to escape would indicate that he knew in advance where to get help in removing those handcuffs:

William Hendricks, convicted of horse stealing at the last session of the County Court in this place, and sentenced to two years imprisonment in the State penitentiary, made his escape by jumping from the stage several miles north of the Pleito Station, in Monterey County, on Saturday night last, 14th instant, while en route for San Quentin. Mr. Mauk, the gentleman who had him in charge, informs us that Hendricks complained of being, and was, to all appearances, very sick, caused by the motion of the coach, and had violent fits of vomiting in consequence. When about seven miles north of Pleito Station, as above stated, he was again taken with a desire to unload his guilty conscience, and, during his feigned or compulsory retchings, his head protruding from the window, he managed to drop his hat. The stage was brought to a halt by one of the passengers, for the purpose of procuring it, to which Mr. Mauk objected, but was finally induced, as it was bright moonlight, to leave the prisoner's side to get it. Mr. Mauk had hardly touched the ground, when Hendricks made a desperate leap over a two-hundred-pound passenger and through the window on the opposite side of the coach, disappearing in the undergrowth that abounds at that point. A general search was at once instituted, but the bird had flown. Mr. Mauk returned rather wiser, but considerable less hilarious than when he started, and assures us that if he undertakes to act as body guard to any more convicts in the future, he will not be so accomodating.[18]

It is a poor rule that does not work both ways; if a stagecoach could be used by horse thieves to escape, it could also be used by the "law" to catch them. The Los Angeles *News* of March 6, 1868, reported the arrival in town of a posse from San Bernardino in hot pursuit of a couple of well-known citizens who had left town with six or seven horses and mules without a bill of sale. When informed by Los Angeles citizens that the culprits had passed through town and headed up the coast ("They went thata way!") one of the pursuers took passage on the stage, passed the robbers en route, and reached San Luis Obispo ahead of them. The unsuspecting horse thieves rode blithely into town with their loot and into the waiting arms of the law. The *News* added that upon their return to San Bernardino, "no doubt they will receive their just deserts."

If there had been no horse thieves, Lucrezia Borgias, pseudo-Countesses, runaways, grizzly bears, or rattlesnakes, to vary the monotony of Coast Line staging, the unusual weather of the country could still have been depended upon to take care of the job. Newcomers to the San Fernando Valley may be slightly skeptical of the following news item printed in the Los Angeles *Star* on November 18, 1871, but thousands of old-timers will remember the sands of the valley before they were covered with concrete, and the horrendous storms that resulted from Santa Ana weather conditions. Those subdivision signs erected in the valley became firewood in a matter of minutes after the first gusts hit.

---

[18] *Ibid.*, Dec. 25, 1872.

The overland stage from San Francisco, was six hours late yesterday morning. The cause of the detention was a terrible sand storm that prevailed in the San Fernando Valley. The driver represents this storm as exceeding anything of the kind that he has ever witnessed. The wind commenced blowing Thursday evening and continued with increasing violence until Friday morning.

The horses refused to face the storm, and the driver had to stop and unhitch, and camp for the night behind the coach. When daylight came, no trace of the road was to be seen; the sand had entirely covered it. At one place on the road near an arroyo, a pile of sand had drifted some ten feet in height, and stands there now as a land mark. The horses were unable to see for several hours after the storm, so full were their eyes of the sand, which had to be dug out like clay.

Sand was not the only thing that had to be dug out like clay or could drift ten feet high. Back in 1882, southern California was visited by a rare snowstorm of unusual intensity. To be truthful, it was only in the other fellow's newspaper that the depth of the snow in one's own town could be found; the snowfall in the other fellow's town was *your* news.

The Ventura *Signal* made no mention of the local snowfall in San Buenaventura, but reported there were ten-foot drifts at Calabasas. The Sacramento *Record* reported the snow was ten inches deep in San Buenaventura, an assertion which brought forth cries of "Foul!" from the Ventura *Free Press;* although McLean conceded that the white stuff *had* fallen in the town, and that the snow had practically obliterated the islands. The *Free Press* then weakened its own case by reprinting a portion of a letter from J. C. Hartman relative to those ten-foot snow drifts at Calabasas:

Mr. J. C. Hartman sends an account too long for our columns [The editor means here that he had to get that stagecoach into Los Angeles County before picking up the threads of Hartman's story] of the trials and tribulations experienced by himself and two fellow-passengers last Thursday and Friday while traveling by the Coast Line hence to Los Angeles. One incident out of many will show why the stage was two days in making the trip:

"When we had got about 1½ miles from the Calabasas ranch house, we found a bridge drifted full of snow. We could not go around it, therefore had to try to go ahead. The driver forced the horses in as far as possible, when they stuck in the snow and laid down. We unhitched them and they wallowed through. We then hitched one horse to the stage with a long rope, using the neck-yoke for a singletree. He could not move the stage, so we hitched the other on, attaching the lugs to the first horse's harness by means of the breast-straps. Together they could not pull it, so we went to work scooping the snow out of the road with a bucket. After an hour's hard labor we released the coach."

The driver, Mr. Van Baker, reports that in places the snow was 10 feet deep.[19]

Snow! Snow ten feet deep at Calabasas. It's your move Bret Harte.

It was the Geiger Grade, a mile and a half from the summit;
Black as your hat was the night and never a star in the heavens.
Thundering down the grade the gravel and stones were sent flying
Over the precipice side – a thousand feet plumb to the bottom.

Halfway down the grade I felt, Sir, a thrilling and creaking,
Then a lurch to one side as we hung on the bank of the ravine,
Then looking up the road I saw in the distance behind me
The off hind wheel of the coach just loosened from its axle and
  following.

One glance I gave – then gathered together my ribbons,
Shouted and flung them outspread on the straining necks of my
  cattle,
Screamed at the top of my voice and lashed the air in my frenzy,
While down the Geiger Grade, on three wheels, the vehicle
  thundered.

Speed was our only chance, when again the ominous rattle;
Crack, and another wheel slipped away and was lost in the
  darkness;

---

[19] Ventura *Free Press*, Jan. 18, 1882.

Two only now were left, yet such was our fearful momentum,
Upright, erect, and sustained on two wheels, the vehicle thundered.

As some huge bowlder, unloosened from its rocky shelf on the
*   mountain,*
Drives before it the hare and the timorous squirrel, far-leaping,
So down the Geiger Grade rushed the Pioneer coach, and before it
Leaped the wild horses and shrieked in advance of the danger
*   impending.*

But to be brief in my tale; again, ere we came to the level,
Slipped from its axle a wheel — so that to be plain in my statement —
A matter of twelve hundred yards or more, as the distance may be,
We traveled upon one wheel, until we drove up to the station.

Then, Sir, we sank in a heap; but picking myself from the ruins,
I heard a noise up the grade, and looking, I saw in the distance
The three wheels following still like moons on the horizon whirling,
'Till circling they gracefully sank on the road at the side of the
*   station.*

This is my story, Sir; a trifle, indeed, I assure you;
Much more, perchance, might be said, but I hold him, of all men,
*   most lightly*
Who swerves from the truth of his tale — No thank you — well
*   since you are pressing,*
Perhaps I don't care if I do — you may give me the same, Jim —
*   no sugar.*

"The Stage-Driver's Story" [20] — Bret Harte

---

[20] Los Angeles *Star*, Jan. 2, 1869. Later reprints of Harte's poem vary to some extent from this early version in the *Star*.

"The Cars Are Coming"

Think of it; in thirty days the last rail will be spiked down. All aboard for Omaha, Chicago and New York! Six days only to span the continent; we can in fancy almost hear the teamster lamenting thus: O, now, forever farewell the dusty roads, the alkali, farewell; farewell the horned bulls and the big trains that made ambition virtue! O, farewell the faithful steers, and the red wagons; the whoa-haws, the ear piercing oaths, the royal swearing; and all quality, pride, pomp, and circumstance of emigrating. And, O, you mortal bullwhips whose rude cracks and immortal Jove's dread clamors counterfeit, farewell! The teamster's occupation's gone.[1]

Thus did the Reno *Crescent* put the lie to the old theory that great moments in history slip by unnoticed, that it is only from a much later vantage point in time the historian can place his finger on a specific week, day, or hour, and say: "This is when the course of human history was altered." The editor of the *Crescent* had put it nobly – but in fancy only. Any Western bullwhacker guilty of such "obscene" language and phraseology would have been committed to the nearest asylum without benefit of trial, or sent packing to New England, there to teach History of English Literature at Boston University for life – without hope of parole.

It will be conceded, however, that the coming of the railroad to any area of the Old West was an exception to the rule. Almost without dissent the newspaper editors, writers, and general population (including cynics) could foresee the tremendous implications of the oc-

---

[1] Los Angeles *Star*, Apr. 3, 1869. Reprinted from the Reno *Crescent*.

casion. Here was an event which drew so sharp a line of demarcation between the old and the new, that so drastically altered a way of life and created such a profound impact upon the economy and the people, it must be forever used if anything is, to define the end of the pioneer period.

There were children born of those pioneers who remembered their mothers flagging down the Coast Line stagecoach to post a letter to relatives in the east. They would live to see man place the American flag upon the surface of the moon, but in all those dramatic years they would never witness an event that was destined to change their lives so profoundly in such a short period of time as the day "the cars" came to usurp the stagecoach.

So far as the Coast Line of Stages was concerned, the graffito on the wall had been clear from the beginning; only the time element was uncertain. It had never been the intention of the Southern Pacific to stop construction at Soledad in August 1873. To be accurate, the proper term would be "The Southern Pacific Branch Railway Company," for such was the name of the offshoot under which actual construction was being conducted. The merger in December 1873, of this hybrid organization with the parent company was the clue that operations had been suspended for an indefinite and probably lengthy period. The reason: financial desperation of the Big Four.

Although the Southern Pacific had intended to continue construction up the Salinas Valley, Crocker was not quite certain in his own mind just *where* the rails were going – except in the general direction of San Diego. It seems probable that heading off Tom Scott, the Atlantic & Pacific Railroad, or some other real or imagined bogy man, motivated the company more than sound railroading principles. This would not be the case thirteen years later when the Southern Pacific Branch Railway was reactivated to build south from Soledad and north from Newhall and San Buenaventura via the Santa Clara Valley and the coast.

In the interim another railroad brainchild was spawned, one with the dynamic intent of building practically everywhere in the United States, but which ended in July 1883, with a terminus at Port Harford on the north and Los Alamos on the south. Later it would manage to crawl southward a few more miles and stake out the townsite of Los Olivos. Today the famed Mattei's Tavern stands across the street from where the narrow gauge tracks of the Pacific Coast Railroad died – a last link with the past, where the stagecoaches for Santa Barbara via the San Marcos Turnpike connected with the cars from San Luis Obispo.

Earlier, with the slim gauge Pacific Coast railhead at Los Alamos, the north-bound traveler's trials and transfers were outlined nicely by Editor Stephen Bowers in the May 30, 1884, issue of the Ventura *Free Press*.

According to Bowers the stage left Santa Barbara at an early hour in the morning, although the editor failed to define what he meant by "early." Pat's Station at the top of the San Marcos Pass was reached in time for dinner (the modern lunch-hour meal) and the Santa Ynez River crossed at the foot of the grade on the north side. Then followed twenty-five miles of pleasant traveling through the grain fields of the Santa Ynez Valley. Los Alamos, sixty miles from Santa Barbara, was reached at six o'clock in the evening and an overnight's rest secured at the hotel kept by Major Durfee. Los

Alamos was departed "early" the next morning via "the cars," which arrived in San Luis Obispo at 9:30 A.M.

Bowers was only traveling as far as San Luis Obispo, but the wayfarer continuing on would have transferred at this point back to the stagecoach for the remainder of the trip to Soledad. Bowers noted that the railroad by-passed Santa Maria because some of the landowners refused to sell rights of way to the company, a statement that may or may not have been true. The editor was obviously laying the groundwork for future ease of land acquisition for railroad purposes in Ventura County when the proper time arrived. It didn't work!

This was the state of affairs travel-wise after 1883 and prior to the completion of the railroad to the head of the Salinas Valley in 1886, and from Newhall to Santa Barbara the following year. With the overnight stop at Los Alamos, it was still faster to travel by stage from Santa Barbara to Newhall, connect with the through trains for San Francisco and arrive in the Bay City well ahead of the shorter but slower route up the coast.

In mid-April 1886, the news came: The Southern Pacific Branch Railway Company was back in business and was starting construction down the Santa Clara Valley from Newhall and up the Salinas Valley from Soledad. Work was to be pushed with all possible speed, and the two forces were expected to meet and join rails within twelve months. After years of an almost constant diet of newspaper pablum on railroading, the general public probably took the news with a cynical, "Oh, yeah!"; but this time it was true, or at least the Southern Pacific's intentions were a reasonable facsimile of truthfulness.

At Soledad work began at once and proceeded with commendable speed. By October 22, 1886, the Ventura

Free Press reported that the road was open for traffic to San Miguel. "It is now possible to reach Paso Robles Springs with only seven miles of staging, and San Luis Obispo with thirty-eight."

The first passenger trains from San Francisco started running to Paso Robles on October 31, 1886; by November 19, the company had published a combination train and stagecoach schedule from San Francisco to Templeton and San Luis Obispo. The rails would be extended to Santa Margarita in 1887 before construction came to a halt. Collis P. Huntington announced in 1889 that it would stay right there until the Southern Pacific obtained a right of way through San Luis Obispo,[2] the inference being that San Luis Obispo had more skinflints per square yard than any other place in California. In truth, the local and national financial and economic outlook in no way justified the costly construction from Santa Margarita to San Luis Obispo down the Cuesta Grade.

For the next seven years the northbound traveler came into San Luis Obispo from Los Olivos on the narrow gauge Pacific Coast Railroad, transferred back to stagecoach to reach Santa Margarita; and only there was he able to secure through train service to San Francisco.

The opposite end of the construction starting at Newhall ran into greater complications. Within a week of the start of work the construction crew of five hundred had disappeared to the last man. The heirs of Henry Newhall[3] had brought the grading to a halt in a dispute over right of way alignment. It was not until late August that word arrived in San Buenaventura the

[2] Ventura *Free Press*, May 15, 1889.
[3] Newhall's death was announced in the Ventura *Signal* of Mar. 18, 1881.

troubles had been settled and construction resumed. The news was brought by stagecoach passengers. From that day until the cars arrived in Ventura some nine months later, every word of published news concerning railroad construction down the Santa Clara Valley came via stagecoach drivers or passengers. There is no indication that any of the Ventura newspaper editors or reporters ever took the trouble to travel to the scene for a first hand investigation.

It was January 5, 1887, when the population of Santa Paula was startled by the shriek of a locomotive whistle. The construction train was only a few miles east of town. On January 19, the editor of the *Free Press* received a telegram from Santa Paula: "The railroad and rain have just reached town and everybody is smiling and happy." Well, almost everybody:

> The days of staging are, for the Santa Clara Valley drawing to a close and the knight of the whips wears a long face as he meditates the prospect. Dispatches received here last night are to the effect that by the 9th inst., passenger trains will be running between Los Angeles and Santa Paula. . .[4]

With the realization of the dreams of two generations of pioneers in sight, the editor of the *Free Press* epitomized in words the ambitions, restless spirits, drives — yes, and *selfishness* — of our forebears: "If a man has some capital and plenty of push and energy he can get on here very well. But if he has none of these qualifications we couldn't recommend him to come to California . . . but to die and get out of the way of others."[5]

Thus began the impact on the environment that continues to this day.

There was still some life pulsating in the old time

---

[4] Ventura *Free Press*, Feb. 4, 1887.   [5] *Ibid.*

manners, however. The rain that arrived with the railroad refused to leave and began "raising hob" with the new roadbed. The construction crew dropped its tools and refused to work until finished with celebrating the Chinese New Year, and the Southern Pacific Branch Railway Company ran out of rails. There was even a newspaper rumor that the Santa Fe had cornered the market on rails to prevent the Espee from building down the Santa Clara Valley!

The first train due to arrive in Santa Paula on Wednesday, February 9, 1887, was wrecked east of Camulos; and the following day's train met a like fate. The passengers, according to the *Free Press,* "traveled under difficulties yesterday evening from the Sespe to Santa Paula on a hand car." [6]

It was not until February 26, that the *Free Press* reported, "Quite long trains of freight and passenger cars arrive daily" in Santa Paula. The Southern Pacific may have a record of when that first train actually arrived in Santa Paula, but the San Buenaventura newspapers never pinpointed the day or time.

During this period of floods, rail shortages, and the Chinese New Year, a flareup of the ever-smoldering feud between San Buenaventura and Santa Barbara occurred which is reminiscent of modern day nit-picking over the naming of freeways. Santa Barbara scratched the scab from the sore by referring to the new railroad line as "The Santa Barbara Extension of the Southern Pacific." The *Free Press* roared back in wrath that it would be just as appropriate to call the new road "The Camulos Extension," or "The Saticoy Extension," or even "The Rincon Extension." Editor Bowers stormed

6 *Ibid.,* Feb. 11, 1887.

on with his sarcasm: "The fact is the railroad will pass through your little city only stopping long enough each day to unload Ventura County products for your people to live on.   . ." [7]

While the Santa Barbara *Press* and the Ventura *Free Press* engaged in childish brawling, Santa Paula basked in the limelight of being the hub of Ventura County. For the next ninety days, packed stagecoaches from up the coast, plus two from the Ojai, arrived and departed daily from the Southern Pacific railhead. Stagecoach agent N. Wines had inserted the first advertisement for the Coast Line Stage Company "connecting with the cars at Santa Paula" on February 5. A new advertisement appeared on February 12, probably due to weather conditions and the postponement of regular train service. With the completion of the railroad to San Buenaventura and the inauguration of regular service on May 18, 1887, Santa Paula returned to something resembling normalcy but without the stagecoach; that was gone forever except for jitney service from depot to hotels, and later to Sulphur Mountain Springs.

The *Free Press* was so excited over the arrival of the railroad that it announced future trains "will arrive at 1 P.M. and leave at 12:05 P.M." [8]

On July 1, 1887, trains began running to Carpinteria, from whence the die-hard Jehus of old vied for customers to haul into Santa Barbara in rockaways, spring wagons, "Yosemite" wagons, or anything else on wheels. This dying gasp of the knights of the lash lasted until August 19, when train service reached Santa Barbara with a gala "whoop and a holler" celebration. All that was left now of the old Coast Line of Stages' itinerary

---

7 *Ibid.*

8 *Ibid.*, May 18, 1887.

was from Santa Barbara to Los Olivos, and from San Luis Obispo to Santa Margarita. Everything and everyone pointed to the following year as the time when the end of the six-in-hand would arrive.

Fourteen years earlier the panic of 1873 had stalled the Southern Pacific at Soledad. In 1887, the great "boom of the eighties" that had raised Los Angeles from *Pueblo* to cityhood burst with even greater repercussions. The outlying counties to the north had not shared to any extent in the expansionism and were looking to the railroad to bring it to them. The economic danger signals and warning lights were ignored and even ridiculed by a new *Free Press* editor: "The sounds reach our ears and we stop to listen, but we are soon convinced that these sounds do not harbinger the approaching storm, they are but the destruction of sunken reefs. . ."[9]

It would have taken more than the eloquent redundancy of the *Free Press* to have stemmed the inevitable aftermath of the boom. The paper profits of the speculator turned back to pulp before his eyes; land that had commanded a double eagle for a handful of dirt soon was begging for the same amount per acre; the business stagnation could be smelled to the east coast; and the Southern Pacific's construction crews came to a discreet halt above Santa Barbara at Elwood, and south of Santa Margarita near the top of the Cuesta Grade. The intervening gap would be one of the fourth estate's best copy sources for the following fourteen years – "Closing The Gap" heading countless articles in the newspapers of the cities and towns affected.

The old Jehus, whips, knights of the lash, or just

[9] *Ibid.,* Sept. 19, 1887.

plain drivers if one prefers, became a bewildered and restless breed, almost incapable of adjusting to the new life and mode of transportation. Oliver Cropper, the veteran whip that had spilled Allman's payload into the plowed ground of the Camulos, tried driving the "bus" for the Ventura hotels: "Nothing pleases that jolly Oliver Cropper more than to have his bus crowded, then his manly chest heaves and his face lights up like a June bug on a ripe strawberry." [10]

Seven weeks later Cropper had had his fill of crowded jitneys, June bugs and ripe strawberries, and filed to run for Town Marshal, a political adventure that ended much like the Camulos wreck – in the plowed ground. The smell of horses and leather was too strong for Oliver's aging nose; and the whip purchased one of the stage lines to Ojai, making the run seven days a week. It was here on January 3, 1888, that the old stager saved the horses, stagecoach, and passengers of his competitor's line in the raging floodwaters of San Antonio Creek.

Three weeks later the restless Cropper sold the Ojai line to Wheeler Blumberg and a C. P. Huntington of Nordhoff. It was announced at the same time that Cropper was starting a new stage line to Hueneme, but by September Watts Haydock was advertised as the owner of the line.

Cropper's restlessness over the new order of things typified the plight of his fellow stagecoach drivers. Gradually the six-in-hand and the owners of those hands faded from the news. Items about "old stagecoach driver visits in Ventura," or "Sam Washburn, old stagecoach driver, suicides in Los Angeles," began to appear.

---

[10] *Ibid.*, Sept. 23, 1887.

In May 1894, the Southern Pacific completed the line down the tortuous Cuesta Grade into San Luis Obispo. Now only on that thirty-five-mile run from State Street in Santa Barbara to the Pacific Coast Railroad in Los Olivos was the old order still to be seen. While the newspaper editors talked of "closing the gap" between Elwood and San Luis Obispo, the mud wagons continued to climb the cruel San Marcos Pass with six straining steeds digging their hoofs into a road washboarded for traction. Everyone agreed that the view from the summit was nice.

After the final closing of the gap in 1901, the grandiloquent prose of Katherine Lynch combined with the *Out West Magazine* of Charles Lummis to preserve the "good old days" as future generations would always want them to be:

> When Joel Fithian flung out the reins over his six splendid bays and tooled one of the veritable old stage coaches up State street, heading for the San Marcos Pass, the bugler beside him making the echoes ring, and he himself on the box – a great splendid pink-cheeked cherub in his flapping sombrero, the heart of every Barbareno thrilled within him. . .[11]

Stephen Bowers and the *Free Press* would have added that a dog fight at State and Anapamu streets would have had the same effect.

---

[11] Katherine Lynch, "The Passing of Old Santa Barbara," *Out West Magazine* (Feb. 1904), p. 158.

Bibliography
and
Index

Sources and Bibliography

W. H. Hutchinson, when introducing his bibliography of *Oil, Land, and Politics* (1965), stated: "I see no merit in displaying my familiarity with the card catalog files of various repositories."

The author of the present work concurs with Mr. Hutchinson, particularly where books relating to stagecoaching are concerned. A truly impressive list could be compiled, but the writer would merely be displaying his familiarity with the various libraries' card files. A study of those books disclosed little of value to the subject matter under consideration, although revealing considerable misinformation and/or "potboiling."

The facts presented in *Stagecoaching on El Camino Real* have been gathered primarily from the United States Post Office Department records at National Archives, Washington, D.C.; the Minute Book of the Overland Mail Company; the minute books of the Boards of Supervisors of Los Angeles and Santa Barbara counties; road records supplied by the Clerk of the Board, Los Angeles County Supervisors; contemporary maps of the staging era; and, most important of all, the files of several newspapers from 1851 to 1889 inclusive.

It is the use of these latter items that the author wishes to explain in detail, since they are directly or indirectly the basis of most of the important data presented.

Specifically, the newspaper files in question are:

1. The Los Angeles *Star,* May 17, 1851 through October 1, 1864, and May 16, 1868, through December 1874. The continuity of the *Star* files for the first four

years is very spotty, but beginning with January 1855, it is excellent.

2.   The Los Angeles *News,* October 1, 1864, through May 15, 1868. The *News,* using various prefixes, was the only newspaper published in Los Angeles during this period, the *Star* having suspended operations on October 1, 1864. There are but few missing issues.

3.   The Ventura *Signal,* April 22, 1871, through April 4, 1885. Possibly a dozen missing issues only mar this splendid file, one which covers the heyday of Coast Line staging.

4.   The Ventura *Free Press,* November 13, 1875, through December 28, 1889. There are frequent gaps during the years of 1880 and 1881, otherwise the continuity is excellent. For a time during the late 1880s, it was published under the name of the *Vidette.*

5.   The Santa Barbara *Press,* July 1, 1869, through November 29, 1873. The continuity of this file leaves much to be desired.

The use of these valuable newspaper files was not one of hit and miss, or spot checks. Rather, the method used was a year by year, issue by issue, page by page, column by column, and paragraph by paragraph search for any item relevant to stagecoaching. The contents of such items were noted or copied and the whole arranged chronologically for a continuity of developments. By this method any errors in one specific news account would be exposed in later issues, the trend of events clarified, and clues to government records that would "officially" confirm or deny the newspaper version be revealed.

Where critical data was concerned and the file of a contemporary newspaper was available for study, a cross-check was made for verification. The Los Angeles *News* during the years it was publishing contemporaneously with the *Star* was particularly valuable in this respect. The Ventura *Democrat* was utilized in a like manner for events of the later stagecoaching era.

It should be noted that the nineteenth century practice by the fourth estate of exchanging their product far and wide resulted in the more important stagecoaching items being reprinted in papers far from the scenes of the events. Thus, little of value was lost to posterity.

The following books were of particular value, even though one or two may have been criticized by the writer:

Brewer, William. *Up and Down California in 1860-1864.* Edited by Francis P. Farquhar. New Haven: Yale University Press, 1930.

Conkling, Roscoe P. and Margaret B. *The Butterfield Overland Mail, 1858-1869.* 3 vols. Glendale: The Arthur H. Clark Company, 1947.

Eggenhofer, Nick. *Wagons, Mules and Men, How the Frontier Moved West.* New York: Hastings House Publishers, 1961.

Fernald, Charles. *A County Judge in Arcady, Selected Private Papers of Charles Fernald, Pioneer California Jurist.* Edited by Cameron Rogers. Glendale: The Arthur H. Clark Company, 1954.

Hafen, LeRoy H. *The Overland Mail 1849-1869.* Cleveland: The Arthur H. Clark Company, 1926.

Ormsby, Waterman L. *The Butterfield Overland Mail.* Edited by Lyle H. Wright and Josephine Bynum. San Marino: The Huntington Library, 1942.

Sawyer, Eugene. *The Life and Career of Tiburcio Vasquez, The California Stage Robber.* Foreword by Joseph A. Sullivan. Oakland: Biobooks, 1944.

Warner, Col. J. J., Judge Benjamin Hayes and Dr. J. P. Widney. *An Historical Sketch of Los Angeles County, California* (1876). Reprinted Los Angeles: O. W. Smith, 1936.

Index